Pope Francis Among the Wolves

Pope Francis
Among the Wolves

THE INSIDE STORY OF A REVOLUTION

Marco Politi
Translated by William McCuaig

Columbia University Press   New York

Columbia University Press
Publishers Since 1893
New York   Chichester, West Sussex
cup.columbia.edu

Library of Congress Cataloging-in-Publication Data
Politi, Marco.
[Francesco tra i lupi. English]
Pope Francis among the wolves : the inside story of a revolution /
Marco Politi ; translated by William McCuaig.
pages   cm
Includes bibliographical references and index.
ISBN 978-0-231-17414-5 (cloth : alk. paper) —
ISBN 978-0-231-54008-7 (electronic)
1. Francis, Pope, 1936- 2. Catholic Church—History—21st century.
I. Title.

BX1378.7.P6513 2015
282.092—dc23   2014046193

Jacket design by Noah Arlow

References to websites (URLs) were accurate at the time
of writing. Neither the author nor Columbia University Press
is responsible for URLs that may have expired or changed
since the manuscript was prepared.

To Riccardo

A cardinal enters the Church of Rome, my brothers, not a royal court. May all of us avoid, and help others to avoid, habits and ways of acting typical of a court: intrigue, gossip, cliques, favoritism, and partiality.

—Pope Francis, homily, 23 February 2014

Contents

Preface

According to legend, Saint Francis of Assisi once met a wolf, to which he addressed a mild sermon. Won over by the saint's words, the fierce animal grew gentle and submissive, lowered its head, and followed him.

The adversaries of Pope Francis, however, are not so quick to yield. The Argentine pope continues to encounter many obstacles in the Roman Curia and in the ranks of the Catholic hierarchy worldwide, obstacles arising from inertia, from a refusal to abandon the habits of the past, and from attachment to rigid dogmatic structures.

Much of the Catholic world and much of secular public opinion too were slow to confront the deadlock into which the successive crises of the government of Benedict XVI had driven the church between 2005 and 2007. It was not just that this refined intellectual and theologian, remembered in the United States for the important speeches he delivered in Washington and New York and before the United Nations in 2008, was temperamentally incapable of exerting leadership over a community of 1.2 billion followers: in those years the world witnessed the radical crisis of an office, the papacy, which still conceived of itself in terms of absolute power, and the crisis of a church always perceived with a finger raised in lofty admonishment.

Joseph Ratzinger had intuited even before he was elected that Catholicism could no longer be governed as a monarchy. But as in so many other cases, he lacked the courage to innovate.

Now in the third year of his pontificate, Pope Francis continues to press on with determination down the road of reform, aiming to reshape the structure of Roman Catholicism, the way of life of its institutions, and the church's approach to the contemporary world. The word *revolution* is not out of place; it is a continuation of the great shift heralded by the Vatican II council.

Jorge Mario Bergoglio ploughs his furrow and scatters his seed with the patience of a Jesuit and the maturity of a priest and bishop who—the first Roman pontiff of which this is true—knows what it means to live and work in a twenty-first-century megalopolis like Buenos Aires. The city from which he comes is a melting pot of the most disparate nationalities, social levels, religions, and currents of thought, and in that respect he is not at all a newcomer "from the ends of the earth." On the contrary, he has lived and operated at the epicenter of globalization and its discontents.

The Argentine pope is aware that he has launched an undertaking that will span the whole arc of his pontificate. It doesn't make him uneasy. One cardinal who sits on the pope's privy council of eight cardinals asserts that the pontiff listens tirelessly but gives the impression "of having his own goals clearly in view."

His objective is to involve bishops, clergy, and laity in his project for change. Yet it is difficult to reform the Catholic Church and even more difficult to change its long-standing mechanisms of command. The opponents are tenacious, and behind the scenes their aggressiveness has provoked a growing campaign to make the pope look illegitimate. Their hope is that the Bergoglio pontificate will end soon.

In concluding the episcopal synod of October 2014 and celebrating the mass for the beatification of Pope Paul VI—the pope who brought the council to a successful conclusion in the 1960s—Francis made an allusion to these modern pharisees, "who experience qualms of conscience, particularly when their comfort, their wealth, their prestige, their power, and their reputation are in question."

And he stressed that they have done so throughout history.

Marco Politi

Rome, October 2014

Acknowledgments

I thank in particular the colleagues who helped me to understand the Argentine reality from which Jorge Mario Bergoglio came forth: E. Piqué, M. De Vedia, M. Varela, J. M. Poirier, G. Valente, P. Loriga. C. Martini Grimaldi all guided me wisely.

The aid of M. Rust was precious.

H. Fitzwilliam drew my attention to illuminating publications. At Rome, I have always been able to count on the friendship of S. Izzo and I. Scaramuzzi, the only one to guess, a day ahead of time, who the new pope would be.

A. Szula, S. Garpol, and P. Trico have given constant assistance.

When Francis was elected, a debate exploded about the future pontiff's role during the Argentine dictatorship: in this regard, it is indispensable to consult *Bergoglio's List: How a Young Francis Defied a Dictatorship and Saved Dozens of Lives* (St. Benedict Press, 2014) by Nello Scavo.

Translator's Note

The Vatican website, www.vatican.va, presents the texts, including interviews and speeches, of the pontificate of Pope Francis and those of his predecessors in Italian, English, and other languages. To locate any papal document, whatever the language, a reader merely needs to know the date of the document (in the day/month/year format used throughout this book) and the category into which it falls: audiences, homilies, letters, speeches, and so on. The Vatican website also provides easy access to documents emanating from the cardinalatial congregations and other departments (or "dicasteries," to use the preferred term) of the Roman Curia. The Official Vatican Network website, www.news.va, is a multilingual hub from which it is possible to access a number of news sources, including *L'Osservatore Romano* and Vatican Radio. A great many news items of significance for the Catholic Church, for which the author cites Italian sources published in print or on the web, may likewise be found on the web in English translation.

At the Vatican website, the Italian text is always the authoritative one and sometimes the fullest one for the papal interviews and speeches. If the pope switches from Italian to Spanish, the Italian text will report the Spanish wording and furnish an Italian translation inside square brackets. Occasionally, the official English text of the less formal remarks Francis has made in speeches and interviews veers a little bit off the mark in passages quoted in Italian by the author to make a precise point that depends on the original wording, so I adapt the English translation to match. For the pope's "morning meditations" at mass in the Santa Marta residence, the website supplies English summaries from *L'Osservatore Romano* that are much briefer than the corresponding Italian reports, and quite often there is no official English translation for a passage quoted by the author, so in these cases the translations are my own. In every case where I have intervened in any way to translate on my own or recast an official English translation, I render a full account of my intervention in the notes.

Pope Francis Among the Wolves

1

The Smell of the Sheep

In Buenos Aires, the Bolívar subway station is very close to the cathedral. Jorge Mario Bergoglio walks down the stairs and into the bowels of the city. He boards the E line train, heading for Plaza Virreyes. It takes a long time to get there; the metal groans, the wagons are covered with graffiti. The archbishop chooses a seat near the exit and sits down with his habitual expression, grave and slightly melancholic. He is wearing clerical black, and nobody recognizes him, for he appears infrequently on television and avoids official receptions. The metropolitan area of Buenos Aires contains 13 million inhabitants, the city itself almost 3 million.

It is hot in the wagon, which is packed with commuters. The people around Jorge are lost in their thoughts: some gaze fixedly at the walls of the tunnel and the neon lights that flash past at regular intervals; others let their heads droop sleepily or stare into the emptiness with resigned expressions. The gaze in the eyes of some is hard and ferocious, despite their youth. Jorge is surrounded by mothers with bundled children, old folks struggling to keep their footing in the swaying car, a swarm of young people engrossed in their cell phones.

At every stop, the train shudders to a halt amid the deafening shriek of the brakes. Forty minutes underground amid the assortment of races, origins, and stories that is Buenos Aires: children and descendants of immigrants from Spain, Italy, Russia, China, Africa, Germany, and France as well as native people from Central America, and South Americans from every nation of the continent. The wagons are crammed with middle-class people focused on the family budget, young people holding onto a job, any job, by their fingernails, and masses of people struggling merely to survive.

Archbishop Jorge Mario Bergoglio doesn't have a car or a driver, nor has he chosen to live in the elegant archiepiscopal residence, choosing instead to inhabit two rooms on the third floor of the diocesan curia. The archbishop knows how to drive: when he was the provincial superior of the Jesuits—in the 1970s, during the Videla dictatorship—he transported politically persecuted individuals in search of a refuge or an escape route more than once. Now he no longer uses a car. From the moment in 1992 when he became auxiliary bishop, going on to become primate of Argentina, he has submerged himself in the daily flux of humanity on public transportation, using the subway or the *colectivo*, the urban bus network. It is not unknown for a woman seated beside him, upon seeing his black habit, to ask him: "Padrecito, will you hear my confession?" and to receive the answer: "Yes, of course." Once on a bus he finally had to interrupt a man whose catalog of sins was interminable with the polite remark, "Bueno, I get off two stops from here."[1]

At Plaza Virreyes, the thirty-five steps back to the surface aren't all that easy for him, with his slightly fallen arches and the painful spot in his leg. At the top of the staircase, there is a little Madonna of Fatima adorned with fresh flowers. Now Jorge finds himself beneath a large shelter where the air is muggy in summer and cold and humid in winter. Everyone is patiently waiting for the dilapidated regional train that will carry them to the outlying districts. There is not a single curial prelate in the Vatican or a single cardinal president of an Episcopal Conference or even a bishop in any of the numerous countries where the Catholic Church is established who is accustomed to such a fatiguing routine. Or if there is, it is a well-kept secret.

Two stops out on this secondary line, Bergoglio arrives at Villa Ramón Carrillo. *Villas miserias* is the local term for the outlying residential quarters haphazardly thrown together, *villas de emergencia* the more polite equivalent, and *shantytown* the standard English expression. At the station, the rails are littered with cardboard and tin refuse. The slums begin only a few steps away, dwellings for which no construction permit was ever issued, some half finished and others that totter at a precarious height. Where the asphalt road ends, no man's land commences: packed earth and perpetual rivulets that smell like sewers. No writ runs here. A few groups of better-maintained houses with vases of flowers in the windows bring to mind the *borgate*, the clusters of habitation on the outskirts of Rome beloved of Pier Paolo Pasolini. But most of the place is just a shantytown, a site of crude and anarchic urbanization where the visitor's dominant sensation is that of having lost any point of reference. "The state is absent here," according to the parish priests, even though Villa Ramón Carrillo does have a primary school and a clinic.

The parishes are often located around the rim of the agglomeration, as though to keep open an escape route back to the "normal" city. At the edge of another agglomeration called Villa-21, there is even a guard post manned by tall young men wearing body armor and the khaki uniform of the naval forces. Paradoxically, their presence heightens the feeling of insecurity. Many taxi drivers won't go to the villas so as not to get "beaten and robbed." Pedro Baya, parish priest of the Church of the Immacolata in Villa Ramón Carrillo, doesn't try to pretend otherwise. "Sometimes I've heard the bullets whistling around me," he declares calmly.[2]

Jorge, as the priests informally call their archbishop, comes out to the shantytown, to every parish in the shantytown, year after year. Several times a year in fact—for the feast day of the patron saint, a procession of the Madonna, a spiritual retreat, some special occasion, the annual gathering of the priests or the teachers in the zone's Catholic schools. He takes part in the procession, stopping to talk with the people, many of whom have emigrated from Paraguay, Bolivia, Peru, or the inlands of Argentina. He is so remote from the traditional image of the august archbishop that the members of the Peruvian community were disappointed the first time they saw him because, says Father Pedro, "he didn't arrive in a limousine with fanfare."

Bergoglio knows every one of the eight hundred priests in his diocese. From the time he took charge of the archbishopric, he aimed to reinforce the presence of priests in the outlying shantytowns. Every parish in the villas has two or three. There was a total of eleven when he took charge of the diocese, now there are twenty-three, and they can reach him on a direct telephone line. He follows them closely, listens to them, helps and assists them in moments of personal crisis. He is more of a companion than a judge. He knows (and Pepe Di Paola, for years his vicar for the shantytowns, testifies to this) that his priests trust him, confide in him in a way they would not with other archbishops, tell him sincerely what they are experiencing, and often show up at the cathedral, "not because they have to, but to hear his spiritual word."[3]

It used to be that priests would pay visits to the archbishop at the curia in the center of Buenos Aires; now it is the archbishop who goes to visit them. This makes the "Bergoglio difference," the priests say; he is "close by" whatever their problems—even the big problem, the moment when a priest arrives at an existential crossroads and asks himself whether the time hasn't come to give it up and live openly with a female companion. At Buenos Aires, there is a tale about a priest who goes to Jorge to say that he has decided to live with a woman. Agreed then, says the archbishop, we'll do the paperwork for you to abandon the clerical state. "But why not wait a year or two before having children." Two years go by, the relationship falls apart, the former priest returns and confesses that he now sees that his true vocation is the priesthood. Agreed then, says the archbishop, we'll start the paperwork for you to be readmitted. "But first you must live in chastity as a layman for five years." Today, they say, he is one of the most respected priests in the capital.

Jorge knows the dusty streets of the shantytowns, the trees that have turned gray, the expressions of those who dwell there, now affectionate and festive, now diffident and impassive. He knows the streets that are full of holes and littered with the battered wrecks of cars that have been repaired a thousand times. He recognizes the children who play by the rivulets, a mother picking fleas off her child, and the stray dogs that plod lazily from one clump of houses to another. Once in a while a little house with barred windows bears the pretentious sign "Drinks, ice cream, bread, detergent." Farther on, above a closed door, there is a hand-written sign advertising a connection to the Internet.

Jorge knows the iron grilles installed everywhere to protect doors, windows, verandas, and even the minuscule courtyard of the vegetable seller. In Villa Ramón Carrillo, even the little shrine of San Gaetano, patron of bread and work, is covered with metal netting so dense that the image can't be seen. All the other shantytowns are the same. Jorge is accustomed to the disorderly succession of shoddily built houses, where the ground floor with plastered walls unsteadily bears the weight of second and third stories made of brick. Improvised balconies, unfinished rooms lacking a roof that remain uncovered for years at a time and serve as terraces for drying laundry. Trash cans, pieces of ironwork, the skeletons of tables and beds thrown into the street. On the far side of an overpass, an even more precarious shantytown called Villa Esperanza has grown up, where the streets are so narrow that a single person can barely squeeze through. A cement cell bears a "for sale" sign.

At Buenos Aires, the archbishopric has been a totem of power for centuries. The Plaza de Mayo symbolically brings together the power centers of the nation's capital: the Casa Rosada (the presidential palace), the cathedral, the city hall, the Ministry of the Economy. But, says Father Di Paola, "Bergoglio never viewed reality from the vantage point of the Plaza de Mayo, but rather from places of pain, misery, and poverty. From the depths of a shantytown, from a hospital."

Jorge insists that a priest must not be a civil servant, that he must treat consciences on the basis of their concrete situation, use "much pity in the confessional," facilitate access to the sacraments, "give the things of God to whoever requests them right away." And give them without charge because the priest is not the proprietor of the things of God, but their transmitter. As the priests know, Jorge is hard on those who burden their relationship with the faithful with regulations, obstacles, and ecclesiastical bureaucracy.

The archbishop, who mingles with the crowd in the subway like any other priest, is personally convinced that the relationship with the poor represents spiritual wealth, that among them may be found an authenticity and a particular sensitivity to God. This option in favor of the poor, sanctioned by the great assemblies of the Latin American Episcopate over the past fifty years at Medellín, Puebla, Santo Domingo, and Aparecida is fundamental for him, not for ideological reasons but for profoundly religious ones. As he puts it, the shepherds must "have the same smell as their sheep."[4]

Jorge also knows that the shantytowns are a world of violence, where brutality hangs in the air despite the calm appearance of the women seated on their doorsteps, the men slumped in seats drinking and chatting, the babies splashing about happily in little plastic tubs at Christmas time (midsummer in Buenos Aires). He knows all this perfectly well, but he doesn't shrink from it and has no fear.

At Villa Ramón Carrillo, not far from the parish center, the blackened entrance to a house is the mark of a punitive expedition carried out by the family of a boy killed by a stray bullet in a gang war. Worse things than that take place. A bourgeois Buenos Aires family who adopted a baby daughter from the shantytowns discovered from her drawings and from the psychological treatment she needed that the little girl had witnessed an abortion and seen the fetus thrown to the dogs to be devoured.[5]

The parish priest Pedro Baya has stamped in his memory one particular day when he was performing baptisms. While he was administering the sacrament beside the altar, a thief fleeing pursuit paused, gasping for breath, at the door of the shed that is the church. His pursuer grabbed him and began beating his head with the butt of a pistol. "The kid was on his knees screaming, and at a certain point his pursuer gripped the pistol in both hands and aimed it at him, saying, 'I'm going to kill you.' I left the newborn and ran in terror to stop him." The kid, his head bloodied, was rescued in extremis and taken to the hospital. A large pool of blood was left at the entrance to the church, "blood infected with AIDS," the priest recalls. "We put on our gloves and began to clean it up."

Jorge has stepped across that threshold with its green wrought-iron door many times. The priest didn't have the courage to tell him that particular story, but the archbishop has heard many like it, in places with which he is perfectly familiar. It is not a world he has learned about on television. He knows the smells and the faces; they are a part of his life.

Drugs and violence are rooted in the shantytowns. The bosses of the criminal syndicates live elsewhere, in the upscale part of town. But the *peones* of the drug trade live here. This is the world of *paco*, a cheap street drug (five pesos or a bit more) obtained from a derivative of cocaine that "splits your brain," as they say in Buenos Aires. It creates dependency very quickly and is sold to adolescents as young as thirteen or fourteen or even younger. The parish priest sometimes feels the hard shape of a concealed handgun when these kids embrace him with affection at a funeral. They start by breaking into houses to get money to feed their habit and wind up as twitchy, aggressive perpetrators of muggings in broad daylight.

Drugs are a major problem because they lead to the use of firearms by minors. In 2009, the *curas villeros*, shantytown priests, took a provocative stance in the national debate on decriminalization, a policy option they fiercely reject. "In the shantytowns the liberalization and depenalization of drugs already exists de facto," they wrote. The problem isn't the slums, they said, but the drug trade that exploits them and grows rich off them. Their letter made a strong impression on public opinion. The reaction of the drug lords was immediate. "Disappear or you're a dead man" was the message delivered to Father Pepe Di Paola by a masked criminal who stopped him one April night in an alleyway in Villa-21.[6]

The archbishop was in full agreement with his priests about the drug trade and broadcast the same message. Two days later during a mass celebrated in the square in front of the cathedral, he publicly attacked the "powerful merchants in the shadows" and recounted the threat made to his priest. Father Pepe, the man behind the anti-decriminalization stance, felt that he and the other shantytown priests had cover: "I prefer to die myself rather than see them kill you," the archbishop told him. The narcotics traffickers did not carry out their threat, although Father Pepe was subsequently forced to leave Villa-21.

Descending into the tunnels of the subway or clambering onto buses clasping his black briefcase, Jorge bears the memory of all of it with him. He is not oblivious, not a fatalist. He is merely convinced that if he is to exercise his function as a "shepherd following his flock," then he cannot opt for the palatial residences, the official cars, the chauffeurs, and the armed escorts. He is aware that the drug traffickers will stop at nothing, not even an assault on a prince of the church. In 1993, the Mexican cardinal Juan Posadas Ocampo was assassinated at the Guadalajara airport in a massacre carried out by ruthless killers from the Tijuana cartel. The official investigation labeled the event a tragic coincidence, as though the cardinal had just happened to be in the wrong place at the wrong time as rival gangs were shooting it out. It later emerged that government insiders had warned Ocampo to keep his mouth shut about the ongoing collusion between the drug cartels and local politicians.

Archbishop Bergoglio has received warnings too. Some trade unionists alerted him in 2012 to be careful because there were groups who had it in for him, and perhaps it would be better not to go about the city on foot without an escort. "I'll never leave the streets" was his reply.[7] His reaction was the same when his priests in the shantytowns pointed out to him that there was a risk of being kidnapped.

Jorge has experienced both faces of the urban periphery: uncurbed violence and great humanity. He knows that in these chaotic agglomerations there are masses of simple folk, famished for a bit of hope, animated by solidarity, filled with intense popular devotion, happy on feast days. It is a lot easier to arrange a community meal in a shantytown, Father Pepe always maintains, than in a wealthy quarter of town. "The women cook, the men set the tables and chairs up, the kids act as voluntary helpers." Amid the gaping houses, endlessly under construction, where the state is an abstraction and the civil registry has always turned to the priests to find out who lives where, the parishes are centers of social assistance and the promotion of citizenship.

At Villa-21, people living in poverty come by in the early afternoon to pick up a bit of food: bread, something to go with it, and a piece of fruit, already prepared in little bags. Toto De Vedia, the parish priest who succeeded Father Pepe, receives everyone in a tiny room covered with photographs, reminders, and hand-written announcements. Two mobile phones, a perennial cup of *mate*, the fragrant and bitter national drink, an agenda filled with appointments. The procession never ends: mothers who come to pick up a school snack for their children, mothers in a panic because their sons have taken to drugs and to the street, mothers seeking a job for their daughters, youths trying to decide on a trade, a woman who needs a wheelchair. Someone wants to organize a festival in the seniors' residence; there are visits to be made to families and the sick, a supply of food to be arranged for persons with special needs, a mass to be celebrated in the nearby psychiatric hospital, a school to be constructed for the shantytown, confessions to hear, and yet more masses to celebrate.

In metropolitan Buenos Aires, the villas, for which the archbishop set up a dedicated vicariate, are not neighborhoods; they are small cities. Villa-21 has forty thousand inhabitants—"twenty-five or thirty acres," as Toto De Vedia puts it, "under no institutional control." On Archbishop Bergoglio's watch, the church has provided or sponsored institutions in the shantytowns to help dropouts complete secondary school, centers for seniors, antidrug centers, centers offering training for the job market. There are sports facilities to give kids something to do other than take drugs and after-hours activities at schools so that children are not abandoned to their own devices. The creation of the vicariate demonstrates the vital importance the archbishop assigns to pastoral activity in these zones.

Every time Jorge arrives at the outskirts, he witnesses the birth of new initiatives. When he gets off the regional train and walks at a slow pace toward the parish of Villa Ramón Carrillo, the most recent one he has created, he sees how an annex is slowly rising alongside the church, a place meant to serve as a meeting hall and center for after-school activities, job-training courses, and even a small pharmacy. The builders are a group of thirty university students working under a foreman, who arrive every Saturday from the city center. "A group of Jewish kids with their rabbi are helping too," explains one of the volunteers, Mechi Guinle. Even a shantytown dweller who is an evangelical Christian helps, using his truck. The members of his community, who have their own church and a couple of prayer houses, have no difficulty coexisting with the Catholic parish priest. In front of the church, a blue banner proclaims: "Mary, help us to believe that the impossible is possible."

Jorge feels at ease in these outlying shantytown parishes. They are houses of God that he has seen expand or has helped to create. For those who arrive from areas even more desolate, their local church becomes a focus of hope. In Villa-21, where many immigrants from Paraguay fetch up, the parish bears the name of the Virgin of

Caacupé. The church resembles a cement garage and overflows with statuettes of the Madonna, each with its own history and its own power of intercession, starting with the Virgin of Guadalupe. On the back wall, a large mural shows a festive crowd on a pilgrimage to the sanctuary of Caacupé. Then there is a round stained-glass window with the image of Jesus. And a large crucifix. And a statue of Christ pointing to his own pitying heart. And a painting of Don Bosco. And an image of Father Carlos Mugica, the intellectual priest of Villa-31 in the Retiro District, who was active in the Movement of Priests for the Third World and was assassinated in 1974 by the anti-Communist death squads of the AAA (Alianza Anticomunista Argentina). And a statue of Saint Roch with his dog. And in a corner behind the altar, a sort of grotto surrounded by colorful paper flowers, which shelters a Baby Jesus standing before the cross, with photos of members of the parish all around him.

Jorge warms to this outpouring of popular faith, smiles at the wooden plaque that records "the baptism of the church, performed on October 8, 2009, by the bishop, Father Jorge Mario Bergoglio." Jorge loves the sight of the women in silent prayer on the pews of the church while the children frolic in the space under the adjacent roof. He often tells his priests, "The church is not meant to control people, but to accompany them where they live." Before his arrival, priests who had a parish in the city would also be assigned some portion of the outskirts to look after. Now it is the opposite, he gives parish priests from the shantytowns a second parish in a middle-class quarter.

Already at the age of retirement, Jorge has no idea that his life is about to change. Everyone is "born" in unique circumstances. Karol Wojtyla was tempered in a clandestine theater movement in defiance of the Nazi occupation and by hard labor in a quarry and at the Solvay factory. Benedict XVI was formed in university lecture halls. Pius XII and Paul VI were schooled in the offices of the Vatican Secretariat of State. John XXIII came to maturity among the Orthodox Christians of Bulgaria and the Muslims of Turkey.

Jorge Mario Bergoglio is reborn in his trips on the subway, observing the innards of the city, measuring the distance from one tumbledown slum dwelling to the next with his steady tread.

2

Francis's Fear

I t was raining on the apostolic palace of the Vatican, and the air was saturated with humidity on the afternoon of Wednesday, 13 March 2013. St. Peter's Square was dotted with umbrellas. Everyone's gaze was trained on the Sistine Chapel, where 115 cardinal electors were choosing the successor to Benedict XVI.

A seagull alighted on the chimney from which the smoke would rise and remained there for hours. Seagulls bring to mind the vast expanse of the open sea. More prosaically, they have been descending on the eternal city for years, following the Tiber inland in search of food. At daybreak, Rome resounds with their squawking as though it were a seaport.

This conclave looked like a long one. Shortly before it began, the archbishop of Paris, Cardinal André Vingt-Trois, had spoken of "roughly half-a-dozen cardinals" who were still viable candidates.[1] At the head of the list was the archbishop of Milan, Angelo Scola, but a pope from Brazil or Canada or Hungary was not out of the question.

The crowd in the square waited, patient but tense. On the previous afternoon, Tuesday, 12 March, the solemn procession of cardinals clad in purple had wound its way into the Sistine Chapel. They swore themselves to maintain secrecy and "not ever to lend support or favor to any interference, opposition, or any other sort of intervention" on the part of secular authorities, groups, or individuals. "I promise, bind myself, and swear. Thus may God aid me and these Holy Gospels which I touch with my hand,"[2] each of the cardinals recited, and at 5:39 p.m. the papal master of ceremonies, Guido Marini, intoned the words, "Extra omnes" (Everybody out), and the great door to the chapel was bolted shut.

Inside there are no windows at eye level. The only apertures are set very high, just below the ceiling, and they had been covered over. In the large space dominated by Michelangelo's *Last Judgment*, the cardinals were seated in four rows, two on either side of the chapel, before long benches covered with red velvet. There was still a smell of fresh wood. The elegant chairs had cushions the color of champagne.

No other inner sanctum of power can stand comparison, not even the Kremlin or the Forbidden City at Peking. No emperor ruling countless subjects is elected with similarly sober yet mysterious rites in such a perfect hall, covered with such impressive frescoes. As Cardinal Angelo Bagnasco put it, "The impact, with the Christ of the Last Judgment, makes one shiver. When the door is closed, we are alone: we and Him."[3]

At each round of voting, every cardinal secretly writes the name he has chosen on a ballot, folds it to keep it private, and slowly strides to the end of the chapel. He walks past the reading stand bearing the Gospels and reaches the table of the presidency, on which stand the three urns of the conclave: one to receive the ballots as they are deposited, one for the ballots that have been counted, and one to be brought, if necessary, to any cardinal whose infirmities may have confined him to his bed.

Behind the table of the presidency stands the antique altar of marble, turned in the bygone manner to face the wall where Michelangelo's fresco blazes forth. There Benedict XVI deliberately celebrated a mass in Latin as an implicit challenge to those who opposed the ancient preconciliar rite, and there the ring signifying papal power slipped from his finger and rolled across the floor. A presage.

In the vestibule, which is bounded by a grating of marble and wrought iron, are located two stoves, a round one for burning the electoral ballots and a square one for the chemically prepared candles that will ensure brilliant white or dark black fumes.

The steps that separate the vestibule from the area where the cardinals are seated are covered with a ramp. Officially it is there to make things easier for elderly cardinals, but actually it conceals electronic equipment installed to detect any mobile phones or other communication devices that might be used to leak information to the outside world. Since the time of Paul VI, the latest technology has been used to ensure the absolute secrecy of the conclave. Electromagnetic waves are generated to block any transmission from the chapel and the adjacent area.

The seagull was still there, as if to suggest that there was not likely to be a plume of white smoke this day. After the first round of voting the previous evening, the smoke signal at 7:41 p.m. was black, as everyone expected: the first round serves the electors as a gauge of the forces in play.

This was a conclave of the undecided. It was they who would tip the balance in favor of the winner. Unlike in 2005, there was no clear front runner as Joseph Ratzinger had been after the death of John Paul II. At the time, Ratzinger was regarded as a distinguished theologian, a close collaborator of the Polish pope, a man of intellect with the capacity to engage with contemporary culture.

While the cardinals were voting, two young female militants from the protest movement Femen staged an event in St. Peter's Square. One of them had "No more pedophilia" written in large letters on her nude torso. That is how things went on the first day.

Wednesday morning, day two of the conclave, the chimney spouted dense black smoke at 11:40 a.m., a sign that the second and third rounds of voting had not produced a result. There were 115 electors, of whom a two-thirds majority, or 77, were needed for victory. Many observers thought that it would take three days to reach agreement on what course the church should set and who should take the helm, as it had for Ratzinger, or something like the eight rounds of voting it took to bring Karol Wojtyla to the pontifical throne. But the papal spokesman, Federico Lombardi, let slip a sibylline utterance: "Possibly in the next few hours we will have the election of the successor."[4]

The afternoon passed slowly. It is when they pause to take lunch in the Santa Marta residence that discreet conversations take place among the cardinal electors. Veiled invitations are issued to abandon one candidacy, allusive hints given that another *papabile* is gaining momentum, rapid computations made about whether to "park" a chunk of votes temporarily with a certain name, last-minute requests for information about a fellow cardinal advanced. A conclave is always an inextricable mixture of spirituality, strategy, religious inspiration, and skill at tactical maneuver. There are the "king makers"—or in this case pope makers—and there are the great consiglieri who can channel votes one way or another.

Cardinal Bagnasco remembered the atmosphere at lunch on Wednesday as being very relaxed. "I didn't detect any urgency to achieve a result as soon as possible." And yet beneath the surface, tectonic plates were shifting. A few cardinals expert at sniffing the breezes that blow through the curia did get a feeling of gathering momentum as the meal ended. Cardinal Antonio Maria Vegliò, who until a few hours earlier had thought a rapid outcome unlikely, suddenly felt certain that one was near: "In the conclave I felt like a pen in the hand of God."[5]

Between the second and third votes that morning, Bergoglio had taken the lead, receiving more than fifty votes.[6] The previous evening his compatriot Cardinal Leonardo Sandri, once his fellow seminary student at Buenos Aires and now prefect of the Congregation for the Oriental Churches, had tried to hearten him: "Prepare yourself, my dear fellow." Seated in the midst of his fellow diners at lunch, Bergoglio felt extremes of emotion: a great and unaccountable feeling of peace along with a "total darkness, a profound obscurity about everything else."[7]

In the forecourt of the Vatican basilica, the afternoon passed slowly, but at around 6:00 p.m. there was a ripple of nervous excitement. The crowd in the piazza realized that a fourth round of voting had failed to yield a winner. At the start of the day, a portion of the electorate had not yet made up their minds. Cardinal Donald Wuerl of Washington, D.C., had forecast earlier that "the conclave will not be short . . . no clear choice of candidate has yet emerged."[8]

From 6:30 on, the crowd grew increasingly restless. With every minute that passed, the feeling grew that a positive outcome was imminent. Under a livid sky, a spotlight illuminated the chimney atop the Sistine Chapel. And then, at 7:06 p.m., a puff of gray smoke appeared, gradually turning white as snow. A roar went up from the crowd, followed by an unnatural silence as everyone held their breath waiting to hear the name of the person elected. The tension rose again as the minutes passed and nothing happened.

The wait was long, extremely long. Tens of thousands of the faithful and the curious, clustered under umbrellas, peered at the balcony of the basilica, waiting for the curtains to be drawn back for the announcement of the new pope. Guesses abounded. The conclave, contrary to predictions, had been very short, virtually a bolt of lightning. Among the observers, some took this as a sign that the winner was Scola.

The patriarch of Milan, before that of Venice, had gone into the conclave propelled by a strong wave of organized support. He was credited with between thirty-five and forty votes from the outset. Scola is a pastor, an organizer, an intellectual engaged in dialogue with the Orthodox and the Islamic worlds through a journal he founded, *Oasis*, and a former rector of the Pontifical Lateran University. Scola was identified with the vision of the church and the world propounded by Benedict XVI. He and Joseph Ratzinger had collaborated on the journal *Communio*, founded to combat the progressive reformism of the theologians of Vatican II, represented in turn by the trimestral journal *Concilium*. As pope, Ratzinger had transferred Scola from the patriarchal see of Venice to the archiepiscopal see of Milan, where, as head of the largest diocese in Europe, he enjoyed high visibility, but many Catholics muttered under their breath that this transfer—which Scola had not requested—had had the effect of diminishing the patriarchal see.

On the Sunday before the conclave, the *Corriere della Sera* came out with the headline "Hope for an Italian Pontiff." The undertone seemed to be that the election of the archbishop of Milan (home city of the *Corriere*) would amount to a providential national redemption and, for the church, a beneficial resolution of the crisis of the Ratzinger papacy. With these hopes in mind, the adherents of Comunione e Liberazione, a Catholic activist movement in which Cardinal Scola had matured, turned out in massive numbers at Rome.

What the crowd in the square did not yet know was that in the Sistine Chapel there had occurred a startling upsurge of votes in favor of Jorge Mario Bergoglio, archbishop of Buenos Aires.

The swell of support was not halted even by an incident that had occurred during the fourth round of voting in the afternoon, when an aged cardinal had mistakenly placed two ballots in the urn. The vote was annulled when the count revealed that there was one more ballot than there were voters, and the electors immediately voted again. Bergoglio had started with twenty or so votes on day one, but his tally had risen steadily with each round of voting, and he was elected with an avalanche of ninety votes,[9] many more than the seventy-seven required and more than the eighty-four votes received by Joseph Ratzinger in 2005.[10] "It was like a tap that kept on opening," one cardinal confided.

In that previous conclave from which Benedict XVI had emerged the winner, Bergoglio had been a protagonist, prominent among the reform-minded cardinals. Their leader, Cardinal Carlo Maria Martini, had not been in contention himself, for he was crippled by Parkinson's disease, the same malady that had ended the life of John Paul II. At the third round of voting in 2005, there had been a total of forty votes for Bergoglio, seventy-two for Ratzinger.[11]

At that point, Bergoglio, unwilling to act as point man for the anti-Ratzinger group to the bitter end, had withdrawn, making way for the German cardinal, who then headed the Congregation for the Doctrine of the Faith. And Bergoglio had been touched by fear. In any case, the internal balance of power in the conclave of 2005 gave him little or no chance.

This time he had not envisaged entering the lists again. Embarking on the Alitalia flight from Buenos Aires to Rome on 26 February 2013, the Argentine cardinal had taken his place in row 26, close to the exit, to have a little more room for his legs. To the friends who had sounded him out about his plans before leaving, he had repeated: "Don't worry. There exists not the slightest possibility of my being elected pope."[12] Yet there were those in Argentina who believed the opposite. Father Alejandro Russo, rector of the cathedral of Buenos Aires, had said to Bergoglio before his departure: "When in the conclave you hear 'most eminent Bergoglio 75,' 'most eminent Bergoglio 76,' 'most eminent Bergoglio 77,' and the applause breaks out, remember what I said."[13] Another member of his staff had confided while saying good-bye, "Perhaps your time has come."[14] Bergoglio didn't think so and replied evasively. Yet in the uncertain period following the resignation of Benedict XVI, he let slip a remark while speaking to a lawyer he knew: "If I were elected, I'd know what to do."

Now, on 13 March 2013, Cardinal Giovanni Battista Re, president of the conclave, was asking him if he accepted his election. Bergoglio answered yes without hesitation, and he added in Latin: "Vocabor Franciscus in memoriam sancti Francisci de Assisi" (I will be called Francis in memory of Saint Francis of Assisi). Still, one participant in the conclave recalls that "only at the last minute did he fully grasp that his election had become a reality."

"During the voting Bergoglio was seated in the front row on his side," recalls another cardinal, "and he wore a serious look, a serene but serious look." A number of cardinal electors were themselves surprised at how unexpectedly their conclave had ended: "At the moment of the decisive vote, we felt joy. The rapidity gave us a sense of relief . . . it wasn't pre-programmed."

No sooner had Bergoglio uttered the name he would take, added another witness, than there was a shiver. "It ran through the rows of men in purple like an electric charge. We realized that we were present at a spiritual turning point. 'Francis' signifies the cross, joy, poverty." Bergoglio himself recounted the crucial moment of the conclave for the benefit of a gathering of journalists: "At the election I had the archbishop emeritus of São Paulo next to me . . . a dear, dear friend. When things were getting a little 'dangerous,' he comforted me. And then, when the votes reached the two-thirds, there was the usual applause because the pope had been elected. He hugged me and said: 'Do not forget the poor.' And that word stuck here [tapping his forehead]; the poor, the poor. Then, immediately in relation to the poor I thought of Francis of Assisi. Then I thought of war, while the voting continued, until all the votes [were counted]. And so the name came to my heart: Francis of Assisi."[15]

In his heart, the newly elected pope also bears another word: *misericordia* ("mercy" or "compassion" in Spanish and Italian). On the first day of the conclave, the German cardinal Walter Kasper, who had recently published a little book entitled *Barmherzigkeit*, made him a gift of the Spanish translation, *La misericordia*. "This is the name of our God. Without mercy we are lost!" Bergoglio exclaimed.

While the conclave was still in session, Francis made his first departures from the traditional rules. In changing his clothing after his election, he rejected the long shirt of white linen called a rochet, the red mozzetta (an elbow-length garment) that goes over it, and the stole. He refused the cross of gold and retained his own iron cross. He demanded to wear only the white papal tunic, known as a cassock or soutane, which John Paul II had transformed into a symbol recognized worldwide.

Wearing the pontifical vestments (liturgical garments), Francis received the homage of obedience from the cardinals while standing rather than sitting on the papal throne. He declined to receive genuflections. "He preferred the embrace," one cardinal noted expressly. But the first thing he did, spotting the wheelchair of the Indian cardinal Ivan Dias sitting in a corner of the Sistine Chapel, was to advance and embrace him.

"May God forgive you" is how Bergoglio vented his feelings to the cardinals who had just elected him, an expression now virtually classic that was uttered by Albino Luciani upon being elected Pope John Paul I.

Before stepping out onto the balcony of the basilica, Francis was suddenly overcome with perturbation, dizziness almost. His state of mind had swung from one extreme to another during the past few hours. Leaving the Sistine Chapel, he passed through the files of cardinals, "looking neither to right nor to left . . . his eyes were lowered, his expression was grave, he did not smile or speak, as though he were bearing an enormous weight," testified Monsignor Dario Viganò, the director of the Vatican television center. He emerged, walked a short distance, and entered the Pauline Chapel, where a sort of scaled-down throne with a kneeling stool had been set up for him. But instead of using it, Bergoglio halted at the last pew, took Cardinal Jean-Louis Tauran and the vicar of Rome, Agostino Vallini, by the arms and drew them to him. Kneeling, he began to pray, "as though he were settling accounts with himself before God."[16]

It was a lengthy prayer. "My head was completely empty and I was seized by a great anxiety," Bergoglio would later confess to Eugenio Scalfari. "To make it go away and relax I closed my eyes and made every thought disappear, even the thought of refusing to accept the position, as the liturgical procedure allows. I closed my eyes and I no longer had any anxiety or emotion. At a certain point I was filled with a great light. It lasted a moment, but to me it seemed very long."[17] After the prayer, Viganò confirms, "he stood up, and he was a different man from that moment on."

In the conclave of 2005, one veteran cardinal recalled, Bergoglio had felt uneasy about his own opposition to Ratzinger, whom he esteemed. And he had felt unprepared to be pope. "Now he was ready," said one of his collaborators from Buenos Aires, who had observed him upon his return from that conclave. "In 2005, he felt summoned by God but was fearful. Now it was like in the Bible, when the Lord calls to a prophet for a second time."

Outside, in Saint Peter's Square, the crowd was at the end of its tether. But they had to wait a little longer while Bergoglio telephoned his predecessor, whom he failed to reach because nobody at the other end heard the telephone ringing: Benedict XVI was glued to the television. Finally, the windows of the balcony were flung open, and the cardinal deacon Jean-Louis Tauran appeared. "Habemus papam," he said with a French accent: "Georgium Marium Sanctae Romanae Ecclesiae cardinalem Bergoglio." The crowd applauded with joy, but the ovation was tempered by uncertainty about the individual in question. Who exactly was "Bergoglio"?

But as soon as Tauran proclaimed the name "Francesco," the piazza emitted a thunderous roar. Everyone knew who Francesco d'Assisi was: he was the *poverello* (the man of humility and poverty), a potent symbol for believers and nonbelievers alike. As the windows of the balcony closed again, the rhythmic chanting started in the piazza below: "Francesco . . . Francesco . . . Francesco."

The first pope from the New World is an Argentine Jesuit whose family emigrated from Piedmont in northern Italy. Never before has a pontiff of Rome taken the name "Francis," a name that signifies the opposite of majesty and power. Nor, right from the start, did he allow the curia to attach a regnal number to his name, as the courts of kings and emperors do. He insisted on being called simply "Francis," not "Francis I."

It was after 8:00 p.m. when Pope Francis finally appeared on the balcony of St. Peter's, pale and undemonstrative, his face serious and curious, framed by eyeglasses, his gaze directed down at the immense bowl of boiling humanity, his right hand barely raised. With a few words, he cast aside the style used by popes for countless centuries. "Buona sera" (good evening) was his greeting, his left hand thrust out as though to touch the crowd. He offered prayers and thanks and requested the prayers of the crowd for him. He was as human as Michel Piccoli in the film *Habemus papam* (We have a pope), as unruffled as a neighborhood parish priest, a contemporary among contemporaries. He referred to the cardinals who had "gone to the ends of the earth" to find and elect him as "brothers," not *signori cardinali* (lord cardinals) or *eminentissimi* (men of the utmost eminence), as Ratzinger and Wojtyla had done. He never qualified himself as "the pontiff."

His first gesture was a Pater-Ave-Gloria (a form of prayer based on the Marian rosary) for "our Bishop Emeritus Benedict XVI." Tens of thousands of men and women prayed aloud with him in the evening darkness, thronged together in the embrace of the Bernini colonnade. "I thank you for your welcome," he said simply.[18]

But the gesture that startled the crowd and transfixed television viewers all over the world was the words he uttered slowly, in a calm, low voice, and with no attempt to charm his hearers, before imparting the benediction *Urbi et Orbi*: "And now I would like to give the blessing, but first . . . first I ask a favor of you: before the Bishop blesses his people, I ask you to pray to the Lord that he will bless me . . . the prayer of the people asking the blessing for their Bishop. Let us make, in silence, this prayer: your prayer over me."[19] A dramatic silence fell on Saint Peter's Square. "I got goose bumps," one priest recalls.

That is how Francis was born as pope. The fear that had gripped him before he strode out into public view and began his reign dissolved. "I like the new pope very much," said a young believer from Germany, the country that had shown its dislike of the previous pope, its own native son. A priest from northern Europe, watching the television screen, recounted the sensation he felt that "a man had appeared down there at the Vatican who was actually like a priest, someone close to members of the priesthood, with their worries and hopes and daily routines." Elsewhere, ordinary believers burst into tears before their television sets.

An Umbrian pilgrim, seeing the new pope enfold a sick man, his body rigid and twisted, in an embrace on the following Sunday and hearing him say in closing, "Have a good lunch," put it this way: "When he said 'good evening,' he put himself on our level. In clasping the flesh of the handicapped, he participates in the pain we all feel. When he wishes us a good lunch, he shows he understands that for many people it is a struggle to put food on the table." "People are breathing again," a Milanese priest remarked.

The nuncio to Venezuela, Pietro Parolin, soon to become the new secretary of state, registered the sudden change of atmosphere: "From a church almost under siege, with a thousand problems . . . that seemed a bit unwell, we have gone to being a church that has opened itself up."[20] Since that day, 13 March 2013, Francis has held his place in the public imagination. Eight years after the death of John Paul II, a pope who can win the hearts and minds of contemporaries has returned to the world stage.

At Castel Gandolfo, a white-haired man, his face haggard and aged, was watching the appearance of the new pope on television. He was Joseph Ratzinger, the pope emeritus. Without him, this election could not have taken place. When he abdicated, the former secretary of Karol Wojtyla, Cardinal Stanislaus Dziwisz, had said, "One doesn't climb down off the cross" of the papacy. As though Ratzinger were somehow a deserter.

That is not the case. Benedict XVI didn't flee. Joseph Ratzinger performed a valiant act that forced open the portals to the future.

3

The Coup d'État of Benedict XVI

Without Ratzinger, we would not have Francis. If Benedict XVI had not resigned, Catholicism would not have reached the historical turning point of choosing a pope from the New World.

On 11 February 2013, during a routine consistory dedicated to the canonization of the eight hundred martyrs of Otranto, reputedly killed by the Turks for refusing to convert to Islam, Benedict XVI abdicated. That evening a spectacular bolt of lightning struck the tip of the cupola of Saint Peter's, a remarkable symbol of an extraordinary event. "A gesture of that kind," admitted the somewhat shaken German cardinal Joachim Meisner, "exceeded the reach of my imagination."[1]

Paul Poupard, a French cardinal who presided for many years over the Pontifical Council for Culture, commented in retrospect: "The shock of the brief pontificate of John Paul I, which lasted thirty days, drove the conclave of 1978 to end the run of Italian popes that had lasted for half a millennium. The shock of the resignation of Benedict XVI gave the cardinal electors the courage to look beyond the ocean."[2]

The eventuality of resignation, maintains Giovanni Maria Vian, church historian and director of the Vatican newspaper *L'Osservatore Romano*, existed in the mind of Pope Ratzinger from the moment he was elected. The earliest signs can be detected in the encyclical *Deus caritas est*, signed on 25 December 2005, barely eight months after he took the throne. Those who are "instruments" in the hands of the Lord, the German pontiff states, will not think of acting in isolation. "It is God who governs the world, not we. We offer him our service only to the extent that we can, and for as long as he grants us the strength."[3] Even as a cardinal, Ratzinger had confronted the possibility. In 2002, as the Parkinson's disease afflicting John Paul II worsened, he had commented: "If the pope [Wojtyla] saw that he was absolutely unable to carry on, then he would certainly resign."[4]

Even earlier, when commemorating the late Paul VI in 1978, Archbishop Ratzinger, as he then was, recalled that, at his seventy-fifth birthday and again at his eightieth, Pope Montini had "struggled intensely with the notion of retiring." And the future German pope had permitted himself some reflections destined to reemerge when he himself ascended the throne of Peter: "We can imagine how heavily it must burden the mind . . . no longer to have a private moment. To be riveted to the end, while one's own body gives out, to a task that demands, day after day, the full and vigorous exercise of all a man's strength."[5]

The idea, almost haunting, of the fatigue of being pope as old age encroaches accompanied Benedict XVI constantly. At no time did Joseph Ratzinger desire the papacy; he did not try to build an electoral base and submitted to the yoke only from a sense of duty. Cardinal Poupard, an elector in 2005, recalls that "as the decisive votes were counted in the conclave, Ratzinger had a despondent smile." To him the event was "like the blade of a guillotine coming down on you," and at the crucial moment he cried out to the Lord: "If you wanted me, then you must also help me."[6]

Joseph Ratzinger is a tragic figure. Beneath his apparently cool comportment, his diffidence at coming into contact with the crowd, there lies concealed a tender and timid personality of great delicacy, endowed with a sense of humor and that fundamentally cheerful temperament that is characteristic of southern Germany. He is a person of "disarming simplicity and rare sensitivity," able to "build relationships without ever making his interlocutor feel ill at ease," recalls his secretary Alfred Xuereb, who remains in the service of Pope Francis.

It is true that as prefect of the Congregation for the Doctrine of the Faith, Ratzinger gave reformist theologians a hard time. But as pontiff his aim was to testify to a faith lived joyously, an expression of love for God and for one's neighbor, not the application of a heap of prohibitions. A faith that abandons no one in the deserts of life and steers persons who are lost "towards friendship with the Son of God."[7] To restore Christ to the center of Christian existence was the objective of his pontificate because God "has not withdrawn into his heavenly dwelling place, looking down at humanity from on high," he is a *tu* (you) with whom a relationship is possible, a real face "visible in Jesus Christ."[8] A few days before resigning, Benedict XVI returned again to the concept that constituted the core of his mission: "The desire . . . to see God's face, is innate in every human being, even in atheists . . . we unconsciously have this wish simply to see who he is . . . who he is for us . . . this desire is fulfilled in following Christ."[9]

His was a dramatic pontificate. Ratzinger, a great theologian, thinker, and preacher, was chained despite himself to the command post of an organization that includes more than 1.2 billion men and women on five continents. Benedict XVI was torn between his responsibilities and an incapacity to master the art of governing, hampered by an absence of collaborators who might have helped him to marry his intellectual gifts to a robust knowledge of the Vatican machinery and of contemporary reality in its manifold aspects. The end phase of his reign saw a church "turned in on itself and prey to desperation," was the assessment of the historian Andrea Riccardi.[10] The historical turn that Francis's election represents is only comprehensible against the background of the arc followed by Benedict XVI and the limitations inherent in the triumphal parade of John Paul II.

Karol Wojtyla interpreted the safeguarding of Catholic identity in dynamic fashion. He did not so much defend the faith as affirm its relevance in the present. He was a geopolitical pope who intuited the process of globalization. His voyages, which at the outset might have been seen as a species of frenetic religious tourism, revived the sense of unity in the church and reinforced the links between the papacy and the far reaches of the Catholic empire. Wojtyla presented himself as the spokesman of human rights, overriding all cultural, religious, and sociopolitical boundaries. He launched a dialogue with the other great forms of monotheism, entering the synagogue of Rome and the mosque of Damascus to cement belief in the One God and to combat religiously based fundamentalism and terrorism.

After the collapse of the Soviet Union and the liberation of his Polish homeland, John Paul II denounced the hegemonic isolation of the United States and fiercely attacked the unfettered capitalism that was corroding the world economy. Gravely ill, he led a diplomatic and religious mobilization against the invasion of Iraq by President George W. Bush, which he assessed prophetically—and subsequent events have proven him right—as a political and humanitarian catastrophe.

Not that there weren't darker sides to John Paul II's papacy. There was the attempt to file and forget the accusations against the founder of the Legionaries of Christ, Marcial Maciel, who was guilty of grave sexual offenses; the repression of liberation theology and innovative theological research; the nomination of bishops whose distinguishing feature was their loyalty; the refusal to allow communion for the divorced and remarried; the refusal to consider a fresh approach to matters of sexuality; the absence of any critical thinking about the crisis of vocations; the continued confinement of women to ancillary roles in the church, notwithstanding fine words in public about the "female genius."

Three major signals directed to the future remain from the Wojtyla pontificate. One was the convocation at Assisi in 1986 of religious leaders from around the world to hold a common prayer for peace—a respectful recognition of the dignity of all human beings and their resort to the divinity in accordance with their own traditions. Another was the famous mea culpa, in the Jubilee Year 2000, for the errors and horrors committed by the church in the course of centuries. Finally, there was the encyclical *Ut unum sint* of 1995, in which for the first time in history a pontiff invited the leaders of the Christian churches to work together on revising the role of the Roman pontiff in light of an eventual ecumenical reconciliation.

After John Paul II, there was stagnation. Joseph Ratzinger adopted a defensive stance vis-à-vis Christian identity, summoning up the image of a church besieged by a swarm of specters: relativism, materialism, libertinism, syncretism, nihilism, consumerism, atheism, individualism, agnosticism, laicism, secularism. The faith, he endlessly proclaimed, is threatened by a context that "tends to delete God from the horizon of life and does not . . . help one to discern good from evil."[11] In his thinking, Western society (with which he was principally concerned) is conspiring to reduce religion to the private sphere.[12]

These ideas hardened into incontestable maxims, the so-called nonnegotiable principles that Catholic laity who were members of legislatures anywhere in the world were in theory obligated to observe: the inviolability of life from conception to natural termination, the indissolubility of matrimony between a man and a woman, freedom of education (or in other words the duty of the state to finance Catholic schools). And some national episcopates, especially the Italian Episcopal Conference, did wield these arms in political debate in their countries.

In the area of liturgy, Benedict XVI propounded a recovery of the sense of the sacred and of ritual mystery, which translated into the full equivalency between the postconciliar mass and the former Tridentine mass, in which the laity are reduced to a passive flock. In pontifical ceremonial, there was a return to paraments (elaborate robes and liturgical hangings) and other objects from the past. Paul VI's processional cross, with Christ hanging in agony, disappeared from view. The imposing miters of Pius IX returned to favor, and in consistories the lofty papal throne, which John Paul II had eliminated as anachronistic, reappeared. Postconciliar reformism came under fire, accused of having interpreted the documents of Vatican II in such a way as to "break" with tradition.

But it was in the area of church government that the Ratzinger pontificate really went down a blind alley. The crescendo of incidents is striking. A year after his election, Benedict XVI provoked a conflict with the Islamic world by an imprudent quotation regarding Mohammed. With Judaism, there was more than one crisis: for revoking the excommunication of the Lefebvrist bishop Richard Williamson, an anti-Semite and Holocaust denier; then for the new Holy Friday prayer in the Tridentine mass, with its allusion to the need for the Jews to convert; and lastly for his veneration of Pius XII. With international health organizations, Benedict XVI clashed over the use of condoms, which according to the pope "aggravated" the problem of AIDS. With the Catholic faithful, there was a split over concessions made to the scismatic movement of Bishop Marcel Lefebvre, which rejects the fundamental documents of Vatican II on religious liberty, freedom of conscience, ecumenism, and relations with Judaism and Islam.

Then there was the explosion in 2010 of revelations about sexual abuse perpetrated by the clergy in the United States, Ireland, Belgium, Germany, and Austria, accompanied by documented allegations to the effect that for years the Vatican had suppressed evidence of this violence and had tolerated the transfer of pedophile priests from one parish to another. The scandal grazed the person of Ratzinger directly on account of his position as archbishop of Munich from 1977 to 1982. He had harbored a pedophile priest, Peter Hullermann, at diocesan headquarters for a period of therapy, but after a few weeks Hullermann had been given a new pastoral assignment, and in 1986 he was convicted once again of sexual abuse.

The year 2010 was the watershed of the Ratzinger pontificate. Advanced age—he was over eighty-three by this point—had sapped his strength, and he came to realize that to remain at the helm was beyond him. His heart was under increasing stress (he had had a pacemaker for some time to combat a chronic atrial fibrillation[13]), his left eye was causing him problems, and getting about on foot was more of a challenge every day. In July 2009, while getting out of bed in the middle of the night, Benedict XVI fell and broke his right wrist in his vacation residence in Val d'Aosta.

But his physical state was not the sharpest thorn in the pope's side: it was problems of church government. The secretary of state, Cardinal Tarcisio Bertone, had shown himself incapable of establishing a productive working relationship with the Roman Curia. Its members accused him of being a centralizer, of not knowing the inner workings of the bureaucracy and lacking diplomatic experience, and of behaving as though he were vice pope and being too much of an improviser.

Cardinals Christoph Schönborn, Angelo Scola, Angelo Bagnasco, and Camillo Ruini requested that Bertone be replaced.[14] The same suggestion reached the pope from a personal friend as well, Cardinal Joachim Meisner, following the media catastrophe of the Williamson case: "Holy Father, you have to dismiss Cardinal Bertone! He bears responsibility, exactly like a minister in a secular government." But Ratzinger, loyal to his collaborators, refused, repeating emphatically: "Enough, enough, enough! . . . Bertone stays!"[15] But the attempt to silence the critics was not enough. Benedict XVI became aware that his pontificate could not go on like this. During 2010, he confided to his biographer Peter Seewald (and authorized the publication of his words in a book) that in the presence of danger "one cannot flee." One may, however, resign "in a moment of serenity, or when one is simply unable to carry on." Indeed, if a pope comes to the conclusion that he is no longer able "for physical, psychic, or mental reasons" to discharge the task entrusted to him, then he has the right and in certain cases even "the duty to resign."[16]

The year before, visiting Aquila, Italy, to console the victims of the earthquake there in 2009, Benedict XVI performed a discrete and symbolic gesture. He left his papal pallium on the tomb of Celestine V, the medieval pope who famously did resign.[17]

During the relative calm of 2011, Joseph Ratzinger gave firmer shape to his intentions. A few hints were dropped. Antonio Socci, a journalist with ties to the organization Comunione e Liberazione, wrote in September that the pope "does not discount the possibility of resigning at the turn of his eighty-fifth year," which would fall in 2012.[18] The article was reposted at the Salesians' website with expressions of alarm: a resignation "would be disastrous in our view."[19] But few were disposed to credit something so unheard of. Benedict said to Cardinal Jean-Louis Tauran, who was promoted in February 2011 to the post of cardinal protodeacon, "You will announce the new pope." Dumbfounded, the French cardinal replied, "No, for the love of God."[20]

While on a journey to Mexico and Cuba in March 2012, Benedict XVI fell during the night in his lodging in the Mexican city of León and cut his head. The wound was not deep, but he lost a great deal of blood. The fact was kept secret, and the papal skullcap hid the swelling, but the pope's personal physician, Dr. Patrizio Polisca, opposed any more intercontinental journeys by the pope.[21] And, indeed, his subsequent visit to Lebanon was his last such voyage.

Back at the Vatican, Ratzinger made an irrevocable decision to leave the papal throne. It was an epochal choice, one destined to change the course of Bergoglio's pontificate and those yet to come. Never in the history of the Catholic Church had a pope resigned of his own free will. Those who had left the throne of Saint Peter had always been forced off it at the will of the Roman emperors of late antiquity or as a result of political and religious confrontations like the one in the fifteenth century that resulted in three competing popes and antipopes abdicating at the Council of Constance. Even Celestine V, the most famous of all because of the scorn his deed earned him from Dante, withdrew under pressure. After reigning for less than four months (29 August to 13 December 1294) he was overwhelmed by political and ecclesiastical intrigues, and on the morrow of his abdication was imprisoned until his death by his ambitious successor, Boniface VIII.

Joseph Ratzinger's decision to resign was utterly different. It was not compelled; it was not influenced by emotion; and it was not even the result of excessive physical frailty. It was the upshot of a precise line of reasoning. Benedict XVI wanted to sweep the board clear of all the entrenched positions of power in the curia. By resigning, he triggered the automatic resignation, as stipulated by canon law, of the other principal office holders of the church's central government. De facto, his decision to abdicate amounted to a sort of coup d'état, a virtual "reboot" of the Vatican.

Ratzinger knew that for more than half a century the possibility of a papal abdication had been floating about the Vatican. Pius XII had contemplated doing so, fearing that he might be taken prisoner by the Germans, and so had Paul VI. John Paul II had assessed the hypothesis, setting up a secret panel to study all its aspects. In the end, he chose not to abdicate, making the passion of Christ the model for his own continued suffering instead and not wishing to set a "dangerous precedent," as his former secretary Cardinal Stanislaus Dziwisz put it.[22]

Ratzinger overcame this hesitation. The explosion in 2012 of the enormous scandal of the Vatican leaks only confirmed him in his intention. The leaked documents made the disorder and the paralysis prevailing in the Vatican public knowledge. Letters from Monsignor Carlo Maria Viganò, the secretary-general of the governorate (executive organ) of Vatican City, to Cardinal Bertone, the secretary of state, were splashed across the international media. Readers learned of accusations of corruption in the letting of contracts inside the pontifical city-state to the tune of hundreds of millions of euros. In response, Bertone fired Viganò and sent him to Washington, D.C., as nuncio. The secretary of state was also engaged in a contest with the cardinal of Milan, Dionigi Tettamanzi, for control of the Catholic University and the Gemelli Medical Center. Cardinal Attilio Nicora, president of the Financial Information Authority, which was charged with inspecting movements of currency inside the Vatican, clashed with Bertone because the policy that such movements should be transparent was being overridden. Ettore Gotti Tedeschi, president of the Istituto per le Opere di Religione (IOR, Institute for the Works of Religion)—otherwise known as the Vatican Bank—and a friend of Pope Benedict, was initially urged to clean up the operation but was then spied on, blocked when he attempted to submit the bank's books to an audit by accountants from Deloitte, and finally driven ignominiously from his post.[23]

What had come to light within the church's central government was a "tangle of crows and vipers," Cardinal Bertone was later to exclaim.[24] Spokespersons tried in vain to reduce the scandal to a case of document theft on the part of Paolo Gabriele, the papal majordomo, who was convicted and then pardoned. Nobody inside the Vatican believed that such a catastrophe could be the work of a "lone gunman."

For the first time since becoming pontiff, Benedict XVI adopted a well-planned strategy. He set up a special investigative committee of three cardinals, all of them more than eighty years old—Julián Herranz, Salvatore De Giorgi, Jozef Tomko—to sift through the Vatican offices and consign to him a secret report three hundred pages long. It laid everything bare: the careerist maneuvering and power seeking that was going on in the Vatican, the profit seeking, the sexual irregularities of a certain number of prelates. Benedict XVI, whose own papacy had begun with a denunciation of "dirt" in the church, felt disgust.

Meanwhile, he had started to let a small circle of persons in on his plans. They included his brother Georg and his private secretary, Monsignor Georg Gänswein, who reacted with consternation: "No, Holy Father, it's not possible." But the time for debate had passed. "It felt like being stabbed," Gänswein recalls. Outsiders suspected nothing. Only a bishop who was a veteran of Vatican II, Monsignor Luigi Bettazzi, confronted with the appearance of a singular document regarding a conspiracy to damage the pontiff, prophesied: "I think that Benedict XVI feels great weariness . . . and faced with the tensions that exist inside the curia, he might consider resigning and letting the next pope deal with these things."[25]

Toward the end of 2012, Benedict XVI had his strategy in place. In October, he ordered work to start on the renovation of the Mater Ecclesiae convent, a shelter for cloistered nuns that John Paul II had created within Vatican City. It was to be his residence as pope emeritus. Meanwhile, the preparation of the *Annuario Pontificio*, the annual papal directory, was delayed for unexplained reasons.

On 11 October 2012, Benedict XVI inaugurated a Year of Faith, knowing that he would not be there when it ended. In November, he created six new cardinals, none of them Italian or even European. They were the American James Harvey, prefect of the papal household; the Latin American Rubén Salazar Gómez, archbishop of Bogotá; the African John Onaiyekan, archbishop of the Nigerian capital Abuja; the Arab Béchara Räi, Maronite patriarch of Lebanon; the Indian Baselios Thottunkal, major archbishop of the Syro-Malankara Catholic Church; and the Filipino Luis Tagle, archbishop of Manila.

The storm of the Vatican leaks gave Benedict XVI a stronger hand to play. Compulsory resignation en masse would strip the Bertone clan and the other curial factions of their influence. Power would revert to the sole organ the Catholic Church possesses where one man/one vote is the rule and the will of the majority is sovereign: the conclave. And in the conclave the worldwide episcopate would be strongly represented. The right man with the best plan for the future would be chosen by cardinal electors from "outside." Abdication by the reigning pontiff would make possible the free and open debate, unconstrained by the papal monarchy, for which the church was yearning.

The date 11 February 2013 was a Monday. In the apostolic palace, the cardinals were meeting with the pope in consistory for the case of the martyrs of Otranto. Everything had been organized with military precision. The dean of the College of Cardinals, Angelo Sodano, had been warned the previous Friday so he could prepare a brief speech in reply to Benedict XVI's announcement. Also in the know were the secretary of state, Bertone, and his deputy, Monsignor Giovanni Angelo Becciu. An alert had been given to those in the Holy See principally concerned with journalism: the papal spokesman Federico Lombardi and the director of the *Osservatore Romano* newspaper, Giovanni Maria Vian.

Consistories of this kind are habitually attended only by the cardinals present in Rome and those who may be visiting. The meetings are routine, and this one too unfolded routinely until the end, when Benedict XVI put on his glasses, picked up a sheet of paper, and began reading from it in Latin. "He's going to resign now," whispered Sodano to the cardinal next to him.

Seated on the grandiose papal throne, wearing the red mozzetta lined with ermine and the stole embroidered with gold, a pallid Ratzinger read out his abdication in a low, restrained voice, his tone monotonous, almost scholastic, and at times imperceptible. Beside him, the master of ceremonies, Guido Marini, maintained an impassive gaze, while a little farther away another prelate was directing perplexed looks at the pontiff.

The unthinkable was happening. In full awareness before God, Benedict XVI read rapidly, "I have come to the certainty that my strengths, due to an advanced age, are no longer suited to an adequate exercise of the Petrine ministry." Although the mission of the pontiff is essentially spiritual in nature, the pope explained, "in today's world, subject to so many rapid changes and shaken by questions of deep relevance for the life of faith, in order to govern the bark of Saint Peter and proclaim the Gospel, both strength of mind and body are necessary, strength which in the last few months, has deteriorated in me to the extent that I have had to recognize my incapacity to adequately fulfill the ministry entrusted to me."[26] In the meeting hall of the consistory, the row of cardinals in purple sat frozen in their seats against a backdrop of tapestry-covered walls. Out of Ratzinger's toneless murmur they caught the phrases "the seriousness of this act . . . with full freedom . . . I renounce." From 8:00 p.m. on 28 February, the reign of the current pontiff would cease, and the see of Peter would be vacant.

At the hour of bringing it to an end, Ratzinger carried out the most important act of his pontificate, the act that will earn him his place in history. It was a gesture at once noble, humble, courageous—and revolutionary. Benedict XVI brought to completion the reform initiated by Paul VI, who had set the age of retirement at seventy-five for bishops and excluded cardinals older than eighty from voting in conclave in order to bring down the average age of the ecclesiastical hierarchy. Benedict XVI demythologized the pontifical station and dispatched to the museum of history the supernatural icon of the pope as a monarch eternal (until death intervenes) and infallible because surrounded by a court ready to swear that he never errs. On the contrary, the German pope made it clear that the headship of the church must fall to a pastor who is not cut off from the rapid transformation the contemporary world is undergoing. At the supreme hour, Joseph Ratzinger rejected the mystique of the infirm pope, his strength slowly guttering out like the wick of a candle, and effected the rational choice of a man of government. "I believe that what I have done may be enough," he had confided to his biographer a few months previously.[27] For that matter, he had always said that he was not a mystic. He declined an appeal from Cardinal Bertone that he should remain in office at least until the conclusion of the Year of Faith.

Incredulity and bewilderment resounded in the response uttered by the cardinal deacon Angelo Sodano. Benedict XVI, serious, strained, and pallid of countenance, embraced him and then took his leave in silence. Left to themselves, many cardinals crowded around the cardinal deacon. Quite a few had not even fully grasped what the pope had said softly to them in Latin; many did not take it in until they heard Sodano's response. "You could have thrown a bucket of cold water over me, and I wouldn't have noticed," remembers one of those present. "I was speechless, wordless, couldn't form a thought," confessed Cardinal Giovanni Battista Re. That morning and for many mornings to come the disorientation would be total.

4

The Secrets of an
Anti-Italian Conclave

The conclave of 2013 was anti-Italian. Juan Luis Cipriani, cardinal of Lima and a member of Opus Dei, felt it right away upon arriving at Rome. Cardinal Scola was Opus Dei's first choice, but the organization doesn't like to go to the wall for lost causes. Cipriani detected an "anti-Italian sentiment" especially among the cardinals arriving from the United States, along with the "fixed idea" that the new pope ought to be Latin American. This coldness toward potential Italian candidates, he later said, "was present among Italian cardinals too."[1]

The Rome upon which cardinals from beyond the Alps and beyond the oceans converged to decide the succession of Benedict XVI was a strange place: a Rome without a pope but with the former pope still around. There was no coffin, no mourning, no apotheosis to draw a curtain over the past. The pontiff emeritus was alive and well, following the preparations for the conclave from Castel Gandolfo.

The ecclesiastical hierarchy was still in shock from the resignation. There were cardinals who, speaking off the record, judged Ratzinger irresponsible for having opened the door to a resignable papacy.
One or two cardinals with a niche in the curia hid their uneasiness
by adopting a bantering tone: "I would have said to him: 'Your Holiness, take a month's vacation and then cut down on your workload.'
As things stand, he has created problems for his successors." Cardinal
Ruini, speaking on the record, put it more sagely: "The pope's decisions aren't matters for debate; they are accepted, even when they
cause pain."[2]

It didn't take long for Catholic believers in general, on the other
hand, to absorb the blow. They understood Ratzinger on a human
level, however much they may have felt that popes ought "to stay right
to the end, if they feel they can." One text message conveyed their
distress: "Will God resign now too?" The people of Rome let instinct
be their guide, as they often do: "I say he did it to get rid of all of them.
Am I wrong?" exclaimed Signora Tiziana, who runs the newspaper
stand in front of St. Peter's Square.

The timetable set by Benedict XVI meant that the period before
the conclave was unusually long. There are generally about three
weeks between the death of a pope and the start of a conclave, but
now the scheduled interval between the announcement of the abdication and the moment the Sistine Chapel would be sealed off from
the world was an entire month—and it seemed to go on forever. Two
key turning points were the actual departure of Benedict XVI on 28
February 2013 and the start of the general "congregations" of all the
cardinals of the church on 4 March. The purpose of these meetings
was to discuss the state of the church.

As the cardinals from around the world gradually began filtering
into Rome and before the meetings had even begun, the maneuvering started. "They want a pope we don't care for. We'll do everything
to block him," affirmed an Italian curial cardinal. He was referring
to Scola, the archbishop of Milan. A cardinal from north of the Alps
said, for his part, "The Italian self-candidacies created annoyance."
Cardinals from outside Italy balked at accepting a candidacy stitched
up in advance. A singular document, sent by Cardinal Castrillón
Hoyos to Benedict XVI personally in December 2011 and revealed

during the Vatican leaks scandal, had poisoned the atmosphere well in advance. This bizarre composition appeared to denounce a plot against the German pontiff, but its true purpose was to suggest, two years in advance, that Ratzinger should retire "within twelve months" and to attack Scola. One journalist paraphrased it this way: "In secret the Holy Father is supposedly arranging his own succession, and . . . slowly but inexorably preparing him [Scola] . . . to take over the papacy."[3] Similar intrigues have featured throughout the history of papal conclaves.

The number of Italian cardinals entitled to vote in the conclave was twenty-eight, enough to exert considerable pressure if they had been united. In any case, there had been a rising tide of ill will against the Italians in recent years. Foreign cardinals had had enough of the disarray in the curia and the battles going on inside it, flaunted before the world thanks to the secret papers published by the international press.

This time there were no personalities with the kind of high public profile enjoyed by Ratzinger and Martini in 2005, and the cardinals had to assess what kind of pope the times required in a climate of uncertainty. For more than a century, the prestige and influence of the Catholic Church had waxed —from Leo XIII to Pius XII, from John XXIII to Paul VI, down to John Paul II. Then came the reversal of the Ratzinger pontificate, with the explosion of one crisis after another. In 2012, Benedict XVI's approval rating had sunk to 39 percent even in Italy, according to a poll conducted by Eurispes.

The College of Cardinals had to undergo yet another ordeal while it was gearing up to select a successor to Ratzinger. A sexual scandal broke in the United Kingdom featuring one of their brotherhood, Cardinal Keith O'Brien, archbishop of Edinburgh and primate of Scotland. Three serving priests and one former priest accused him of inappropriate sexual conduct in the 1980s. He had allegedly propositioned one after evening prayers, even though he was the man's spiritual director; used duress on another in a parish; and invited a third to spend a vacation in the archiepiscopal residence and approached him in the middle of the night after a bout of drinking. They all claimed they had gratified him because they feared for their careers.

It was 23 February, five days before Benedict XVI was due to step down. O'Brien initially contested the accusations. Twenty-four hours later the papal spokesman, Federico Lombardi, stated: "The pope has been briefed, the matter is before him." Benedict XVI acted with extreme rapidity. The allegations had been made in confidence to church officials earlier and had been transmitted to the papal nuncio in the United Kingdom, Monsignor Antonio Mennini, a week before the pope had announced that he would resign, so there was no suspicion that the scandal had been staged in order to influence the imminent conclave.

The German pontiff compelled the Scottish cardinal to accept an exemplary solution. "Cardinal O'Brien will not take part in the conclave," announced the website of the Vatican news service on 25 February. Instead he left the diocese of Edinburgh and on 3 March made an official apology for "sexual conduct that has fallen below the standards expected of me as a priest, archbishop and cardinal." One of the four accusers, it is worth noting, had been in regular contact with the cardinal for years and had been a habitual guest at the official residence in Edinburgh.[4]

The cardinals arriving in Rome were shaken by the O'Brien affair and the punishment visited on him. It felt as though the sensational news stories breaking one after another, above all the papal resignation, were laying bare for all to see the emergency situation in which the Catholic Church found itself. In January 2013, another cardinal elector hit the headlines: Roger Mahony, archbishop of Los Angeles from 1985 to 2011. While he was in charge, more than 120 cases of sexual abuse by clergy had been reported to the diocese. When the courts forced the archdiocese to release correspondence between Cardinal Mahony and Thomas Curry, his episcopal vicar, the public learned how Mahony had maneuvered to keep law enforcement out of the picture.

The new archbishop of Los Angeles, Monsignor José Gómez, reacted by stripping his predecessor of any public function, calling it a "brutal and painful" experience to read the file. The Vatican subsequently compelled Gómez and Mahony to keep the peace in public.

Among the cases imputed to Cardinal Mahony was the failure to report the priest Kevin Barmasse to the police. Barmasse had systematically plied underage boys with alcohol and then taken advantage of them, a twofold crime under California law. Then there was the case of the priest Michael Baker, subsequently defrocked, who confessed in a meeting with Archbishop Mahony in 1996 that he had molested two young brothers for almost seven years (starting when one was ten, the other fourteen). Baker had been sent to New Mexico for therapy, but then returned to Los Angeles, where he was assigned pastoral duties involving contact with adults only, but he had begun abusing two underage boys again.[5]

In the United States, the group Catholics United circulated a petition requesting that Mahony be barred from the conclave. In Italy, the magazine *Famiglia Cristiana* polled its readers about whether he ought to be allowed in, and a large majority answered no. Even in the Vatican, there were those who suggested he step back. "Mahony might be counseled not to attend the conclave," commented Cardinal Velasio De Paolis, the man delegated by the Vatican to superintend the Legionaries of Christ after problems had emerged in that organization.[6]

The American organization Survivors' Network of Those Abused by Priests (SNAP) entered the fray, naming a "dirty dozen" cardinals in the United States and elsewhere who, it claimed, ought to be barred from consideration as papal candidates and perhaps even barred from voting in the conclave for having protected the predators. Vatican spokesman Lombardi responded stiffly, "SNAP doesn't get to decide who should participate in the conclave." But the novelty of this interregnum was that there was no longer any churchman above the fray. The mass media, public opinion, and investigative journalism were factors the Catholic Church could not go on ignoring forever. Bertone, the secretary of state, reacted edgily, with a note denouncing the attempt to influence the papal election, but Sodano, the dean of the College of Cardinals, kept silent.

The O'Brien and Mahony cases reinforced the will to open a completely new era in the history of the church. The general desire was for a successor to Benedict XVI capable of taking the helm and steering the ship. All camps were agreed on that. "We need a man of government," said the English cardinal Cormac Murphy-O'Connor.[7] The Australian George Pell, a Ratzinger ally, declared: "The next pope will naturally need to be a good theologian, but I would prefer someone really capable of guiding the church and reuniting it."[8] The Cuban cardinal Jaime Ortega called for a man "equipped with knowledge of the world of today, from the philosophical and political points of view."[9] The church needs to rebuild its credibility, said the South African Wilfrid Fox Napier.[10]

The absolute priority was the reorganization of the church's central government, the Roman Curia. The cardinals from beyond Italy complained about an organization that they saw as both suffocating and uncoordinated, weakened by the drop in the quality of its personnel, not to mention by financial scandals. They weren't alone. Even inside the curia there was discontent for various reasons. The majority of curial prelates were against the excessive degree of power that over the years had come to inhere in the office of the secretary of state and saw the change of popes as the occasion for reducing it. Many cardinals complained of a lack of regular access to Pope Ratzinger. They criticized the negative effect on church government of the isolation of a pontiff who toward the end was not meeting regularly either with those in charge of the departments of curial government or with individual bishops paying their visit *ad limina* or even with papal nuncios when they touched base in Rome.

Benedict XVI himself, in his last statements, pushed for renewal. At the Ash Wednesday rite, he denounced the rifts in the church and pointed the finger at "individualism and rivalry."[11] In his farewell speech on 28 February 2013, he urged courage: "The church is . . . a living reality . . . she lives through the course of time, in becoming, like every living being, in undergoing change."[12]

Age played a part in the effort to identify the best successor. Many cardinals revealed that they preferred a candidate between sixty and seventy years old. The church could not permit itself another excessively brief reign, they believed. That of Paul VI was ideal: fifteen years. Twenty years, as with Pius XII, was rather long, and the twenty-seven years that John Paul II lasted was way too long. "We want a Holy Father," they said jokingly, "not an Eternal Father."

It was agreed that they needed a pope with the gift of command, but for many days observers detected a proliferation of candidates. "Electors are few and *papabili* many," was the ironic comment of the French cardinal Philippe Barbarin, whom the Romans saw riding his bicycle to the Vatican every morning.[13] The candidates ranged from the Canadian Marc Ouellet, prefect of the Congregation for

Bishops, to the primate of Hungary Péter Erdö, the African Peter Turkson, and the Italian Gianfranco Ravasi, the Vatican's minister of culture.

Erdö and Ouellet came from the same school of thought as Ratzinger, the journal *Communio*. That was a handicap because most of the cardinals were looking for signs of a clean break as they began their formal assemblies on 4 March 2013. "The sessions were dominated by criticism of the curia," recalls one cardinal. "No names were mentioned, but the question kept coming up. Only three or four speakers were prepared to defend it."

Veteran cardinal Roger Etchegaray, John Paul II's roving ambassador to crisis zones, described the state of mind of many cardinals: "You could feel that this change of pope represented a chance to make changes to things." A European cardinal put it this way: "Most of the talk was about making a break. After the events of recent years, the general feeling was 'never again!' They wanted fresh air, there was a desire in the room to step outside what felt like a cramped little space."

Their outsider status and their warm humanity earned sympathy for the cardinal of Boston, Sean Patrick O'Malley, with his white beard and frank countenance, who went about wearing sandals and the robe of a Capuchin friar, and the Filipino Luis Antonio Tagle, nicknamed the "Roncalli of Manila" because he called to mind Pope John XXIII. But Tagle was not even fifty-six years old; better for him to wait a round, prophesied some.

The name "Bergoglio" was not on many short lists in the weeks leading up to the conclave, though he was a well-known and highly esteemed personality. In addition to the votes he had attracted during the conclave of 2005, he had garnered success as the author of the final document issued by the Conference of Latin American Bishops at Aparecida in 2007, and in 2001 he had been elected to the council of the Synod of Bishops with the maximum number of votes. But by now he was regarded as too elderly. He had been born in 1936 and was nearly seventy-seven, about the same age as Joseph Ratzinger when he was elected. "Before the conclave began, I hadn't heard his name mentioned even by my Latin American brothers," confessed Cardinal Renato Martino, former president of the Pontifical Council for Justice and Peace.[14]

Jorge Mario Bergoglio felt that he was nearing the end of his pastoral duties. He foresaw that the next pope would replace him in Buenos Aires since the two-year extension habitually granted to archbishops who reached the term limit of seventy-five was about to expire. His collaborators at Buenos Aires found him depressed at times. "Recently I saw him looking tired and dejected because he was near retirement," said his former spokesman, Father Guillermo Marcó.[15] When Don Pedro Baya saw Archbishop Bergoglio arriving at Villa Ramón Carrillo the November before Benedict XVI abdicated, he found him so "exhausted and weary" that he decided to take a picture of him: "I was afraid I would never see him again." Bergoglio happened to remember a priest who had once worked in the shantytown, Father Vernazza. They brought him a photo of the man, and he, generally so reserved, began to cry as he stroked the photo.[16] Psychologically prepared to leave office, Bergoglio had already reserved a room for himself in the residence for elderly priests in the Flores quarter of Buenos Aires, where he was born. He had come to Rome with the ticket for the return flight in his pocket and before leaving had pre-recorded the archbishop of Buenos Aires's traditional Easter message for the diocesan broadcaster Canal-21.

The archbishop of Buenos Aires had his own candidate in mind: Cardinal O'Malley of Boston, who had distinguished himself in his own diocese for his firmness against pedophile clergy. Even before departing for Rome, Bergoglio had formed a precise idea of what sort of man the next pope should be: a man of prayer, a pontiff convinced that Christ, not he, was the top man in the church, a bishop with the capacity to "show affection to persons and create communion." Last, "he should be able to clean up the Roman Curia."[17] He confided these views to a group of religious from the Schoenstatt movement.

Conversely, there was a cardinal from the United States who arrived in Rome with the thought in mind that Bergoglio was a prime candidate for the office: Sean O'Malley. The archbishop of Boston, who speaks perfect Spanish and had founded a social services agency for Spanish immigrants, knew that his opinion was shared by three of his South American brothers: the Brazilian Cláudio Hummes, who was sympathetic to liberation theology and very cool toward the Roman Curia after having spent four years there, from 2006 to 2010, as prefect of the Congregation for the Clergy and finding himself hampered at every turn; the Honduran Oscar Rodríguez Maradiaga; and the Chilean Francisco Javier Errázuriz.

A web linking these two poles gradually took shape in the fragmented atmosphere that characterized the preconclave period of 2013. O'Malley's view was shared by the energetic and very active archbishop of New York, Timothy Dolan, a leader of the group of cardinals from the Americas who amounted to almost 10 percent of the electorate. Eleven of them were from North America, and they moved as a team, arriving together in a minibus for the general meetings at the Vatican and organizing a couple of press conferences to inform public opinion about the progress of the discussions in these meetings. After two days, though, the Vatican made them stop, invoking the confidentiality imposed on the debates.

The Americans were split on whom to vote for, but they had a shared program that drew support from many cardinal electors. They were demanding transparency and order in the financial affairs of the Vatican, a radical cleanup of the IOR, a slimmed-down curia with less bureaucracy, and lastly—the other top priority of many episcopates— a rebalancing of the relationship between the Holy See and the Episcopal Conferences. They expected the future pope to consult the bishops of the church more often and more regularly.

This was the principle of collegiality adopted fifty years earlier by Vatican II but never realized. The German cardinal Walter Kasper, who would have been excluded from the conclave for having reached the cutoff age of eighty if it had begun just a week later than it did, stipulated: "We need a new approach to the exercise of the government of the church . . . a more horizontal governance."[18]

Dolan was on excellent terms with the papal nuncio in the United States, Monsignor Viganò, the former secretary-general of the Vatican governorate who had been transferred to Washington, D.C., for his part in exposing financial fraud in the sacred palace. Anglo-American culture has a low tolerance for theft from the community chest, and a year earlier Dolan had praised Viganò in these words to the *New York Times*: "He is a man who is not afraid to speak the truth and not afraid to point out areas that need reform in the church."[19]

The Vatican leaks scandal hung like a cloud over the preconclave, although the cardinals were unable to get any information about the investigation being conducted by Cardinals Herranz, Tomko, and De Giorgi at the behest of Benedict XVI.

There was another group of cardinals searching for a candidate promising change, the reform-minded cardinals from the German-speaking lands. They included Cardinal Christoph Schönborn of Vienna; Karl Lehmann from Germany, for many years the head of the German Episcopate; and Walter Kasper, a German present in the curia and former president of the Pontifical Council for Promoting Christian Unity. In this group could be counted the Belgian cardinal Godfried Danneels.

Over the thirty-five years during which Wojtyla and Ratzinger reigned, the strongest calls for reform of the church had come from the Germanic world. Again in 2011, when Benedict XVI paid a visit to his homeland, a memorandum prepared by German theologians, male and female, had stressed the urgency of launching a season of reform and participation in the church. In Austria the same year, parish priests were summoned to engage in "disobedience" by Catholics in favor of clerical marriage, the ordination of female priests, and participation of the laity in the running of parish communities that lacked a priest. Cardinal Schönborn had been urging the Vatican for some time to confront such hot-button issues but had been hushed.

The hour for change had come. Although uncertainty still prevailed in early March about the best candidate, Cardinal Lehmann detected a radical change of atmosphere in the discussions among the cardinals, compared to the conclave of 2005. At that time, the Ratzinger candidacy had been imposed on the conclave by the cardinals based in the curia, and the centrality of Europe had been unquestioned. Not in 2013: "Europe doesn't play the same role as before. . . . [A]t the conclave of 2005 the cardinals from Europe were more self-confident and swung more weight; now things are different," Lehmann confided to his collaborators. "Among the non-Europeans there are many outstanding figures . . . speaking English, French, and Spanish, and who are perfectly acquainted with European church problems, the abuses, the leaks."

Although, with the conclave a week away, the German group had not yet coalesced around a particular candidacy, they had a clear idea of what kind of pope they wanted. "There is a need for a man of faith, who can show what believing means. Someone detached from any interest group, belonging to the reasonable, modern, open and positive 'center,' . . . and not a prisoner of his own monologue."

For all that, it would represent an epochal turn for the conclave to cut the papacy loose from Europe, from the matrix in which Christianity had grown and matured, where Catholicism had erected its fortress on organizational and juridical foundations laid by imperial Rome. The princes of the church in whose hands the outcome of the conclave lay still needed a period of contact with one another and reflection before making such a break. As the conclave drew closer, the Bergoglio candidacy was not lifting off. Cardinal Pell, the Australian, was still convinced that the papacy would not abandon Italy: "If there is a well-prepared Italian cardinal, I believe he will always be the favorite." Pell relegated any change to the distant future: "The election of a Latin American pope should happen sometime in the next hundred years."[20]

Inside the Roman Curia itself there was plenty of movement that gave impetus to the gathering drive for change. Contrary to the stereotypical image projected by the media, the Roman Curia is far from being a stronghold of conservatism and is anything but monolithic. Each of the various groups within it moves on its own. Not all in the curia were favorable to the Italian candidate, Scola. Important cardinals openly urged the necessity of making a courageous leap beyond the confines of Europe. Cardinal Giovanni Lajolo, former foreign minister of the Holy See, stated frankly: "Nothing says there cannot be a non-Italian pope and a non-Italian secretary of state at the same time."[21]

Lajolo belonged to the circle within the curia, trained in diplomacy, that drew sustenance from the teaching of Paul VI and Cardinal Agostino Casaroli. These "diplomats" intended to pursue the internationalization of the central church government initiated by Pope Paul VI. Following the Slavic pope and the German pope, who together had symbolically bridged the European fault line created by the Cold War, they believed the hour had come to give a voice to transatlantic Catholicism.

The group centered on Cardinal Bertone was also well aware of the urgency of making a fresh start. Unwillingness to change is a recipe for irrelevance. Bertone had a South American candidate of high caliber in mind: Odilo Scherer, archbishop of São Paulo, Brazil, the largest city in the country with the largest number of Catholics in the world. The son of German immigrants and just the right age for the conclave (he was sixty-three at the time), Scherer is a man of strict orthodoxy, alert to social problems, and committed to the defense of the Amazon basin against agribusiness speculators. At the same time, he had a strong foothold in the curia, being a member of the Congregation for the Clergy and—above all—a member of the supervisory committee for the IOR, the Vatican Bank.

It was the latter connection that ultimately harmed his chances. When in the final conferences among the cardinal electors prior to the conclave debate flared up about who was responsible for the bank's mishaps, Scherer defended the curia's work, thus leaving others with the impression that he was not the right man to reform the Vatican administration.

Scola or Scherer. As 12 March approached, the date that had meanwhile been set for the first round of voting in the Sistine Chapel, these two candidates were regarded as the front runners. Receiving the bishops from Lombardy in the Vatican a few days before stepping down, Benedict XVI had exhorted them to be "the believing heart of Europe . . . a light to all."[22] His words were interpreted as a boost to the Scola candidacy. "Around the Ratzinger hearth," his brother Georg later confided to the newspaper *Münchner Merkur*, "it was rather assumed that the successor would be an Italian."

The cardinals from the United States had in any case taken a strategic decision. They too had one or two high-caliber *papabili* in addition to O'Malley: Cardinal Dolan and Donald Wuerl of Washington, D.C. But they decided not to vote for either of them, preferring to play the role of king makers. Cardinal Wuerl, basically speaking for all of them, explained the political motivation: "A pontiff coming from the American superpower would encounter great difficulty in presenting a spiritual message to the rest of the world."[23] With this in mind, O'Malley and Dolan focused their attention on Maradiaga.

It is safe to say that the idea of backing Bergoglio again after his second-place finish in the 2005 conclave gained consistency fairly late in the game. One of his backers recalls that "only in the wake of the first two preconclave meetings did we really focus on him because we realized that none of the current front runners would be able to reach the required majority." But assessments of this kind remained highly confidential, and there was no public buzz about a Bergoglio candidacy.

The watershed moment came on Thursday, 7 March 2013, at the halfway point of the preconclave debates. Bergoglio spoke off the cuff during the morning session, leaving aside his prepared notes. He evoked a church "stepping outside its own bounds . . . and heading for the outskirts—both geographical and existential." Many of the afflictions of church institutions, he said, "are rooted in self-referentiality, in a species of theological narcissism." A church turned in on itself "falls ill." The archbishop of Buenos Aires presented the purple-clad gathering with two models: an "evangelizing church, that steps outside of itself . . . and a worldly church that lives within itself, by itself, and for itself." Bergoglio alluded to the suitability of "possible changes and reforms to be carried out for the salvation of souls" and concluded by sketching the profile of a dynamic pope with a cheerful countenance and of a church with the countenance of a "fecund mother of the sweet and consoling joys of evangelization."

The speech made a deep impression; the Cuban cardinal Jaime Ortega immediately asked Bergoglio for his notes so he could disseminate them. Many cardinals liked the Argentine's style: his humility and simplicity, his remoteness from curial machinations and preconclave coteries. The ascent of the Bergoglio candidacy began then. Two evenings later, in the apartment of the Lombard cardinal Attilio Nicora, there was a meeting of the Italians Francesco Coccopalmerio and Giuseppe Bertello, the Englishman Murphy-O'Connor, the Frenchman Tauran, and the German Kasper. There it was decided to launch the Bergoglio candidacy and to seek the backing of the U.S., Latin American, and German cardinals who were or might be favorable; Murphy-O'Connor undertook to approach his fellow Anglophones.

Bergoglio sensed that the interest of the electors was starting to build around his name. On Sunday, 10 March, strolling through Piazza Navona in the evening, he ran into Tom Rosica, a priest and the director of the Canadian Catholic multimedia broadcaster Salt + Light. "Pray for me," Bergoglio exclaimed. "Are you nervous?" Rosica asked. "A little bit . . . I don't know what my fellow cardinals are cooking up for me."[24]

And yet, at the first round of voting in conclave on Tuesday, 12 March, Bergoglio received scarcely twenty votes (only sixteen according to some sources), which dismayed the group that was backing him. "We were disappointed and fearful he would not be able to stay the course," recalls one of them. In conclave on Wednesday morning, though, both the Scola and the Scherer candidacies ran aground. The former, who went into the conclave (according to some whispers) with a packet of between twenty and thirty votes, including ones from North and South America, had no idea how much damage his adversaries were doing to him by bringing cardinals from outside Italy into the picture about some of the shady business dealings in which Comunione e Liberazione had engaged and the cynicism of this activist movement's alliance with the politician Silvio Berlusconi.

As for the adversaries of the Brazilian Scherer, they spread the word that if elected he would retain Secretary of State Bertone—a bête noire in the eyes of many cardinals both in the curia and abroad—in his post for a year and then replace him with Mauro Piacenza, the ambitious prefect of the Congregation for the Clergy and a hidebound conservative. (Disinformation is a tactic typically employed at papal conclaves. On the eve of this one, the word went round that Bergoglio had just one lung, forcing Cardinal Maradiaga to go round the tables of diners in purple at the Santa Marta residence, informing them that it wasn't true: only the upper part of his right lung had been surgically removed.)

From the third round of voting, Bergoglio's rise was uninterrupted. Scola stalled at twenty-seven votes,[25] and the undecided electors began to shift their votes to the archbishop of Buenos Aires. His spirituality made an impression on many. An Italian cardinal said: "I had only seen Bergoglio once, and I sought information . . . they told me that he is a man of prayer, that he spends the night praying." It was what this particular elector wanted to hear; that is how votes are won.

The break with the past came at the fifth round of voting. "Right to the end the outcome was uncertain," testified a cardinal from northern Europe. "One-third was all it would take to block his election." But the undecided made up their minds, and lumps of frozen votes began to thaw and trickle toward Bergoglio. Support came from Europe (the cardinal of Paris, André Vingt-Trois, and the patriarch of Lisbon, José da Cruz Policarpo), from Africa (the Congolese Monsengwo Pasinya), and from the Philippines (Tagle).

In the final surge, as often happens in papal conclaves, those present had the sensation of being transported by an overriding impulse. The realization that the Catholic Church was about to have a pope from the Americas provoked euphoria in many.

The 115 elderly men dressed in violet purple revealed an extraordinary farsightedness. The senate of the church showed that it could think big. The papacy was casting off the bonds of Europe, leaving behind the cradle of the Mediterranean and venturing out onto the boundless ocean, setting course for the peripheries of the third world and the globalized twenty-first century. "I felt the hand of God guiding the church," confessed Cardinal Bertello, today a member of the privy council created by Pope Francis. "To exit from Europe after twenty centuries . . . was a breath of fresh air." Peering at Bergoglio's serious and emotionally stirred countenance at the moment when the threshold of two-thirds was reached, Cardinal Salvatore De Giorgi thought to himself: "He's a Latin American, he comes from a continent where people go hungry . . . it's different there from consumerist Europe."

In the final tally, Jorge Mario Bergoglio received more than 90 of the 115 votes. "This is your fault," Pope Francis said to Cardinal Murphy-O'Connor two days after his election.[26]

During the mass *Pro eligendo pontefice*, celebrated prior to the locking of the Sistine Chapel doors, Cardinal Sodano had spoken during his homily of the kind of pope the church needed: a man animated by a "mission of mercy," a man who could create unity in collaboration with all the members of the body of the church, a person with a "generous heart." The description fits the man. But Francis showed immediately that he was and intended much, much more than that.

5

The End of the Imperial Church

The image of a new pope jells in the space of a few minutes. When Albino Luciani (John Paul I) appeared before the faithful for the first time on the Vatican balcony in 1978, he struck them by his disoriented smile and the almost childish manner in which he greeted them. He wanted to speak, but the master of ceremonies told him it wasn't done. The sight of Joseph Ratzinger's black sweater peeping out from under the white sleeves of the papal cassock aroused a certain tenderness. John Paul II immediately displayed his seductive charm with the celebrated remark, "If I err, you'll correct me."

They were curious about Bergoglio as he advanced with a slightly undulating pace to the balustrade, where he remained a moment in silence, waving discretely as though catching sight from a distance of a group of relatives and friends.

His body language was discursive rather than lofty, and he didn't stop speaking after introducing himself as a man summoned "from the ends of the earth" by the cardinal electors. Francis immediately outlined a new perspective: "And now, we take up this journey: bishop and people," he repeated, stressing the commonality between the pope and the faithful and the "trust among us." The Church of Rome, he stated, "presides in charity over all the churches."[1]

With a few strokes, he had already indicated the style of a more community-oriented church: bishop and people walking together. Rome is not a bureaucratic power center but a link binding together the Catholic communities of the world, not in the juridical sense but on a foundation of love. This had been the message of Saint Ignatius of Antioch at the dawn of Christianity. Francis prefers above all to be called "bishop of Rome"; on that first evening he never referred to himself as the pontiff. From the balcony there hung not his coat of arms topped by the triple crown, the symbol of regality, only a dark red drape with a white rectangle.

Francis alluded again to the image of wayfaring the following day, during the mass celebrated in the Sistine Chapel with the College of Cardinals. He spoke not from a seated position on the small papal throne but standing erect, like a parish priest delivering a sermon, and emphasized three concepts: wayfaring, edification, and confessing Christ. Life is a journey, he said, and "when we stop moving things go wrong." And on this journey we bear a cross because if Christ is proclaimed without the cross, then the church is just another nongovernmental organization, and then "we are not disciples of the Lord, we are worldly: we may be bishops, priests, cardinals, popes, but not disciples of the Lord."[2] While addressing the cardinals who had just elected him, the pope paused several times for breath; his sciatica was tormenting him.

Bergoglio's style was evident from the very first: the immediate, almost down-home way of speaking, the intense spirituality, the idea of a dynamic church. One or two cardinals wrinkled their noses at the contrast with the elevated oratory of Benedict XVI. But Bergoglio's simple and frank diction springs from a wish to make waves. Pope Francis is an icebreaker, the American Catholic writer Michael Novak would later comment. Introducing reform means shattering hardened attitudes. Francis wanted a church prepared to take to the streets, not a church huddled within a gated enclave for fear of trouble: "But I am telling you: I would prefer a thousand times over a bruised church than an ill church! A church . . . with the courage to risk going out."[3] It is an image that would recur in his speeches over the coming months.

His standard outfit was the plain white cassock. It was a choice that drew the earliest criticism of him. While donning papal dress following his election, he rejected the red shoulder cape (mozzetta), and rumor has it that he said to the master of ceremonies, Monsignor Guido Marini, "No thanks, you put this on. Carnival is over." The phrase is apocryphal, put about by his detractors. It is hard to imagine any Jesuit, let alone a Jesuit pontiff, using such discourteous language.

The day after the election the Romans spotted the fact that the new pope was not wearing the classic red shoes, the violet Pradas for which Ratzinger had been tormented by the media. Francis's shoes were old, black, and rather shapeless—orthopedic shoes suitable for a parish priest, of the kind he had worn in Buenos Aires both in the archiepiscopal curia and out in the shantytowns. On his wrist was an ordinary watch. He wore an iron cross on his chest and rejected any gold jewelry: the "ring of the fisherman" given him by Cardinal Sodano in the name of the College of Cardinals was of simple silver.

Twenty-four hours after being elected, the pope insisted on going back to the international residence for clergy in Via della Scrofa, where he had stayed before the conclave, in order to pack his bags and settle his bill in person. A photo seen round the world showed the Roman pontiff, dressed in white, waiting at the reception desk while the clerk made out the bill. When he paid a visit the same day to the basilica of Santa Maria Maggiore, he rode in an ordinary car belonging to the Vatican gendarmerie, refusing the official automobile with the license plate SCV1. For an official visit to the president of the Italian Republic, Giorgio Napolitano, at the Quirinale, on 14 November 2013, he used a Ford Focus for transportation. No sirens blared, and there was no motorcycle escort or mounted guard of honor. As he got into the car, he lifted his white cassock and viewers glimpsed his black trousers underneath.

At Lampedusa, where he landed in July 2013 to meet refugees from Africa and pray for their companions lost at sea, Bergoglio used a four-wheel-drive Fiat loaned by a Milanese resident of Sicily. At Assisi the following October, his car was a simple blue Fiat Panda. When a Veronese priest made him a gift of a Renault 4, the pope accepted but sent it to the museum of papal automobiles. If he could, he would have gone to Lampedusa on a regular commercial flight, but security wouldn't permit it. He did succeed in preventing any cortège of dignitaries from turning the visit into a photo op; government ministers were barred. At lunch after mass, he ate a sandwich on his feet and sampled a slice of *cassata* out of courtesy.

The days passed, yet the pope from Argentina did not move into the papal apartment in the apostolic palace. He stayed where he had stayed during the conclave, in the Santa Marta residence located in Vatican City. Was this just a temporary solution while the traditional apartment of the popes was set up to his liking? At one point, rumor had it that he was going to live at the Lateran palace, the ancient seat of the bishop of Rome. But it was the very concept of "palace" that Francis rejected. After two months, the monsignori had to face the facts: Santa Marta was where Francis was going to live. Conservatives were naturally shocked, but there was muttering among some of his electors as well. The first faint signs of opposition began to emerge. Some accused him of breaking with tradition for demagogic reasons, to cast his predecessors in a negative light.

The pope preferred his small Santa Marta hotel suite (number 201). He preferred eating in the common dining room, seated at one of the tables like anyone else, with whomever happened to be there. "That way it'll be harder to poison him," was the joke in Buenos Aires. "I am visible to people and I live a normal life . . . I go to public mass in the morning and I eat in the dining hall with everyone else . . . I'm not isolated," he wrote to an Argentine priest.[4]

Every morning at 10:00 a.m. Francis would arrive at the apostolic palace for the day's meetings, but in the afternoon he would remain in his study at Santa Marta. There it was possible to run into him riding in the elevator or going to get an espresso from the coffee machine, groping for coins in his pockets. Two priests who found themselves sharing an elevator with the pope during these early days stuttered out a greeting, uncertain whether to scurry away or kiss his hand.

To be cut off from the world is bad for him: "I cannot live in isolation . . . I just can't . . . for psychiatric reasons," he says with a self-mocking laugh. During a question-and-answer session with pupils from the Jesuit schools, one little girl asked him whether he had wanted to become pope and received this answer: "Do you know what it means when a person does not really love himself? A person who wants, who has the wish to be pope does not love himself. God does not bless him. No, I did not want to be pope. Is that okay? Come, come, come."[5]

Speaking to reporters on the return flight from Rio de Janeiro to Rome following World Youth Day, he repeated: "I need people, I need to meet people, to talk to people."[6] To Antonio Spadaro, S.J., he gave this telling explanation of why he had chosen not to live in the papal apartment: "It is like an inverted funnel. It is big and spacious, but the entrance is really tight. People can come only in dribs and drabs, and I cannot live without people."[7] In Vatican jargon, the wishes of "the Apartment" bear the weight of supreme authority. By choosing to reside at Santa Marta, Francis at one stroke undercut the charmed circle of insiders who, in every pontificate, claim to relay snippets of the papal thinking thanks to their privileged access, real or pretended, to the apostolic apartment. With a pope who speaks to those he encounters in scandalously direct fashion, it becomes rather pointless to go around dropping veiled hints that you are one of the few acquainted with the intentions of "the Mind" (another curial circumlocution for the seat of ultimate power).

The pope's doggedly sober style upsets tradition. Sometimes he shows up for solemn ceremonies like any other bishop, carrying his own miter bag. At his first mass with the cardinals in the Sistine Chapel, he was still wearing his old miter from Buenos Aires. If he needs to put on his glasses during his homily, he extracts the case laboriously from his pocket instead of having a secretary hand them to him respectfully, like his predecessor. He climbed the steps to board the airplane for Rio de Janeiro clutching a black briefcase, and when asked about it, he said, "That's what I've always done . . . inside there was a razor, a breviary, an agenda, a book to read."[8]

Those in the Vatican inclined to look askance at this novel conduct called it "the South American style," but that is not accurate. Latin America has produced bishops and cardinals of every sort, including some who practiced extreme poverty, such as Hélder Câmara, who left his palace to the poor; others with middle-class habits; and yet others haughty enough to pass for aristocrats of Old Castile. Francis's humility is not folklore; his unconventional ways reflect his personality. For Cardinal Ruini, they hark back to the "austerity of the Jesuit schoolmasters, who possessed nothing but their books."

Above all, the idiosyncratic style is part of a coherent design to dismantle the imperial character of the papacy, its Caesarean absolutism, semidivine and fed by the aura of infallibility that has clung to the papal court. The formal title of the successors of Peter is itself pagan, for the *pontifex maximus* was the chief priest of ancient Rome.

Within a few days of the papal election, Francis rocked the image of Vatican power in the most forceful way. Referring to the saint of Assisi who gave him his own regnal name, Bergoglio paused and murmured in a low voice and with a marked sigh, "Oh, how I wish for a church that is poor and for the poor!"[9] The words were greeted with a burst of applause from the auditorium, and the *Osservatore Romano* used the phrase as a front-page headline. A church of that kind is not the first thing most people think of when asked by pollsters. Those who were present in the audience hall that day will remember the powerful impact of hearing these words uttered and the intent they revealed.

The "sacred" and grandiloquent character that has become attached to the bishopric of Rome does not derive from Christianity, much less from the Gospel, but from the later Roman Empire. "Everything having to do the emperor Diocletian was defined as 'sacred': his edicts, his bedchamber, his bodyguard, the palace chancellery," writes the historian Giovanni Filoramo, evoking the heightened rituality of the late imperial court. "Those granted an audience with the emperor were admitted to the 'adoration of the purple,' the hem of the imperial mantle."[10]

This is the origin of the red shoes and red shoulder cape of the popes. It has nothing to do with the redness of blood or with any symbolic readiness for martyrdom. It is the red of absolute power. The custom of prostration before the pope and cardinals corresponds to the self-effacement of subjects in the presence of the Roman emperor and his great imperial counterpart and model, the Persian king of kings. The "Sacred Rota," the "Holy Inquisition," the "sacred palaces" of the Vatican, the "audience of kissing the hand," the "sacred congregations," the "kissing of the pope's slipper"—all are descended from the practices of the absolute oriental monarchies, where the sovereign's mere nod was the supreme law.

"Heads of the church have often been narcissists, flattered and thrilled by their courtiers. The court is the leprosy of the papacy," Francis confided to Eugenio Scalfari, founder of the newspaper *La Repubblica.*[11]

Half a century ago it was still possible to see the pontiffs being carried on the gestatorial chair (a portable throne borne on the shoulders of footmen) with large fans flapping about their ears—a ceremonial custom dating back to the pharaohs of ancient Egypt. The triregnum, the high triple crown that symbolically laid claim to papal supremacy over all the kings of the earth, was only set aside by Paul VI. John Paul II abandoned the use of the gestatorial chair, as his timid successor John Paul I had lacked the nerve to do. The mild Benedict XVI went a step further, removing the triregnum from the papal crest and replacing it with a simple bishop's miter. Pope Francis has set about stripping away non-Christian symbols even more rapidly and visibly.

Soon after John XXIII was elected in 1958, he was astonished to have the vice director of the *Osservatore Romano*, Cesidio Lolli, fall to his knees in his presence. "What on earth are you doing?" exclaimed the pope, inviting him to sit. "I can't, Your Holiness. Etiquette forbids it," Lolli replied. "One gets down on one's knees to pray, not to work," responded Pope Roncalli, threatening to leave.[12]

Vatican prelates were scandalized when Bergoglio kissed the Argentine *presidenta* Cristina Kirchner on the cheeks and bowed as if to kiss the hand of Queen Rania of Jordan. He is also the first pontiff to allow himself to be kissed regularly by the faithful.

It all serves to break down the mythology of pontiff-emperor. John Paul II was warm, human, sometimes merry, and sometimes irate, but he always remained an "emperor." Francis is turning his back on the aura of monarchy once and for all. A pope is a bishop and ought to speak as a priest. The shift is evident in the annual pontifical directory. "Francis, Bishop of Rome," is how the first page dedicated to the pope reads; his other baroque titles (vicar of Jesus Christ, successor of the prince of the Apostles, highest pontiff of the Universal Church) have all been relegated to the next page.

Three months after his election, Francis failed to appear at a concert dedicated to him in connection with the Year of Faith. In the Paul VI Audience Hall, his conspicuously empty seat was promptly photographed. Surprised, Monsignor Rino Fisichella, president of the Council for Promoting the New Evangelization and organizer of the event, announced that Francis had been called away by "pressing commitments." At that very moment, Bergoglio was actually immersed in studying the paperwork of the IOR, the Vatican Bank, and his mordant remark that he was not a "Renaissance prince" was allowed to leak from Santa Marta. In November 2013, the pope cancelled the final concert scheduled for the ending of the Year of Faith altogether. The concept he strove to hammer home as the months passed, to the utter scandal of those enthralled by papal majesty, was that the pontiff was a normal person, who "laughs, weeps, sleeps soundly, and has friends like everyone else."

The elimination of the trappings of monarchy could be observed in little things. No special bonus was paid out to the Vatican's employees for the new pope's election. Honorific papal distinctions and medals were no longer awarded except to foreign diplomats, and no more laymen were elevated to the rank of "papal gentlemen." The granting of the title *monsignor* to priests younger than sixty-five was abolished.

The retirement of Benedict XVI made it easier for Francis to start taking apart the icon of the imperial church. The abdication brought the papacy down to a human level and desacralized it. While still a cardinal, Ratzinger had intuited that the papal monarchy was no longer sustainable in its inherited forms. "A church of worldwide dimensions, and with the planet in this state," he said to me a few months before he was elected, "cannot be governed in monarchical fashion."[13] But once he became pope, he found the task of reform too much for him.

Francis went to the root of the problem. He tackled the church's steeply perpendicular structure, with the Roman Curia perched at the top: a general headquarters and locus of command, where the very surroundings, with all their impressive pomp and stunning beauty, ooze the conviction that this is the "center" and the "whole" of the Catholic world. Such arrogance is a relic, according to the church historian Alberto Melloni.[14] As Francis sees it, the moment has come to make the collegiality stipulated by Vatican II—the principle that pope and bishops together, like Peter and the apostles, share the responsibility of governing the universal church—into a reality. He and they alike are vicars of Christ. This was the "turn" at the core of Vatican II: no more bishops operating like prefects subordinated to a pope-monarch, but apostles to whom, as to the pope, the care of the entire church has been entrusted.

For such an objective to be attained, an intake of bishops less tainted by careerism is a prerequisite. To the nuncios abroad, whose task it is to supply the Holy See with profiles of potential nominees to bishoprics, Bergoglio addressed the following warning: "Take care that they be pastors who are close to the people . . . that they love poverty . . . and do not have the psychology of 'princes.' Be attentive that they aren't ambitious."[15] A bishop must be "neither prince nor functionary," he often says. And nor should he be a bureaucrat "attentive mainly to discipline, the regulations, the organizational mechanisms."[16]

The great popes have had a set of goals in mind from the morning after their election. Indeed, John XXIII summoned Monsignor Domenico Tardini to tell him that he was about to be named secretary of state on the very evening the conclave ended on 28 October 1958. He was discussing with his inner circle the idea of holding the council that became Vatican II barely ten weeks later and indeed had already alluded privately to the necessity of convoking one when he was nuncio in Turkey between 1934 and 1944.[17]

Four days after his election, Bergoglio had already decided on a replacement for Cardinal Bertone as secretary of state.[18] The man he chose was Monsignor Pietro Parolin, fifty-eight years old, then the nuncio in Venezuela and previously, from 2002 to 2009, undersecretary of foreign affairs for the Holy See. He had been formed in the great school of diplomacy of Cardinals Casaroli and Silvestrini. Before being dispatched to Venezuela in 2009, he had negotiated the accord between the Holy See and the Socialist Republic of Vietnam, opening the way for the two parties to enter into diplomatic relations and, from 2010, for the Vatican to nominate Vietnamese bishops by presenting the government with a short list of three from which to choose (the procedure that had been followed with the states of eastern Europe during the Cold War). Francis intended Parolin to become secretary of state in a curia both slimmed down and opened up to collaboration with bishops all over the world. Parolin has a gift the Argentine pope considers indispensable: sacerdotal commitment. Those who know him say he is a good priest.

The replacement was carried out methodically. Pope Francis waited a courteous interval of seven months, during which Bertone sought in vain to obtain a year's extension. But the pope had made up his mind in March 2013 that the changing of the guard would take place when summer was over, and so it did. Parolin was elevated to the purple and officially took charge of the Secretariat of State on 15 October, although an unforeseen liver operation kept him from effectively doing so until 18 November.

Thirty days after the conclave, the pope initiated his revolution. With a press release on 13 April, he set up a new organ to work with him, a group of eight cardinals from the five continents: from Latin America the Honduran cardinal Oscar Rodríguez Maradiaga, who was appointed coordinator, and the Chilean Francisco Javier Errázuriz; from North America, the U.S. cardinal Sean Patrick O'Malley; from Europe, the German Reinhard Marx; from Asia, the Indian Oswald Gracias; from Africa, the Congolese Laurent Monsengwo Pasinya; and from Oceania, the Australian George Pell. Their far-flung origins reflect the globalized church that Francis has in mind. The eighth and last member is the only one from within the curia, Cardinal Giuseppe Bertello, the president of the governorate of the state of Vatican City. Another Italian acts as secretary, Marcello Semeraro, former bishop of Albano. The group includes several personalities, including Monsengwo, who had worked in the conclave to assure radical change by securing Francis's election.

A privy council (to give it an informal label familiar from the history of political institutions) flanking the pontiff was such a stunning novelty that the Vatican spokesman Federico Lombardi hastened to issue a clarification to the effect that it was merely a working group, not an encroachment on the role of the Roman Curia. But the text in which its membership was announced goes much further. The eight cardinals, it states, would have the tasks of studying a reform of the curia as well as "advising the pope on the government of the universal church." It was the first step toward making collegiality into a reality.

Five months passed, and Francis broke fresh ground. On 28 September 2013, he made the new organ into an institution, denominated the Council of Cardinals, and specified that its task would be "assisting me in the governance of the universal church." The pope reserved the power to structure the council as circumstances dictated and to enlarge it if he saw fit. He desired a permanent consultative organ at his side, directly representing the bishops of the world, and made a point of stating that he was putting into practice "suggestions" advanced during the general meetings prior to the conclave.[19]

In fact, the council is a step toward shedding the ecclesiastical model of absolutist monarchy and giving the Catholic Church a communitarian structure in which the national episcopates will be able to take part in determining a strategy for the contemporary era, including the ways Catholics live their faith in modern society. With summer behind him, the pope accelerated the pace of change. The privy council of cardinals was convoked in rapid succession in October and December 2013 and then again in February 2014. The top agenda items included the drafting of a new statute for the Roman Curia, meant to reorganize it radically, and the decision to confront, in a Synod of Bishops, the whole tangle of problems around the family, contraception, sexuality, and same-sex relationships.

Francis is more than a charismatic personality; he is a political actor. His working methods are based on listening to and carefully assessing a range of proposals. During the first year of his pontificate, he took no vacation—not a visit to an Alpine village in the manner of Karol Wojtyla, not even a real period of repose in August in the papal villa at Castel Gandolfo. It was as though he felt that the time at his disposal was not unlimited.

He spent the early months of his government systematically consulting with all the branches of the curia and the representatives of the principal Catholic organizations. Maria Voce, the president of the Focolare Movement, had occasion to meet him during this period and was left with the impression of a personality "very mild yet at the same time endowed with an extraordinary force of character. He is prudent, not a gambler, but if he feels the inspiration of the will of God, he doesn't stop until the job is done."[20]

A political actor, a man of government, has to be flexible. The remaking of the curia is Francis's long-term priority, but the ongoing damage being done to the church by financial scandal has forced the question of money to the top of his agenda. During the summer of 2013, he created a set of organs aimed at bringing transparency and reviewing expenditures. On 24 June, he nominated a committee to look into the IOR: the Vatican Bank would have to "align itself" with the church's mission. The committee included Mary Ann Glendon from the United States, an academic and the first woman to head a diplomatic delegation of the Holy See at the United Nations (UN) Conference on the Status of Women at Peking in 1995, a former president of the Pontifical Academy of Sciences, and subsequently the U.S. ambassador to the Vatican during the second term of President George W. Bush.

A month later, on 18 July, a committee was created to "simplify and rationalize" the economic and administrative structures of the Holy See, with the aim of containing costs and outlays. On August 8, a "committee on financial security" was launched to check on the possible laundering of dirty money in all sectors of the Vatican. This body was headed by an American, Monsignor Brian Wells, an assessor in the "general affairs" section of the Secretariat of State, and brought together representatives of the relevant departments of the Holy See: the Prefecture of Economic Affairs, the governorate, the Vatican prosecutor, the Financial Information Authority, the security service.

In the composition of these new bodies, the pontiff followed an inclusive strategy. There was no Argentine faction or Jesuit faction or faction made up exclusively of his friends. Francis was aware that he was attempting in-depth reform of the structures and profile of the church—in fact, as both his supporters and his adversaries understood, a revolution. He knew that he needed to create the largest possible base of involvement and consensus for his innovations. The chairmanship of his privy council of eight cardinals may have been entrusted to the reformer Maradiaga, but there was a place on it for the conservative Pell of Sydney, for a Ratzinger man like Marx of Munich, and for a curial insider like Bertello, regarded until the conclave as Bertone's man. The secretary of the Committee for Financial-Administrative Reform was a member of Opus Dei, Monsignor Lucio Angel Vallejo Balda, who came from the Prefecture of Economic Affairs. Fernando Vérgez Alzaga, a legionary of Christ (but one untainted by the scandal surrounding the legion's founder, Marcial Maciel), became secretary-general of the governorate of the state of Vatican City. The American Wells was in fact named to two of these bodies, the anti-money-laundering committee and the committee to reform the IOR—a reflection of the strong pressure coming from the U.S. hierarchy to clean up the Vatican.

This range reflects the range of tendencies existing in the Catholic Church, precisely as Bergoglio wanted it to. In dismantling the imperial church, the pope knew he needed to harness allies and collaborators from different backgrounds. The electoral coalition that had backed him wanted a reform of the curia above all else, and what he had in mind was much more than a shakeup to make it run more efficiently.

Until the end of the Ratzinger pontificate, the Roman Curia had always been seen as an instrument in the service of papal government. Francis changed that; he proclaimed his intention to remake it into an instrument in the joint service of the pope and the bishops of the world. That this would entail severe disruption was perfectly clear to him because the curia, operating in the name of the supreme pontiff, had become a species of idol in its own right over the centuries, a center of power governing Catholic communities everywhere.

Bergoglio defends and praises the personal commitment of all who labor in the curia. But its limitations are starkly clear to him. Its defect, he said in his colloquy with Eugenio Scalfari, is that it is "Vatican-centric. It sees and looks after the interests of the Vatican, which are still, for the most part, temporal interests." The privy council of eight cardinals, he explained, "is the beginning of a church with an organization that is not just top down but also horizontal." These were strong words because they were explicit. The conversation between Pope Francis and Scalfari was published on 1 October 2013 in *La Repubblica*, reprinted the same day in its entirety by the *Osservatore Romano*, and posted online at news.va, the Vatican news website.[21] Nevertheless, the interview created a great deal of resentment inside the apostolic palace, and on 15 November 2013 it was taken down from the Vatican site. Federico Lombardi, the papal spokesman, let it be known that the article had not been carefully checked word for word and was therefore to be regarded as "reliable in its overall import, but not as regards the specific wording." The interview has not been included among the official texts of the pontificate.

This odd reversal, coming a month and a half after the fact, was an alarm signal, a symptom of the hidden conflicts generated by Bergoglio's revolution. The ninety-year-old founder of La Repubblica, who had written up the interview afterward from memory (as, for that matter, the Corriere della Sera journalist Alberto Cavallari had done after his first interview with Paul VI), reported a spoken phrase that well expresses the thought of Pope Francis: "The church is, or should go back to being, a community of God's people, and priests, pastors and bishops who have the care of souls, are at the service of the people of God."[22]

The extent of the revolution Francis had in mind emerged clearly in the controversial interview he gave to the director of the Jesuit journal La Civiltà Cattolica, the specific wording of which is not in question and in which his assessments and intentions appear even more radical in certain respects. He even avoids using the word curia in order not to foreground it. What he says is: "The Roman dicasteries [government departments] are at the service of the pope and the bishops. They must help both the particular churches and the bishops' conferences. They are instruments of help. In some cases, however, when they are not properly understood, they run the risk of becoming institutions of censorship."[23] To make the point even more explicit, Francis clarifies: "The Roman dicasteries are mediators; they are not middlemen or managers."[24] No pontiff since the Council of Trent in the sixteenth century has called so radically into question the role of power in the Roman Curia.

Francis's revolution is not an operation that can be carried out in the space of a few months. Cardinal Maradiaga, coordinator of the privy council of cardinals, has already forecast that to rewrite the statute of the curia "will take time" and require a great deal of consultation, first of all with those who work in the curial offices.[25] No perestroika, as the career of Mikhail Gorbachev demonstrates, can be effected if it mounts a frontal challenge to the very structure of the organization within which individuals have spent their whole lives.

In the cathedral of Salerno, inside a glass casket, may be seen the remains of Pope Gregory VII, who died almost a thousand years ago. His body is wrapped in a mantle of purple and gold, and purple is also the color of his slippers. The *Dictatus papae*, a declaration of papal absolutism, was compiled during his reign. In it we read "that the Roman pontiff alone can with right be called universal . . . that he alone may use the imperial insignia . . . that this title [*pope*] is unique in the world . . . that a sentence passed by him may be modified by no one; and that he alone may modify the sentences of anyone." There is a direct line running from this totalitarian presumption and the encyclical *Pastor aeternus*, with which in 1870 Pius IX asserted as dogma that the pope, speaking ex cathedra in matters of faith or morals, enjoys infallibility, and "such definitions of the Roman Pontiff are of themselves, and not by the consent of the church, irreformable." Any who would dare to contradict this stance deserve excommunication.

Infallibility subsequently turned out to be such a two-edged sword for the church that, except for the dogma of the assumption up to heaven of the Virgin Mary "body and soul," proclaimed by Pius XII in 1950, the papacy has avoided invoking it. The principle of collegiality decreed by Vatican II was conceived expressly to offset the overbearing quality of formal papal power.

The notion of an omnipotent hierarchy that never errs is profoundly embedded in the self-understanding of the Catholic Church. In the exercise of his power, Pius XII liked to say, "I don't want collaborators, I want executors." Cardinal Giuseppe Siri, archbishop of Genoa from decades before the Vatican II council until decades after it (1946–1987), maintained that "my successor will have nothing to do, I have thought of everything . . . the diocese of Genoa will run itself."[26]

Fifty or one hundred years are no more than the bat of an eyelash in the history of the church. The language may change, but the concept of the hierarchy as a pyramid continues to pervade the organization. The revolution of Pope Francis aims to restore vitality to the Synod of Bishops, an institution created by Paul VI to play a consultative role and keep alive the experience of the council. Over the half-century of its existence, the episcopal synod has taken on the character of a major conference, usually held at the Vatican every three years to address general topics. The bishops are allotted a few minutes each to make their points. Groups of bishops who are users of the same language then prepare a series of final statements; these are then filed and forgotten.

Pope Francis has decided to make radical changes to the way the synod works, rendering it truly consultative. For the assembly of October 2014, he insisted on a precise agenda so as to give the representatives of the national Episcopal Conferences from the different continents the opportunity to state their opinions forcefully on specific points. Francis is a strong believer in the value of participation. When an attack by the Western powers on Syria seemed imminent, he consulted a wide range of persons in the curia before taking a public stand against the idea. "God doesn't speak to one person in isolation; he speaks when people are together," he confided to Maria Voce of the Focolari.[27] Not everyone in the curia agrees, and autocracy does have its supporters. Francis responds: "But now I hear some people tell me: 'Do not consult too much, and decide by yourself.' Instead, I believe that consultation is very important."[28]

Yet the Argentine pope does not see his role as *primus inter pares* or the president of a sort of multinational. He made this clear to journalists on the return journey from Brazil. His implicit model seems to resemble that of the Society of Jesus, where the superior general governs with the aid of ten assistants nominated by the general congregation. In the end, though, his word is law.

Cardinal Parolin gave this interpretation of the idea of participation Francis has in mind. "We are always reminded that the church is not a democracy, but the times do require a more democratic spirit, in the sense of an attentive heeding. . . . Collegial leadership of the church [signifies] that all positions may be defended. Then it falls to the pope to make a decision."[29]

Francis has a hard head, says a cardinal who knows him well. He acts with determination. During his first year, he achieved the right mixture of keeping some in their posts, appointing others for fixed terms, and letting yet others go. Heads have rolled. In September 2013, he removed the powerful head of the Congregation for the

Clergy, Cardinal Mauro Piacenza, spearhead of the conservative forces in the curia, who during the conclave was thought to be destined for the post of secretary of state if the Brazilian cardinal Odilo Scherer were elected pope. In the Vatican, as elsewhere, ambition exacts a price.

Piacenza, who at sixty-nine was a relatively youthful player, was moved over to head the Apostolic Penitentiary, the department concerned with indulgences, absolutions, and dispensations. In October 2013, Bertone lost the Secretariat of State, and in January 2014 he was stripped of the only operational portfolio he retained, his place on the committee of cardinals supervising the IOR. With him went Cardinal Domenico Calcagno, the president of APSA (the patrimonial treasury of the Vatican), and Cardinal Scherer, the Brazilian *papabile*, undermined by his close links to Bertone.

Two other men considered *papabili* in 2013 were, however, advanced. The Canadian Marc Ouellet was confirmed as head of the Congregation for Bishops, and the Hungarian Péter Erdö was named rapporteur for the Synod of Bishops in autumn 2014.

Step by step Francis took apart Bertone's system of power in key economic sectors. Another ecclesiastic linked to Bertone, Monsignor Giuseppe Sciacca, lost his position as general secretary of the Vatican governorate. In 2014, the pope removed Cardinal Antono Canizares from his post as head of the Congregation for Divine Worship and the Discipline of the Sacraments at the end of his mandate. Canizares, a follower of the Ratzinger theological line and a former primate of Spain, was dispatched not to the diocese of Madrid but to a see of lesser importance, Valencia.

Last, the prelate who had accompanied Francis onto the balcony of Saint Peter's on the evening of 13 March 2013 disappeared noiselessly from the scene: Monsignor Franco Camaldo, dean of the Papal Masters of Ceremonies. Camaldo had been the subject of much chatter on the web for his connections to a lobby involved in wheeling and dealing and headed by Diego Anemone and Angelo Balducci, a former "gentleman of His Holiness." The pope sidelined him by naming him a canon of the Vatican basilica.

Francis is mild-mannered, but he plays for keeps.

6

The Face of a Parish Priest

Francis lets himself be embraced. He seeks contact with people, touches them, and allows them to touch him. When the American cardinal Timothy Dolan placed a companionable hand on the pope's shoulder in the Sala Clementina two days after the election, Vatican insiders raised their eyebrows, but Francis just smiled.

Physical proximity is part of his way of communicating, as it is in South American culture generally and for that matter in African and Mediterranean culture, too. He doesn't want to be a statue. The faithful embrace him whenever they can, clasping him tightly and sometimes, like one Italian soldier returning from Afghanistan, at length. "John Paul II came to see, Benedict XVI to hear, and Francis to touch," is how Cardinal Tauran put it.[1]

On 28 July 2013, 3 million people gathered at Copacabana on four kilometers of beach to take part in the pope's final mass for World Youth Day. On the eve of his first Christmas in the Vatican, more than 1.5 million believers and pilgrims had already taken part in his audiences in St. Peter's Square.[2] There is no distance between them and the pope. Francis doesn't lean down while keeping aloof, as protocol would dictate. He takes them, draws them to him, caresses them, lets them surround him. He converses with the faithful and listens to them, looking them in the eye. If it is raining, he remains bareheaded, like all the other pilgrims.

Back in Buenos Aires he wasn't like that. Only when he put on the white cassock did the carapace of timidity and modesty he had worn all his life split and fall away. "He was quieter and more introverted," said Pepe Di Paolo, the shantytown priest. Something inside him has changed. The director of the Argentine cultural journal *Criterio*, José María Poirier, remembers him back home as "almost sad, preoccupied, saying little, but smiling." Even at Jesuit headquarters in Rome, one or two fellow Jesuits recall that he sometimes gave the impression of being "self-contained and self-sufficient."

In the Vatican, they refer (with a play on words) to the special aura that descends on new popes as the "grace of state," as though the Holy Spirit had caused new capacities to descend upon the chosen one. Indeed, at paragraph 2004 the Catholic catechism guarantees that it does. The fact of the matter is that from his first encounter with the crowd in St. Peter's Square and especially in the wake of his trip to Brazil, Jorge Mario Bergoglio has felt the swelling enthusiasm of the faithful, and this has caused him to express more openly (to his own surprise) the tenderness that he used to recommend to his priests in their dealings with people.

Francis is "near." Karol Wojtyla, who was mourned like a father or grandfather at his death, gave the sensation that he was addressing every individual amid the crowd while never losing his regal authority and even in face-to-face contact he never abridged the difference of status. Francis annuls all barriers. He is as close as a relative; the sincerity with which he reminds hearers of the evangelical precepts is disarming. He preaches compassion and invites them not to be afraid of tenderness. Little children will run toward him while he is speaking at a papal audience. He ruffles their hair like an uncle and doesn't mind if one or two scramble onto his lap. The only authority that exists and reigns in the church (he lets it be felt) is Christ, of whom he is a disciple.

He doesn't want a screen of protocol around him. Francis tolerates the papal gendarmes and appreciates their loyalty but would prefer to do without them. "I don't need bodyguards; I'm not defenseless," he would grumble in the early days. The day after his election he went to Santa Maria Maggiore to pray before the image of the Madonna, "Protectress of the Roman People," and expressed the desire that the basilica should remain open to the faithful and to tourists during his prayer. On the altar he left a bouquet of flowers, like a small-town priest. When Francis returned to the great Roman basilica after his voyage to Rio de Janeiro, he left a colored soccer ball and a jersey at the altar—ex-votos unheard of from a pontiff.

His message on Christmas Day 2013 was: "Let us not fear that our hearts be moved. We need this! Let us allow ourselves to be warmed by the tenderness of God; we need his caress."[3] His magic lies in the way he brings out the deep needs hidden in the souls of millions of persons. Even before Bergoglio stepped out onto the balcony on that historic day, March 13, there was an intermittent vein of expectant desire within Catholicism for a "Francis." The name had begun to circulate some time before the conclave. Masses of believers, no longer trusting a church that felt like a distant stepmother to them, were awaiting a figure like him. When he visited Assisi in October 2013, a banner along the road greeted him affectionately: "1226–2013. Francis, we've missed you."

Artists are prophets in their moments of creative felicity, capturing the spirit of the times and the soul of the multitudes. By pure coincidence, right after Benedict XVI announced his resignation, the Catholic film director Ermanno Olmi published *Letter to a Church That Has Forgotten Jesus*. He characterized the official church as a "disattentive mother, more concerned with pomp and ceremony," attached to its worldly possessions, shaken by scandals and intrigues, and forgetful of the springtime represented by Vatican II. "And what have we learned, and neglected, from the *poverello* of Assisi?" Olmi asked. "And you, O Catholic Church, are you truly the house open not only to obedient Christians, but also to those who seek God in liberty, beyond their doubts?" Touching on themes that would soon be associated with the future Pope Francis, Olmi implored: "Show us, O church, that in your heart you have the weak, the majority who are born but to die."[4]

Two years earlier, at the Cannes Film Festival, the director Nanni Moretti, culturally a secularist, had presented a striking portrait of a newly elected pontiff who does not want to reign over a church in which he no longer recognizes himself. Michel Piccoli, the actor who plays the reluctant pope, bears an extraordinary physical resemblance to Pope Francis, right down to the timid wave of the right hand. Among his lines are these: "At this moment, the church has need of a guide, someone with the strength to bring about immense changes, who seeks to encounter all, who has love for all and a capacity to understand."[5] Without being famous, countless other simple believers, questioned during the Ratzinger era in St. Peter's Square about the kind of faith they had in their hearts, answered as did one believing midwife: "For me Jesus is mercy [*misericordia*] above all else."

Pope Francis is on the same wavelength as the majority of Catholics. If the shepherd, as he maintains, must have "the smell of the sheep," then his flock will recognize in him their own odor. There is something instinctive in the way a touch is exchanged between him and them. This is how Francis characterized his mission in the early months of his pontificate: "I see clearly that the thing the church needs most today is the ability to heal wounds and to warm the hearts of the faithful; it needs nearness, proximity. I see the church as a field hospital after battle. It is useless to ask a seriously injured person if he has high cholesterol and about the level of his blood sugars! You have to heal his wounds. Then we can talk about everything else. Heal the wounds, heal the wounds. . . . And you have to start from the ground up."[6]

It is telling that four days before Bergoglio's election, while the prevailing climate was still that of a metaphysical church superior to anything and anyone, one member of the Catholic hierarchy in Italy—a group fossilized by its own emphasis on doctrinal certainty and its own self-defensiveness—launched a frontal attack on precisely this image of healing. "It appears that for Ermanno Olmi, the church is only strong if it is supplying accompaniment, nearness, and assistance. The church as the world's Red Cross nurse, close to the sufferings ancient and modern of mankind," wrote Monsignor Alberto Carrara, episcopal delegate for culture in the diocese of Bergamo, indignantly. Ah no, he countered, the "perspective of faith is quite different."[7]

Francis has proclaimed a church that does not "lock itself up in small things, in small-minded rules," does not "long for an exaggerated doctrinal 'security'," does not transform religion into ideology but concentrates on the essential message: "Jesus Christ has saved you."[8] The pope speaks of a church that is "mother and shepherdess," and he makes the point clear and explicit: "Have one dogmatic certainty: God is in every person's life. . . . Even if the life of a person has been a disaster, even if it is destroyed by vices, drugs, or anything else—God is in this person's life. You can, you must, try to seek God in every human life."[9]

The reason for the extraordinary support he enjoys lies in this message. "Thank you, thank you!" was the cry reaching him from the crowd in Saint Peter's Square on the day of the inaugural mass for the pontificate. "Thanks," not "Long live the pope." Thanks for his way of speaking, of presenting himself, of being. Among simple believers one hears the most intuitive judgments: "Did you see? We have a pope," said an elderly mother to her daughter, a manager. On the streetcars of Rome the day after the election, what one heard was: "We have a pope who makes himself understood." The mother of one monsignor from the national Conference of Italian Bishops said to him: "Now the pope is going to straighten you out!" Don Alberto Ponzi, the vicar of Anagni, said that laity have begun prodding their priests and mentioning Pope Francis as they do so: "The pope said this, the pope did that," they admonish. It happens in other regions and nations. Men and women who are agnostic have admitted that they suddenly get interested in the news on television when there is reportage about the pope, and these are people who never normally bother with the church and the priesthood.

The frame of mind of the masses is summed up in words uttered frequently in a wide variety of situations: "I'm not an atheist, but not a practicing Catholic either. I had drifted away from the church. Francis has revived my interest." Marco Tarquinio, director of the newspaper of the Italian bishops, Avvenire, testified: "One reader wrote that he had long since ceased to pray. Now he prays every day for Francis. The pope warms the hearts of the faithful, reaches the lukewarm, and lures those most remote." Bergoglio's frankness about his own human frailty helps to win over public opinion. Speaking of himself, he said: "Even the pope makes confession every two weeks because even the pope is a sinner! My confessor listens to what I have to say, counsels me, and pardons me because we all need this pardon."[10] Other popes have called themselves sinners, but in their mouths the word savored of sacred rhetoric. Coming from Pope Francis, it is an authentic admission that takes him down off the pedestal.

His frankness in pointing to the rot in the church without beating around the bush captivates folk. He doesn't like clergy who are not up to their job and lose themselves in the hunt for material goods: "It truly grieves me to see a priest or a sister with the latest model of a car: but this can't be!" he exclaimed to a group of seminarians and novices to whom he gave an audience. "I think that cars are necessary because there is so much work to be done, and also in order to get about . . . but choose a more humble car! And if you like the beautiful one, only think of all the children who are dying of hunger."[11] At times he lashes out: "And you are all disgusted when you find in us priests who are not authentic or sisters who are not authentic!"[12]

Sobriety to Francis does not mean going around with a lugubrious countenance fit for Lent—what he calls a "chili pepper face." There is no sanctity in gloominess, he stresses. If a seminarian or a novice shows the world a sad visage, something isn't right. At Assisi, he stated to the cloistered Poor Clares that contemplation ought to bring joy, humanity, a smile. But not the smile of an airline hostess! The smile that comes from within. And he teased the sisters a bit: beware those whose behavior is extravagantly spiritual. The best advice for them is Saint Teresa's advice: "Feed them a beefsteak."[13]

The films a man prefers are an indicator of who he is. Francis's favorite movie is *Babette's Feast* (Gabriel Axel, 1987), the story of a Frenchwoman who winds up in a remote Danish village, bigoted and mean. One day news arrives from Paris that she has won a lottery prize of ten thousand francs. She spends the whole sum to offer the community a French banquet, a jubilee for the palate—turtle soup, quails, vol-au-vent, caviar, wines, champagne, dessert, exotic fruit—that slowly thaws the souls of the diners, a handful of men and women burdened with a sense of sin, fearful of the Last Judgment, made melancholy by rancor, and terrorized by the very thought of enjoying themselves.

Their faces are gradually transfigured under the impact of the flavor and smell of the food; the diners' spirits rise, and they start to breathe again. Set free, they come to a vision of life they had never imagined before. "Mercy and truth have come together, rectitude and felicity have exchanged kisses," concludes one of the guests, raising his glass. "Because God," he adds, "doesn't impose conditions. One must wait with faith and greet with recognition." Bergoglio believes in the joy of giving and in a faith as a life of happiness under the sign of the Gospel, not tormented by visions of God as policeman.

During an audience, a Spanish mother whispered to him: "Thanks for being another Jesus on earth." Francis grew red in the face, paused a few seconds, then burst out laughing: "But I'm a devil!" Bergoglio's humanity is woven out of his lifetime of experience. He and John Paul II are the only pontiffs who know what labor is. At age thirteen, he was earning a living in a sock factory and was later employed at a chemical plant. "I was a bouncer" in a discotheque, he confessed to the surprise of the parishioners of San Cirillo Alessandrino on the outskirts of Rome.[14]

Bergoglio had a girlfriend when he was seventeen and danced the *milonga* and the tango—not the insipid Mitteleuropean version that even Wojtyla learned to dance, along with the waltz, as was customary among youths of good family during the interwar years. He danced the Argentine tango, full of sensuality. "A sad thought that dances," according to Ernesto Sabato. "A man's hands around a woman's waist, a woman's hands around a man's neck, irresistible legs, one arm guiding the steps, one bearing the partner's weight, hips moving and stiffening . . . the invitation and the rejection, solitude and its remedy."[15]

For Bergoglio, it is essential that the choice of the religious life be rooted in total personal authenticity. "What can I do for my grandson, who wants to become a Franciscan?" a woman asked him at the parish of San Cirillo. Pray that he has the perseverance to pursue his goal, answered the pope, "but also the courage to turn back if he comes to realize that this is not the right road for him."

Francis likes to speak in parables. At his first Angelus, he spoke of the time he met a woman more than eighty years old, who said to him with an air of certainty, "The Lord forgives all things." Bergoglio said to her, "But how do you know, madam?" Back came the reply: "If the

Lord did not forgive everything, the world would not exist." Stories serve Francis to send out a message that erases the paradigm of the church as a judge on the bench and the faithful as criminals in the dock. "God never ever tires of forgiving us! We ourselves tire, we do not want to ask . . . but He never tires of forgiving."

God is a merciful father; he has so much patience. God is greater than sin. No one should lose heart. The appeal to divine tenderness goes together with tenderness toward one's fellow man. The Christian, who asks from God, must be ready to give to others. "People today need words, certainly, but above all they need us to testify to mercy, the tenderness of the Lord that warms the heart, reawakens hope, and draws us toward the good," Francis exclaimed one Sunday.[16] We must never be hard-hearted.

Addressing the heads of the religious orders and speaking once more in striking imagery, the pope insisted that they should not form their recruits through rules and doctrines. "Formation is a work of craftsmanship, not of policing. We have to form the heart. Otherwise, we are forming little monsters. And then these little monsters form the people of God. That really gives me goose flesh."[17]

His appeal to the heart at a time when an economic and existential crisis has entire continents in its grip, including vast areas of the West that are no longer shielded from poverty, caused an upsurge of approval in the polls. In Italy, 87 percent of the population are with him, a Eurispes poll at the beginning of 2014 revealed. Right after his election, a Demopolis poll registered a 95 percent approval rating among Catholics. What people like are his simplicity (72 percent), his spontaneity of language (67 percent), his attention to the weakest in society (65 percent). Fifty-eight percent believe that, thanks to him, there will be significant change in the church.

Time magazine named him Person of the Year for 2013, a recognition previously awarded among popes only to John XXIII and John Paul II. "He has not changed the words, but he's changed the music. . . . Rarely has a new player on the world stage captured so much attention so quickly—young and old, faithful and cynical," wrote Nancy Gibbs,[18] paraphrasing an opinion often expressed in the United States in the era of John Paul II. Then it was said that young people admired Wojtyla the "singer," but not his song, meaning the doctrine he preached. With Francis, that is not how it is: the music is decidedly different. In the multireligious United States, he was given a 79 percent approval rating among Catholics and an ample 58 percent among the overall population.[19]

Seventy-one percent of Russians, of whom the great majority are either Orthodox or nonbelievers, wish him to visit their country.[20] Even in China, fifty members of the media, journalism associations, and the most important diplomatic delegations named him the third-ranking personality of the year in the China international press forum. Never before in the history of Communist China had a religious personality figured on this list.

At Rome, the Wednesday audiences have expanded into major events. They sometimes last more than three hours. The entrances to St. Peter's Square are barred on Tuesday evening, and on Wednesday Via della Conciliazione is closed off entirely. The pope gets around in an automobile without bulletproof windows and sometimes "enters" Italian territory by stepping outside the piazza. Grown-ups and children cry out, "Francesco, Francesco," in the hope of touching him. They give him scarves; they offer him canned drinks, which he tastes; they exchange white skullcaps with him. When a cry reaches his ears, he turns, leans out of the car, and waves "ciao" with his hand, as though he has spotted an old friend. Often he gets out of the car. Faced with a lady in a wheelchair whose purse had fallen to the ground, he bent over to pick it up and put it delicately back in her lap.

Television viewers will not soon forget the image of the papal automobile at Rio de Janeiro, blocked and surrounded at the exit from the airport by an unstoppable crowd: thousands and thousands of persons who overran security, while the most determined shoved their hands through the windows of the minivan in which Francis sat smiling. Three days later, on 25 July 2013, while visiting the Varginha di Rio favela, Francis abandoned his vehicle and set off for a walkabout in the rain through the muddy streets of the shantytown. He prayed in the church dedicated to the Madonna and then knocked at the door of number 81, entering the humble dwelling of Manoel José and Maria Luisa de Penha, just as a local priest would do. They chatted and prayed together. He blessed all the children in the house and picked them up, including the newborn. "I wish I could have knocked at every door, said 'hello,' requested a glass of cold water, taken a coffee, a *cafezinho* . . . not a *cachaça* (a spirit distilled from sugar cane)," he said later from the dais at the neighborhood soccer field. And the people knew it was true.[21]

Francis suffers from not being able to move around freely. Wojtyla needed the outdoors; Bergoglio desires human contact. "You know how often I've wanted to go walking through the streets of Rome, because, in Buenos Aires, I liked to go for a walk in the city. I really liked to do that!" he confessed to journalists.[22] His desire not to be kept in a cage is irresistible, manifesting itself at morning mass, which he does not celebrate alone but rather in the chapel at the Santa Marta residence before a group of the faithful. Through his morning meditations, he engages in almost daily dialogue with the world: many important messages receive their first formulation there.

He finds an outlet for his urge to communicate in writing and telephoning. He lifts the receiver, asks the Vatican switchboard for a number, and greets his interlocutor personally. He called the newsstand owner in Buenos Aires to cancel his subscriptions; he called his usual shoe repair shop and joked about the red shoes he doesn't wear; he may call the shop assistant in a bookstore or a group of prisoners with whom he maintains regular contact. The first time he placed a call, a switchboard operator said to him, "If you're the pope, then I'm Napoleon."[23]

Francis needs to hear unofficial voices around him, voices from everyday existence. He answers the many messages he gets. He telephoned the parents of Andrea Ferri, a gas pump attendant from Pesaro who was killed in a robbery. He called a pregnant girl who had been abandoned; a child who sent him a drawing; a woman who had been raped; a parish priest; a couple with two sick children; an Argentine former drug addict ("Hi Corvo, how's it going?"); the mother of Elisa Claps, the young student from Potenza who disappeared for sixteen years and whose body was discovered in 2010 in the attic of a church. For the pope, making these calls is a way to feel like a parish priest again —for that matter, a *cura callejero*, a street priest. "Thank you, Holiness," said Elisa's mother to him, embittered by the reticence of the late Mimì Sabia, the priest of the Church of the Trinità where her body was found, "for giving us back the church we believed in."

In the Vatican and among ecclesiastical hierarchies around the world, satisfaction at the pope's popularity, which casts a glow of approval on the church as a whole, is enormous. Yet behind the scenes dislike has been aroused at how day by day Francis is dismantling Catholicism's cherished icon of inviolable sovereignty, the papacy. His way of doing things is described as too "common." The same was said more than half a century ago about John XXIII, whose folksy good humor was derided in comparison to the hieratic solemnity of Pius XII.

It was not long before criticism, fed by the dislike of the most conservative sectors of the curia, began to appear in some newspapers. In *Il Foglio*, Giuliano Ferrara accused the new pope of "excessive tenderness," lack of concern for the "slaughter" of abortion, and failure to grasp that globalization and free markets guarantee "emancipation and liberation" for the masses of the third world. Marcello Veneziani suggested that he risks becoming an "oddball," and the sociologist Gianfranco Morra stigmatized his absence from the concert in the Vatican and claimed that his message to the public is fraught with "populist archetypes."

The Catholic writer Vittorio Messori, interviewer of Ratzinger and Wojtyla, ironized about the papal appeals to poverty. "The poor church is a piece of nonsense: Jesus wasn't a starving beggar . . . he had economic resources, even a treasurer who later betrayed him, Judas Iscariot." Indeed, he said, Jesus wore an expensive tunic; "the guards rolled dice for it because it was costly. . . . Jesus wore Armani."[24] On television, Messori distilled subtle poisons in the early months: "The less the pope says, the better. Certain interviews on airplanes, certain off the cuff remarks, can give rise to erroneous interpretations." He recommended a return to "sobriety."[25]

Conservatives were extremely annoyed at Francis's decision not to celebrate his first Holy Thursday at the Basilica of San Giovanni in Laterano and to perform the rite of the washing of the feet in the juvenile prison at Casal di Marmo instead, breaking traditions of long standing. Even more irritating to them was his choice to wash the feet of two women, one of them a Muslim. How can a woman, a follower of Islam, play the part of one of the apostles at the Last Supper? commented traditionalist prelates in the apostolic palace. "Previously in Buenos Aires, Cardinal Bergoglio admitted girls to this rite. And we proposed a feminine presence this time. The Vatican, after some resistance, accepted," explained the prison chaplain, Father Gaetano Greco.[26] It was a sign of the instinctive bond between the pontiff and those Catholic clergymen best acquainted with the struggles of daily life.

To the twelve juveniles—Catholic, Orthodox, and Muslim—Francis said simply: "Now we will perform this ceremony of foot washing, and let each person ask themselves: Am I really prepared to serve and aid my fellow man? Let each be thinking only of that, and this sign is a caress from Jesus."[27] Francis refers to Jesus, but he is ready to encourage the followers of other religions to live their own faiths well. At Lampedusa, where he arrived in the wake of the tragedy in which seven shipwrecked persons died and dozens survived by clinging for hours to a tuna cage, the pope expressed the wish to fifty or so Muslim refugees that their religious fast during Ramadan would bring them "plentiful spiritual fruits."

Francis doesn't much like traveling. Lampedusa was by choice his first trip outside Rome. The mass held on the little sports ground was celebrated on a boat that served as an altar. The wooden chalice used during the rite and the wooden pastoral staff in the pontiff's hands were carved from the remains of one of the death boats. The pope was not assisted by a master of ceremonies; during the homily, Francis held the microphone himself, as he had done so often in his life as a bishop in Argentina. "Welcome among the last and the least," read one sign posted on the wall of a house. Another expressed more bitterness: "The pope brings hope, the politicians eat." Or else they make shameless promises. Former prime minister Silvio Berlusconi, who came to Lampedusa in 2011, had offered the prospect of a tax holiday, an extra effort to boost tourism, the creation of a duty-free zone, gambling casinos and golf courses, and, to top it all off, the nomination of Sicily for the Nobel Peace Prize.

In contrast, at Lampedusa Francis used harsh language. " I felt that I had to come here today, to pray and to offer a sign of my closeness, but also to challenge our consciences lest this tragedy be repeated." And he added in a low voice, "Please, let it not be repeated!" The homily was among the most vibrant of his pontificate. "How many of

us, myself included, have lost our bearings; we are no longer attentive
to the world in which we live. . . . Who is responsible for the blood of
these brothers and sisters of ours? Nobody! That is our answer: It isn't
me; I don't have anything to do with it; it must be someone else, but
certainly not me. Yet God is asking each of us: 'Where is the blood of
your brother which cries out to me?' Today no one in our world feels
responsible; we have lost a sense of responsibility for our brothers and
sisters." Francis described a world in which every person is shut up
inside his or her illusory "bubble of soap" that encourages indifference
toward others — indeed, the "globalization of indifference." He urged
his hearers to weep at the cruelty that has spread across the planet "and
[the cruelty] of all those who in anonymity make social and economic
decisions which open the door to tragic situations like this."[28]

The destinations the pope instinctively prefers are sites of suffering.
At Assisi, a town he had never seen before, he began his pilgrimage
early in the morning, arriving at the Istituto Serafico for handicapped
persons at 7:30 a.m. For more than an hour, he caressed, kissed, and
hugged a hundred people with multiple disabilities. Children and
adults with marked bodies, who "don't speak, don't hear, and don't
vote" and hence are forgotten by society, affirmed the institute's president, Francesco Di Maolo.

The pope, his skullcap awry, moved back and forth among the
patients and stopped before each: limbs contorted by seizures,
bodies shut up in autism, dead eyes, heads that oscillated obses-
sively. Francis's hands did the speaking for him. His fingers grasped
outstretched arms, ruffled heads of hair at length, caressed cheeks,
enfolded shoulders, traced minute signs of the cross on foreheads
shaken by tremors. Stopped by an autistic child, the pope patiently
followed the gestures of the little one, who kept mechanically clap-
ping the palms of his hands. The minutes passed, and the room began
to resound with uninterrupted cries, groans, and moans. Francis
advanced slowly from one chair to the next. When speech is unavail-
ing, he transmits his nearness body against body.

7

Walking with Unbelievers

basilica on an October morning, a newspaper office on a
September morning: the trajectories of two pontiffs attempting
to throw a bridge across the river to the far shore of unbe-
lief pass through Santa Maria degli Angeli at Assisi and the editorial
offices of *La Repubblica*.

It was 27 October 2011, and in the entrance to Santa Maria degli
Angeli Benedict XVI was exchanging handshakes and offering a welcome to representatives of organized religions who had come to Assisi
to participate in a day of reflection, dialogue, and prayer for peace and
justice in the world. Pope Ratzinger had, with some hesitation, taken
up John Paul II's idea of convoking an interreligious summit in the city
of St. Francis. Along with dignitaries from the Christian churches, there
were Jews, Muslims, and representatives of the Oriental creeds and
African tradition. And there was something new. For the first time, the
German pope decided to invite personalities who were not believers:

Julia Kristeva, the French semiologist and psychoanalyst of Bulgarian origin; the Mexican philosopher Guillermo Hurtado; the Austrian economist Walter Baier; and the Italian philosopher Remo Bodei.

Even earlier in September 2009, on the occasion of his visit to the Czech Republic (among the European countries where the atheism of indifference is most prevalent), Benedict XVI had decided to launch a confrontation with "searchers for truth," men and women interested in asking questions about the meaning of existence, oblivious of the chasm between immanence and transcendence.

Ratzinger went on to give firm shape to the idea of arranging a meeting between agnostics and believers in a speech to the curia, maintaining that, "in addition to interreligious dialogue, there should be a dialogue with those to whom religion is something foreign, to whom God is unknown and who nevertheless do not want to be left merely Godless, but rather to draw near to him, albeit as the Unknown." Benedict XVI proposed to choose a place for this encounter, which he called, referring to the area in the temple of Jerusalem open to non-Jews, a "court of the gentiles."[1]

At the basilica of Assisi, Julia Kristeva said: "We must dare to bet on the continuous renewal of the capacity of men and women to listen and learn together." The semiologist invited the audience to discern the "complicity" between secular humanism—with its origins in the Renaissance and the Enlightenment—and Christian humanism. Her approach reassessed the great moral codes of our tradition: the Bible, the Gospels, the Koran, the Rigveda, Tao. The most important thing, she stressed, was the criterion of liberty. In that perspective, she alluded to the struggles for women's liberation, loving care for others, care for the earth, concern for the young, the sick, the aged, the disabled. Kristeva stressed that we have to prevent the destruction of the planet, something that *Homo sapiens* is now in a position to bring about in the name of beliefs, religions, and ideologies. But for us to dedicate ourselves to the common objective of saving the planet, she asserted, it is indispensable to engage in "continuing questioning of our personal, historical and social situation." The psychoanalyst proclaimed that "Man with a capital M does not exist. . . . Man does not make history, we are history." Men and women with all their specificity and individual diversity.[2]

Kristeva, a nonbeliever, accepted the offer of a critical dialogue, while directing an appeal to Pope Ratzinger against any temptation to transform thought and faith into ideology. Benedict XVI replied, manifesting the will of the church to join with all "pilgrims of truth, pilgrims of peace," and confirming its "decisive stand for human dignity and a . . . common engagement for peace against every form of destructive force."[3]

Two years later, on 11 September 2013, Italians saw this headline splashed around their newsstands: "Pope Francesco Writes to *La Repubblica*: 'An Open Dialogue with Nonbelievers.'" During the two intervening years, the Pontifical Council for Culture, headed by Cardinal Gianfranco Ravasi, had organized a number of meetings between Christians and nonbelievers in various nations of the world. Ravasi spoke of a church that recognizes the existence of "diverse visions of reality" and is prepared to accept the fact that both the believer and the atheist are bearers of an existential message to be reckoned with.[4]

No sooner was he elected than Pope Francis ignored protocol yet again and sent a signal of profound respect for the universe of the unbelieving. In a meeting with journalists accredited to the conclave, he terminated the audience not with the habitual formula, "I cordially impart to all of you my blessing," but went on to add delicately (switching from Italian to Spanish), "I told you I was cordially imparting my blessing. Since many of you are not members of the Catholic church, and others are not believers, I cordially give this blessing silently, to each of you, respecting the conscience of each, but in the knowledge that each of you is a child of God."[5]

The Argentine pope intended to go further—to engage on equal terms with those who not only do not believe, who do not seek God, regarding him as a consoling product of the imagination, but who have spent their lives directing explicit criticism at Catholic dogma and all forms of clericalism and ecclesiastical interference in public life. Eugenio Scalfari, founding editor of *La Repubblica*, is a species of secular pope in Italy, an acute observer of the weaknesses and contradictions of the ecclesiastical hierarchy, albeit expressing admiration for the person and the message of Jesus Christ.

During the summer of 2013, Scalfari directed a series of questions to Pope Bergoglio in two opinion pieces. He ranged from the rigid monotheism of the other two Abrahamic religions, Judaism and Islam, to the contradictory doctrine of the incarnation and from the conflict between Christ's preaching and the practice of power by the church to ultimate questions about the next world and the extinction of the human species. It was a genuine "dispute" that he was proposing to Bergoglio, a dispute of the kind that in centuries past took place between Christians and atheists, between Catholics and heretics—an intellectual match measuring two contenders and their basic points against each other.

Scalfari showed undisguised sympathy for the new pontiff, stating that he was "good like John XXIII, fascinates like Wojtyla, was raised by the Jesuits, and has chosen to call himself Francis because he wants the same church as the *poverello* of Assisi." But he did not spare him an array of insidious questions. Modernity, Scalfari remarked, has called into question the concept of absolute truth: the believer believes in revealed truth, the nonbeliever thinks in terms of subjective and relative truths—Is the nonbeliever not therefore in a state of sin? Or again: "If a person has no faith nor seeks it but commits what the church defines as sin, will the Christian God pardon him?" And the prince among secularists concluded: "What is the answer, most reverend Pope Francis?" Scalfari added a provocative comment. The model of the church preached by the Argentine pontiff is good for the world, and the new pope pleases everyone immensely, but "I don't believe there will be a Francis II" because the Catholic Church is a bastion of strength and has lasted for centuries precisely to the extent that it has never surrendered power.[6]

"Dear Doctor Scalfari," began the pope's reply, which arrived on Vatican letterhead. He then proceeded to sweep away the image of God as a customs agent, a bureaucratic divinity scrutinizing the practices of the nonbeliever and weighing the pros and cons of granting him the stamp of absolution. Francis went further; he did not even speak of pardon as descending from on high. He spoke of the God of Jesus, whose "mercy has no limits," and stressed a principle endorsed by Vatican II and profoundly rooted in secular morality: "There is sin, *even* for those who have no faith, when conscience is not followed. Listening to and obeying conscience means deciding in the face of what is understood to be good or evil. It is on the basis of this choice that the goodness or evil of our actions is determined."[7]

This long "letter to a nonbeliever" displays the inner freedom that Francis refuses to renounce. He knew perfectly well—and the whispering that went on in the corridors of the Vatican proved him right—that his gesture would be looked at askance by some prelates of the kind who detect the mark of the Antichrist in any criticism or interrogation directed at the church and who abhor the notion that a pontiff should engage in dialogue with the likes of Scalfari. But the pope's heart is in a strategy of engagement with all the men and women of our time, without distinction—especially those who regard the church as abstract and distant.

Thus, while responding with amiable courtesy to Eugenio Scalfari, he stepped outside the framework of an oratorical duel between the Enlightenment man and the Jesuit, between the Rationalist and the Believer. The frontal opposition didn't interest him. His letter was an updated version, in modern language, of the "good news" of the Gospel. He stated: "Therefore it is necessary for us to face up to Jesus, as I would put it, in the concreteness and roughness of his lived experience."[8] Francis announces a Christ who came to bring his listeners "freedom and fullness of life." The pope speaks of a faith that generates not arrogance but humility: "Clearly, then, faith is not intransigent, but grows in respectful coexistence with others."[9] Such a faith rules out any "search for dominance." This faith, which valorizes obedience to one's own conscience, "enables witness and dialogue with all." The church is the community of faith "in which I lived and thanks to which I gained access to understanding Sacred Scripture. . . . Without the church—believe me—I would not have been able to encounter Jesus."[10]

The pope made a direct link to Vatican II, proposing a dialogue without preconditions. Then, rendering account of his faith before the world of the nonbelieving, he faced the knottiest question head on: absolute truth. It is actually misleading, he explained, to speak of "absolute" truth, as though conjuring up the idea of a truth cut loose from all relationship. No, Francis responded, "truth, according to the Christian faith, is the love of God for us in Jesus Christ. Therefore, truth is a relationship." And every person grasps it and expresses it in the context of his or her own history, culture, and personal situation. There is nothing subjective in all this, Francis observed, merely the awareness that truth "comes to us always and only as a way and a life," it is the same thing as love. And it demands humility and openness if it is to be sought for, heeded, and expressed.

In this light, Francis expressed the wish for a serious encounter with nonbelievers in the hope of finding "the paths along which we may walk together." And he admitted frankly that churchmen "may have committed infidelities, errors and sins, and may still be doing so."[11]

The letter resonated internationally. In the Anglophone world, the essayist Ian Buruma commented approvingly that to admit the primacy of conscience amounted to stating that "neither God nor the church is really needed to tell us how to behave. Our conscience is enough. Even devout Protestants would not go that far. . . . Francis's words suggest that it might be a legitimate option to cut out God Himself."[12] Matthew Fox, a U.S. theologian expelled from the Dominican Order in 1993 at the instance of the Holy Office, then headed by Cardinal Ratzinger, asserted that Francis is bringing "a breath of fresh air after thirty-four years of popes who seemed more inclined to supply the answers, and even the questions, while almost never giving the sensation of having anything to learn."[13] The Brazilian liberation theologian Leonardo Boff, who had also been silenced by Ratzinger in his time, reads in Francis's words the intention to bear witness to Christianity without claims to conquer. Boff wrote to the pope proposing a fresh church council—Vatican III—open to all Christians and indeed to atheists in order to confront "the threats looming over the planet."[14]

In Italy, there was a lively debate over the exchange of letters. The former president of the constitutional court, Gustavo Zagrebelsky, detected in Pope Francis's letter a rediscovery of Vatican II. The Catholic essayist Mariapia Veladiano was delighted that the concept of "truth" had been relegated as an idol of the past, along with the whole package of values regarded as nonnegotiable, "a dreadful commercial expression." The monk and theologian Enzo Bianchi stressed that dialogue with persons of different beliefs should be seen as a gain, not as an inevitable sacrifice. But he did warn: walking together entails

accepting that there may be clashes over topics on which both interlocutors believe that their own positions are rock solid.[15]

The letter to Scalfari is typical of Francis's direct approach. Instead
of speaking to nonbelievers as an abstract category, the pope prefers
to engage in dialogue with a person of flesh and blood and to hear
what he or she has to say. He subsequently invited Scalfari to the Santa
Marta residence and spoke to him there with great liberty: "Proselytism
is solemn nonsense; it makes no sense. . . . Clericalism should not have
anything to do with Christianity. . . . [T]here is no Catholic God, there
is God. . . . Often the church as an institution has been dominated by
temporalism [attempts by the church hierarchy to influence public
policy], and many senior Catholic leaders still have this mindset." The
matter of the primacy of individual conscience resurfaced in this face-
to-face exchange: "Everyone has their own idea of good and evil and
must choose to follow the good and fight evil as they conceive them.
That would be enough to make the world a better place."[16]

After the interview was published, there was some debate about
the extent to which it constituted a verbatim record of the pope's
words, and Scalfari conceded that he had written them down from
memory after the fact and had enhanced the force of certain expressions. But this in turn allowed another facet of the pope's personality
to emerge. Francis had declined from the outset to read through the
text after Scalfari had composed it and had given the OK for its publication to his personal secretary, Don Alfred Xuereb, without seeing
it.[17] What counted for him was the colloquy itself and the message
it broadcast to Catholics and nonbelievers rather than the verbatim
accuracy of every single word. The consensus he wished to establish
between those who believe in transcendence and those whose values
are entirely immanent was perfectly clear to both interlocutors: opposition to the swelling egoism and injustice of the world today.

Julia Kristeva, one of the protagonists of the first phase of the dialogue begun by Benedict XVI, has observed that secular humanism
has been challenged by the Argentine pontiff's new approach. "Francis
is the small-town curate on the pontifical throne: unique, surprising, unexpected," she commented. "His warm and popular style of
communication is a political act." He has attracted sympathy from

even the most critical secularists; he played the role of peacemaker on Syria; and he is facing up to the existential crisis of the globe. "He turns toward the misery of populations in a palpable fashion and touches hearts with the revolutionary language of a Trotsky or a Che Guevara. Who is saying it better? It's a challenge for us humanists."[18]

Kristeva, with whom I spoke at her home in Paris, naturally has a psychoanalyst's sharp awareness of the seductive and consolatory spell the church is able to cast. She discerns a strong feeling for the exercise of power and a Jesuit's strategic gifts in the new pope's public stance. She reflects that a personality like Francis was needed to offer people a different image in the wake of the pontificate of Benedict XVI, who gave off a (probably inaccurate) impression of intellectual coldness. "Catholicism is in decline around the world," she added, "but it has a strong card to play: Christian humanism."

A confrontation between the two kinds of humanism is ineluctable—in Europe in the first instance, as the continent undergoes secularization. For the psychoanalyst, crisis in Europe and crisis planetwide are interconnected. "Europe is in chaos," stated Kristeva. "And if it doesn't emerge from chaos, the whole world will plunge into chaos." Europe may be a tired society, but it has enormous historical resources. The power of European civilization is to conjoin identity, multiplicity, and different people living together. "It is a civilization where identity is continually subject to interrogation" through permanent criticism and self-criticism. Thus, it can stimulate other civilizations, such as Islam and China, to interrogate themselves in turn.

As for secularization, Kristeva commented, it has promoted the liberation of women, the oppressed, and the marginalized, while at the same time breaking the thread of the historical and religious patrimony of the past. Yet "we need to know from whence we come." We must not forget the heritage of Greek thought, of the Jewish and Christian traditions, and even, in certain respects, of Islamic civilization. Ignorance is fertile soil for the growth of xenophobic parties and movements, such as the Front National in France, the Lega Nord in Italy, and similar movements elsewhere.

Here, Julia Kristeva maintained, lies the importance of a reawakening of cultures and a revival of the confrontation between secular humanism and religious forms of humanism. "In terms of human fragility, of life, death, birth, and old age, the religions have much to teach us." The human sciences, anthropology, psychoanalysis certainly have their answers to give, but too often they remain shut up in restricted spheres of specialization. "They are not present at existential crossroads."

Kristeva pointed to two areas of dialogue that intersect with the concerns of Pope Francis: the role of the economy and technical and scientific progress on one hand, and the future awaiting the younger generation on the other. "The richness of European civilization demands that the human vision should not adapt itself to technology, but the reverse," she remarked. But it is the problem of youth that interests Julia Kristeva primarily: "Europe today is the sole civilization in which there are no rites of passage into adolescence, and the passage from adolescence to adulthood has been completely forgotten. No one accompanies adolescents, their enormous need for ideals is ignored, nobody offers them the chance to perform service to others, at home or abroad." The world of the young is in a state of abandon. Some slide into indifference, some turn to various spiritual trends, and yet others plunge into "radical evil"—and here Kristeva cites the racist murders committed at Toulouse and Montauban in 2012 by a young Franco-Algerian, Mohammed Merah, who killed three soldiers and massacred three children and a teacher in front of a Jewish school—or into self-destructive drug dependency, psychosomatic illness, and various forms of unhappiness.

"It's the phenomenon of dis/errancy. The refusal of family, the refusal to socialize, the refusal of schooling, work, professional training. In the end, these young people don't know the difference between good and evil, between mine and yours, between who I am and who the other is. They respect neither themselves nor others and are ready to fall prey to violent extremism," Kristeva explained. All this challenges Europe, challenges the politicians who do not acknowledge the urgency of the phenomenon, challenges humanism both secular and religious.

The earliest moves by Pope Francis showed full awareness that the interface with secular humanism is strategic territory for the Catholic Church in the twenty-first century. From Julia Kristeva's memories of the meeting at Assisi in October 2011, one grasps how far forward

Benedict XVI pushed and how Francis is fracturing consolidated mental schemas. "We were listening to Benedict XVI in the basilica of Santa Maria degli Angeli," she recounted, "and at a certain point he stated that the absence of God causes suffering to agnostics and 'leads to the decadence of man and of humanism.' At that point, my friends in the delegation of nonbelievers started nudging me to get me to react." Yet immediately after, Ratzinger declared that followers of the religions must not regard God as their property and that the queries posed by nonbelievers are "an appeal to believers to purify their faith."[19] It was an extraordinary moment, Kristeva recalled: "The pope recognized that no one is proprietor of the truth and that believers must put questions to themselves, as we do . . . . [I]t was the first time."

There is one point on which the thought of Francis diverges radically from that of his predecessor. The notion that to be atheist causes suffering and leads to human decadence is entirely foreign to the Argentine pope. As a cardinal, he took part in a dialogue with Abraham Skorka, a rabbi of Buenos Aires, about the principal points of faith in the contemporary epoch, during which he stated: "I would never say [to an atheist] that his life is condemned, for I am convinced that I have no right to judge the honesty of that person. All the less so if they display human virtues of the kind that make a person great and do me good as well."[20]

In his letter to Eugenio Scalfari, Francis wrote that the time had come to surpass the barrier of incommunicability that has arisen between the Catholic church and culture oriented to Christianity on one hand, and modern culture, bearing the stamp of the Enlightenment, on the other. For a faithful follower of Jesus, he stated, "this dialogue is not a secondary accessory in the existence of those who believe, but is rather an intimate and indispensable expression." To the Jesuits of *Civiltà Cattolica* he recommended dialogue even with "those who do not share the Christian faith" but who cultivate other human values in accordance with the conciliar document *Gaudium et spes*.

Julia Kristeva maintained that the confrontation between the genius of Christianity and the other philosophies leads to a crucial node in the formation of the individual. "There is a constitutive need to believe that is pre-religious and prepolitical," she said. Freud calls it *Besetzung*, investment. "At the beginning the child is in its mother's arms, body against body. Then the father appears and 'recognizes' the babe, who in its turn 'recognizes' the father. From there, through the work of the psyche, arises speech and communication. That is the investment." It is no accident that the root of the term *believe* in Sanskrit links faith to economic credit.

Reciprocity of giving is the basis of the human bond, Kristeva clarified. "Focused on combating the abuse of faith on the part of religion, we secularists have forgotten the beneficial basis of belief, the pact of faith with the other. It is something we ought to teach in school to combat the 'radical evil' that is the rupture of linkage. Because it is proper to criticize credulity, but it is necessary to believe in what one does."

8

The Hidden Women Priests

It takes eight hours to get by train from the Vatican to Effretikon in the canton of Zurich. Francis could depart from the station located in Vatican City (now transformed into an exclusive shopping center as well), and he would find himself in a reality light-years distant from that imagined by the prelates of the apostolic palace. At Effretikon, the priest of the Catholic parish is a woman. True, she cannot perform all the rites, but it is she who has the care of souls there.

The town has fifteen thousand inhabitants and is a cluster of modern houses surrounded by woodland. Getting off the train, a visitor from Italy finds the Stazione restaurant, the Aida bar, the Pomodoro pizzeria, and the Tosoni butcher shop. A pregnant Muslim woman walks behind a tricycle ridden by her blond-haired daughter.

There are two churches, the Protestant one and the Catholic parish of Sankt Martin. The latter is a very modern design, built in 1982: blank white walls, a small tower with cement striations. The clergy house resembles a social center: conference room, offices, notice boards, numerous staircases, a coffee machine. There are plenty of windows, so plenty of light and a welcoming atmosphere.

And there she is, Monika Schmid, born in 1957, in black jeans and black sweater, a gold chain around her neck, a simple ring on her finger, her chestnut-brown hair worn in a pageboy cut, like so many northern European women who seem to pass unchanged from adolescence to maturity. Under the title of *Gemeindeleiterin* (in the feminine; *Gemeindeleiter* in the masculine), "guide" or "leader" of the parish, this lady cares for six thousand Catholic parishioners. Her bishop doesn't care for the term, though it is in widespread use in German-speaking countries. Actually the Vatican doesn't like it either and, after having allowed it in recent decades, has begun to block its use. The bishop and the Vatican are affronted by the connotations attached to the term *leader*, so the word is likely to be replaced by the more bureaucratic *Gemeindebeauftragte*, "individual placed in charge of the parish."

But that doesn't alter the substance. Monika Schmid studied religious pedagogy then theology at Luzern and Salzburg and is now taking a course in interreligious spiritual theology, focused on points of contact between Christianity, Jewish mysticism, and Islam. She arrived in the parish as a pastoral assistant and in 2001 took over leadership of the community on an interim basis, subsequently receiving the full canonical mandate. The document officially entrusts the parish to her, although its titular incumbent remains a male priest. But is an empty formality because there are next to no priests. In the deaconate to which Effretikon belongs, two-thirds of a total of around forty parishes have been put in the care of laypersons.

Still, the bishop at the time, Amadeus Grab, did not want a woman leading the parish. "He came here to discuss the matter, and the parishioners stood up one after another and said that they wanted me," recounted Schmid. "After three-quarters of an hour, the bishop replied that he would not stand against the wishes of the flock. It is also the case, historically, that in Switzerland the parish community engages its curate."[1]

The crisis of vocations to the priesthood is as grave in Switzerland as it is elsewhere in the Western world. The bishops, like their counterparts in Italy, have created so-called pastoral units: a number of parishes are entrusted to a small team of priests, laymen, and nuns. It is a system that consumes the energy of the few remaining priests, who are forced to hustle continuously from one parish to the next to celebrate mass and hear confessions—a solution that masks the crisis rather than solving it. "The priests hereabouts," says Monika Schmid, "are age ninety-two, ninety-one, and eighty-seven. Thanks to personal acquaintance, one or two come here to celebrate mass twice a month and for the rites at Easter and Christmas." For the other 250 days of the year, more or less, the de facto parish priest is she.

On Sunday, dressed in white with a scarf of the liturgical colors, she leads the procession of ingress, followed by five choir boys (thirty at high feasts), and goes to the altar to celebrate the "liturgy of the word." The first part of the rite is like a normal mass. The parishioners do the readings, Monika and the pastoral assistant (also a woman) take turns for the reading of the Gospel and the sermon. "I also preach when there is a priest to celebrate mass, but the current bishop, Monsignor Huonder, wants to put a stop to that."

The liturgy of the Word omits the consecration of the Host. That aside, Monika does advance to the ciborium, take the consecrated wafers contained therein, and distribute them to the faithful before the altar. The mass concludes in exactly the same way as when a priest officiates: the Lord's prayer, the sign of peace. "Yes," Monika adds, "I celebrate baptisms too. It is a sacrament, but one that any Christian may administer in case of need, so we have the bishop's authorization. I celebrate funerals; I take care of liturgies in the old folks' homes; I give the standard hour of religious teaching in the local school and the courses for adults." She holds so-called pastoral colloquies because no layperson can administer the sacrament of confession. But when a parishioner is deeply anxious or gripped by doubt, there is no use telling him or her that the priest will be here in a few weeks, so come back then. "We give advice, we help people in crisis. I always supply the address of a priest and make a date for an appointment. Sometimes I suggest couples therapy because marital crises are fairly common. But people need to unburden themselves, and sometimes they say, 'It's like I really need to make confession.' Then I answer: Shall we pray? We may recite the kyrie eleison together, and I tell them that they are accepted before God and that it's a good thing to have laid their pent-up troubles before the Lord. It is the next thing to the sacrament of confession, so the bishop frowns on it."

Sources of anguish for parish laity include "conjugal difficulties, mothers who think they are being too irascible with their children, despair at the death of a partner, feelings of inadequacy, fear of failure." I am reminded of the image of the field hospital that Pope Francis uses when he talks about the church's primary task: giving assistance without requesting blood tests or identity cards. According to Monika Schmid, anguish provoked by the classic sense of sin is uncommon nowadays among the Catholic laity.

The parish is basically run by women. In addition to the parish leader herself, there is a female pastoral assistant and a female religious pedagogue. These three are flanked by an administrative employee and a social organizer for summer projects—both women. The only man invested with direct responsibility is a lay pastoral helper. There is also the choirmaster, Stefano Lai, who comes from Sardinia. The people are content. Questions still considered thorny in other parts of the Catholic world, such as how to deal with same-sex couples, have already been silently dealt with in many Swiss parishes. Monika Schmid won't go on the record, but it is well known that in quite a few places priests and lay leaders of parishes do discreetly bless homosexual couples in front of the altar.

Rome is remote, and the sluggishness with which the church has confronted the woman question over the past half-century looks remote too. The pastoral constitution *Gaudium et spes* that came out of the Vatican II council in 1965 was the first sign of any awareness of it. The conciliar fathers regarded women's freedom "to embrace a state of life or to acquire an education or cultural benefits equal to those recognized for men" as a sign of the times. The document states that "where they have not yet won it, women claim for themselves an equity with men before the law and in fact."[2]

Paul VI was the first pope to admit female "auditors," twenty-three of them—thirteen laywomen and ten nuns—to the conciliar debates. Since then the female presence has gradually expanded into animating catechistic and educational activities in parishes, and beyond the confines of Italy they have also taken part in directing committees at the diocesan level. But at the higher levels, the posts of decision and command, the church remains male. Access to holy orders, the diaconate, and the priesthood remains systematically blocked for Catholic believers of the female sex.

John Paul II was an ardent supporter of the "genius" of women in the belief that they were endowed with a charisma of "entrustment." In the apostolic letter *Mulieris dignitatem* of 1988, he put it this way: "God entrusts the human being to her, always and in every way, even in the situations of social discrimination in which she may find herself." Karol Wojtyla highlighted the active and important part that women played in the construction of the earliest Christian communities and then, over the centuries, in the transmission of the faith as martyrs, saints, nuns, and mothers of families. He maintained that the genius of women ought to manifest itself in our time by "ensur[ing] sensitivity for human beings in every circumstance: because they are human!"[3]

In the apostolic letter *Ordinatio sacerdotalis* of 1994, however, the Polish pope reasserted in solemn fashion: "In order that all doubt may be removed regarding a matter of great importance, a matter which pertains to the church's divine constitution itself, in virtue of my ministry of confirming the brethren (cf. Lk 22:32) I declare that the church has no authority whatsoever to confer priestly ordination on women." Wojtyla was tempted to stamp this veto with the seal of papal infallibility but was dissuaded by Cardinal Ratzinger, who suggested the barely attenuated formulation: "and [I declare] that this judgment is to be definitively held by all the church's faithful."[4]

A decade later, Cardinal Ratzinger, in a *Letter to the Bishops of the Catholic Church on the Collaboration of Men and Women in the Church and in the World*, proclaimed that "women should have access to positions of responsibility which allow them to inspire the policies of nations."[5] But with respect to the church as an institution, both Ratzinger and Wojtyla always forced Catholic women into the likeness of Mary of Nazareth. Wojtyla stated that the fact that Mary received neither the mission of the apostles nor sacerdotal status proves that their inadmissibility to ordination as priests is not discriminatory but rather "faithful observance of a plan to be ascribed to the wisdom of the Lord of the universe."[6] And Ratzinger followed up:

"The reservation of priestly ordination solely to men does not hamper in any way women's access to the heart of Christian life."[7]

The refrain in the Vatican has always been that the priesthood is not a power but a service. In that case, many female theologians reply, it cannot but be open to all. The theologian Lilia Sebastiani comments that as long as women are excluded from the diaconate and the priesthood solely on the basis of their sex, they will "inevitably be excluded from any governing and magisterial function" and will thus exert very little influence, however important they may be in other respects. "They will be ignorable."[8]

In the Roman Curia, there are just two women in positions of authority: Sister Nicoletta Spezzati, undersecretary of the Congregation for Institutes of Consecrated Life and Societies of Apostolic Life (in common parlance, the Congregation for Religious), and Signora Flaminia Giovanelli, undersecretary of the Council for Justice and Peace. Benedict XVI specified the obstacle that stands in the way of anything more for as long as the traditionalist viewpoint prevails: "There's a juridical problem: according to canon law, the power to take legally binding decisions is limited to sacred orders."[9]

Pope Francis has opened a breach in the wall. A few months after his election, he sent a concrete message: "It is necessary to broaden the opportunities for a stronger presence of women in the church. . . . The feminine genius is needed wherever we make important decisions. The challenge today is this: to think about the specific place of women also in those places where the authority of the church is exercised for various areas of the church."[10] No pope had ever expressed such a notion before.

Cardinal Walter Kasper takes the view that it is feasible to achieve greater participation by women in the Synods of Bishops and has no doubt that in future women may be chosen to head the pontifical councils for the laity, the family, culture, social communications, and the new evangelization.

The church envisioned by the Argentine pope is markedly feminine. It is a theme he often touches on. "I suffer—to tell you the truth—when I see in the church or in church organizations that the role of service, which we all have and should have . . . when a woman's role of service slides into *servidumbre* [servitude, subjection]." The pope, who was speaking in Italian, used this strong Spanish term in a speech commemorating the twenty-fifth anniversary of the apostolic letter *Mulieris dignitatem* at an international symposium in October 2013 attended by more than one hundred women from Catholic associations in twenty-five nations, and he repeated it to convey the force of his denunciation: "When I see women carrying out acts of *servidumbre*, it is because the role a woman should play is not properly understood."[11] Emphasis on the presence of women in the church and the need to place greater value on it are important to him. He believes that women are indispensable for the church — indeed, that "the church cannot be herself without the woman and her role."[12]

But he refuses to contemplate the ordination of women to the priesthood. "That door is closed," he stated, referring to John Paul II and manifesting his opposition to the ideology of feminist power, which he calls "machismo in skirts."[13]

He is preparing to walk a fine line. To appoint women to top positions will generate mute opposition from conservatives in the ecclesiastical hierarchy, while exposing him to criticism from women theologians who demand complete equality since they believe that exclusion from the priesthood is no longer justifiable. His strategic stance is that "we can't imagine a church without women, but women active in the church, with the distinctive role that they play." He amplifies and qualifies that last reservation: "we have not yet come up with a profound theology of womanhood, in the church . . . we need to develop a profound theology of womanhood."[14] It is a reservation that has already generated dissent.

In the United States, the *National Catholic Reporter* sought reactions from women to these statements, including from some who had attended the meeting in October 2013. "Personally, I am not sure why there needs to be a theology of women, and certainly not one written by men," said Marti Jewell of the University of Dallas's School of Ministry. "There is no talk of a theology of men. We are all disciples by virtue of our baptism." Vicki Thorn, founder of the postabortion ministry Project Rachel, noted that "we keep talking about women as if they were just invented."[15]

The latter comment is a pertinent observation. The Catholic Church, seen in the long perspective of history, is just emerging from a patriarchal and entirely masculine mental universe in which its hierarchy remains profoundly immersed. When the *Osservatore Romano* published an insert on the question of women a few years ago, there was a certain amount of smirking and joking in Vatican corridors about the paper's new cooking and gardening pages.

In 1981, Cardinal Carlo Maria Martini had already raised questions that still await answers at a gathering in the diocese of Milan: "Why, women are asking, do we equate the image of God with that transmitted to us by masculinist culture? . . . What signs are there of a global language, including liturgical language, that, in its elaboration will not leave women feeling excluded? Why are there so few and such inadequate responses to the valorization of one's own body, of physical love, of the problems of responsible maternity? Why has the presence of women in the church, extensive as it is, not had any impact on its structures?" Giancarla Codrignani, a Catholic essayist and former member of the Italian Parliament, forwarded Martini's statements to Pope Francis.[16]

Ivone Gebara, a Brazilian religious belonging to the Suore di Nostra Signora, a professor for twenty years at the Theological Institute of Recife, and an activist who works in the favelas, is the most pungent voice of Latin American Catholic feminist theology. In 1995, the Congregation for the Doctrine of the Faith imposed two years of silence on her, which meant she was prohibited from teaching, publishing, speaking in public, or giving interviews.

"How can Pope Francis simply ignore the strength of the feminist movement and its expression in Catholic feminist theology over the last thirty or forty years?" is the combative question the nun, now in her seventies, puts today. "Please, let him use the Internet to find out about aspects of feminist theology, in the Catholic world at any rate." Sister Ivone points out that there are plenty of relevant texts that are not studied in the principal theological faculties and so contribute nothing to the formation of future priests. "Church officialdom hasn't given them the right of citizenship because the intellectual production of women is still considered inadequate for male theological rationality." And that's not the only reason: female theology "appears menacing to the male power that predominates in the churches."[17]

Riding the wave of Francis's other changes, a portion of the female laity is attempting to make fresh inroads. In autumn 2013, a group of theologians, men and women, from Europe and the United States published an appeal for the nomination of women cardinals. Their reasoning is that until the nineteenth century the cardinalate could also be conferred upon members of the laity and the pope does have the power to abrogate the current canonical statute requiring priestly ordination for those making up the College of Cardinals. The idea had already been advanced in 2011 by the journal of American Jesuits, *America*, and was put forward six months into the Bergoglio pontificate by Lucetta Scaraffia, a Catholic historian and editorialist for the *Osservatore Romano*: "It would be a revolution strong enough to shake up the stance of mistrust and lack of interest that a large portion of the clergy adopts vis-à-vis women, whether nuns or laity." Scaraffia, who had earlier been responsible for the paper's insert on the woman question, conceded that the exhortations of John Paul II and Benedict XVI to recognize the presence of women in the church "have yielded modest fruits."[18]

It constitutes a paradox that in the Vatican organizations concerned with the religious orders, with the laity, with the family and health—dimensions in which women play a preponderant role—women are totally absent from the top chairs. Pope Francis probably has plans to step in and remedy that. The hypothesis of a female cardinal has, however, been rejected by Cardinal Maradiaga, coordinator of the pope's privy council of cardinals: "A woman cardinal? I don't think so. There is no point in clericalizing the role of women in the church, though it should certainly be assigned greater value."[19]

Just how exactly? Maria Voce, president of the Focolare movement, suggests that women should systematically be placed in the "organs of consultation, reflection, and decision that are developing in the church." She would wish to see a council of laymen, composed of men and women, flanking the privy council of cardinals and likewise advising the pope. And she believes that in future it would be appropriate for laypersons of both sexes to take part, along with the cardinal electors, in the meetings that precede papal conclaves—personalities who "are performing duties in the church and can contribute from their own experience."[20] The president of the Focolarini judges the challenge of a female priesthood "not insuperable" and regards it as "not impossible" that in future the doors of the conclave may be thrown open to the superiors of the religious orders and the heads of Catholic lay associations, making the election of the pope a more "choral" affair.[21]

While this debate was going on during the first year of Francis's pontificate, in England the Anglican Church adopted, in a synod of 20 November 2013, the principle that women should have access to the epsicopate. The resolution was practically unanimous: 378 votes in favor, 8 against, and 25 abstentions. Women had already acceded to the Anglican priesthood twenty-one years earlier.

At Effretikon, Monika Schmid told me that if she were to ask her parishioners one Sunday whether they wished to have women priests, three-quarters would answer yes. Young people are especially baffled at the exclusion. If she had the chance to address Pope Francis, she would tell him: "Listen to women and dismiss the gratuitous rationale that theological motives bar them from the priesthood." Her dream is that by the time she retires, the Vatican will at least have authorized women deacons. When Francis was elected, Monika was extremely pleased, "but the moat separating the people from the institution is wide. I would wish for a papal audience, not just for me alone, so we could tell him how we are living at the base."

The chokepoint for the church is the crisis of the clergy. The parish was the great invention of Christianity: a territory, a population of the lay faithful, a spiritual leader in close contact with them. This structure, which has sustained the fabric of Catholicism for centuries, is crumbling because of the dramatic decline in vocations. In the United States and northern Europe, churches are for sale. Everywhere in the developed world, parishes are being dissolved into larger units, and daily contact between priest and parishioners is being lost. In the developing world, many parishes are so large and remote from one another that no priest visits for months on end. As this crisis intensifies, the question of women in the priesthood has mutated. If in the 1970s it was perceived primarily as a matter of gender equality, and still is to some degree, in the twenty-first century — with the very survival of the church's territorial structure at stake — the outlook is different. The problem is no longer purely subjective but the objective one of what structure the Christian communities of the future will have.

While at Rome the previous two pontificates were putting obstacles in the way of a leadership role in parishes for laymen in general and for women in particular, these resources themselves were dwindling. Germany in this respect has always been a laboratory where mutations in Catholicism show up first. In recent years, there has been a quantitative and qualitative decline in the new intakes of lay "pastoral assistants." There is still an acute shortage of priests, and there is starting to be a shortage of laity prepared to shoulder the burden of pastoral responsibility. And that includes women. In Switzerland, the parishes seek laureates in theology from Germany. "If you seek to recruit a pastoral assistant nowadays, you run into difficulty," explained Monika Schmid. "There isn't the same wide choice there was thirty years ago. You encounter people with mediocre training. In my time, at the University of Lugano, there was a good large group of women passionate about feminist theology . . . we read books, we debated texts, we did biblical research. Now the women presenting themselves are of a more bigoted kind."

That the female religious orders, the backbone of Catholicism all over the world, are being shunned by women is a matter of established fact. The numbers of nuns and women living under vows are in steep decline: in 2001 their count reached 792,317; in 2011 the number had dropped to 713,206.[22] The rise in vocations in Africa and Asia has not been enough to offset this slump overall, but it does mean that the center of gravity is shifting from the West to the third world, the origin of one-third of nuns today. This shift impels many religious orders to import fresh sisters from Asia and Africa to swell their thinning ranks in Europe—a "trade in novices" of which Pope Francis is critical.

The Bergoglio papacy is striving for change, but no one can predict the form it will take. Benedict XVI left the Argentine pope a poisonous legacy of conflict with the largest and most important organization of U.S. nuns, the Leadership Conference of Women Religious (LCWR). The Vatican has had them in its sights for more than ten years on account of their critical stance toward the exclusively male priesthood and for their positions on abortion, homosexuality, contraception, and the church's claim to supremacy over the other Christian confessions.

In 2012, with Ratzinger on the papal throne, the Holy Office (short for "Holy Office of the Inquisition," as the renamed Congregation for the Doctrine of the Faith, Ratzinger's former fiefdom, is still often called in common parlance) published a harsh assessment of the LCWR, accusing it of "radical feminism," doctrinal errancy, loss of the sense of the church, contrary positions on sexual matters, and "theological interpretations that risk distorting faith in Jesus and his loving Father."[23] The Holy Office decided to appoint a delegate with a mandate to carry out a revision of the statutes of the organization of American nuns within five years and to control its initiatives and publications in order to align them with "the teachings and discipline of the church." The LCWR was requested to rewrite its training manuals. Speakers at events organized by the LCWR were to be subject to approval by the Vatican delegate. It was an outright administrative takeover.

The nuns responded that the accusations were "unfounded and potentially . . . destructive to the continuation of their mission." Since then, negotiations have dragged on between the Vatican delegate, Archbishop Peter Sartain, and the LCWR leadership. The organization's former president, Pat Farrel, said that with respect to sexuality "the teaching and interpretation of the faith can't remain static and really needs to be reformulated, rethought in light of the world we live in. Women religious stand in very close proximity to people at the margins, to people with very painful, difficult situations in their lives. That is our gift to the church."[24]

After his election, Pope Francis had a meeting with the prefect of the Congregation for the Doctrine of the Faith, Gerhard Ludwig Müller, and confirmed the directives given by Benedict XVI. The pontiff let the new president of the LCWR, Florence Deacon, know that "it is not possible for a religious, man or woman, not to feel as the church feels" and that this demands "fidelity to its teachings."[25]

But this opposition between the Vatican and the LCWR, which represents around 80 percent of the approximately fifty-seven thousand women religious in the United States, was at odds with the style of the Argentine pope. On issues such as homosexuality and abortion, the American nuns have progressed to a pastoral rather than ideologicodoctrinal approach that conforms much more closely to the attitude of Francis than the rigid stance of Pope Ratzinger. As 2014 was drawing to a close, the Brazilian cardinal João Braz de Avis, prefect of the congregation concerned with religious orders, made public a Vatican document that brought the dispute to an end. No anathemas were uttered, and the social commitment of the American nuns was recognized: "Since the early days of the Catholic Church in their country [the United States], women religious have courageously been in the forefront of the evangelizing mission, selflessly tending to the spiritual, moral, educational, physical, and social needs of countless individuals, especially the poor and marginalized."[26] A specific communication was subsequently sent to every single religious order.

To face up fully to the role of women in the church constitutes a ford in the stream that the Bergoglio pontificate must cross. The ecclesiastical structure built around the dominance of the male clergy is gradually breaking apart. The question faced by the Catholic Church as it enters its third millennium is: What will be the physiognomy of the communities of believers of the future? Will they still be strongly institutionalized? Will they become more fluid? Or will an organizational form be found that combines the necessary unifying links with a flexibility of lived experiences?

Should Pope Francis happen one Sunday to cross the Tiber, he might arrive at a large shed in Via Ostiense and attend one particular mass. The altar is a table covered by an embroidered white tablecloth. It has wheels so it can be moved around. A bunch of flowers and a small wooden cross are placed at the center, with a little peace flag in rainbow colors beside them. The chalices of everyday wine and two baskets of bread are ready for the rite. From the large windows at the end the daylight filters in.

A bearded young man tunes a guitar and croons, "Christ came to be with us . . . hallelujah . . . he will take away our fears." A woman wearing a sweater steps up to the altar and reads the act of penitence. Another in an overcoat comes forward and reads a passage from Isaiah. Then a woman wearing a wool jacket reads the letter of Paul to the Corinthians, followed by a fourth in a windbreaker who proclaims the gospel.

Since the 1970s, Via Ostiense 152 is the home of the community of Saint Paul, formed after the abbot-bishop of the ancient monastery of San Paolo fuori le Mura, Giovanni Franzoni, was removed from office for having denounced the murky involvement of the ecclesiastical hierarchy in speculative construction projects at Rome.

The walls of the former storage facility are whitewashed; just one wall of the large cubic space has been painted in trompe l'oeil to resemble an old Roman palazzo; I can make out the statue of a woman wearing a mask and the profile of a few columns. Farther along there hangs a poster of Monsignor Juan José Gerardi, the Guatemalan bishop murdered by three military men in 1988 for having published a report on the violations of human rights perpetrated by the army in his country. "Mártir de verdad y paz," it says in Spanish.

A white-haired lady in her fifties delivers the homily. Her attire, like that of the other women, is that of normal daily life. A blue pullover, a beige wool jacket, glasses, earrings, a beaded necklace. Every hour, she reminds hearers, two thousand people die of hunger in the world. The data are from the UN Food and Agriculture Organization. The mass is a shared meal, the Gospel reading is about the wedding at Cana. But no one must be excluded from the banquet. "As long as people are dying . . . we shall not be the joy of God."

A mentally disturbed boy enters and circulates among the faithful, saying loudly, "Where's Mamma . . . I told Mamma . . . Have you seen Mamma?" Nobody is annoyed; they follow him with affectionate glances as he wanders, listening to the reflections about the Gospel and the readings of the day. Many of them stand up to speak. Someone mentions that in the Old Testament and the first Christian communities, the gift of prophecy was shared by men and women.

The moment of the consecration of the Host arrives. Two women approach the altar, one makes a quick kneeling gesture, and together they break a loaf of bread into small pieces, which they place in the baskets. Everyone holds hands in a chain, reciting the Lord's Prayer. They advance toward one another from opposite sides of the storage shed to give the sign of peace. An atmosphere of friendliness prevails. The communion is the meal the believers share. They form two rows at the sides of the altar, and each takes a piece of bread, dips it in a chalice of wine, and eats it. "Your first miracle, Jesus," runs the common prayer, "is a banquet of love."

My mind turns to a singular mosaic I saw in the ancient cathedral of Santa Sophia at Kiev. The altar is a real table, and there are two Christs, one turning to his right to offer the eucharistic bread to Peter, the other turning to his left to offer it to Paul. The Son of Man enfolds every dimension of life in his embrace.

9

Death in Front of
the Vatican

E very week Pope Francis has the research firm Poliarquía send
him a briefing on Argentina. In December 2013, he closely followed the outburst of looting that rocked his country when the
local police went on strike in various provinces. The policemen were
demanding higher wages. No sooner had they shut themselves inside
their barracks than chaos erupted, with assaults on supermarkets, busi-
nesses, and private homes.

At Córdoba, population 1.2 million, the violence of the raids
exploded on the evening of 3 December. After twenty-four hours, one
person was dead and 130 wounded. Over the space of two days, the
violence and looting spread to other Argentine provinces: El Chaco,
Tucumán, Jujuy, Entre Ríos, Santa Fe. The pandemonium of citizens craving food and material goods was intensified by organized
gangs of bikers who launched surprise raids on supermarkets. The
criminal element took advantage of the tumult, encouraged—it was

suspected—by some in the police so that the disorder would force the government to back down and meet their demands.

By 12 December, the number of dead had risen to eleven amid appalling scenes of social collapse and raw fury. Mindless crowds smashed their way into supermarkets and came running out with loaded shopping carts; street-front stores were attacked with iron bars, and household appliances, sportswear, and consumer goods of every description were carried off. Spontaneous individual raids, attacks on private homes, exchanges of gunfire between pilferers and proprietors, fleeing robbers slain by shotgun blasts. Armed shopkeepers mounting guard by turns. A woman named Claudia told reporters from *La Nación* that she, her husband, and their employees spent their nights standing guard over their grocery store in the neighborhood of San Miguel de Tucumán, armed with guns and rudimentary Molotov cocktails. She had already lost everything once during a similar wave of looting twelve years earlier. Hers was just one episode among countless others of rage and desperation in the center of a developed nation. It ended only when the police got their raise.

A local story? It certainly was for the European papers, which, except for the Spanish ones, paid little attention to the events. Or rather a foretaste of what might happen elsewhere, whenever the social contract were broken? John Carpenter describes that outcome in the 1981 science fiction film *Escape from New York*, set in the dystopian future of 1997 and depicting the metropolis in the grip of criminal bands, the survivors engaged in a ruthless struggle of "all against all."

Sociologists have a word for the mental state of nations adrift, where all institutional, social, and even family bonds have lost their grip on the population. They speak of "anomie"—the eclipse of the law, the abrogation of all the rules except the law of the jungle and every man for himself.

Pope Francis is extremely sensitive to the social question. Not a week passes that he doesn't touch on the topics of injustice, hunger, poverty. Strident social disparity can only generate violence, he admonishes. There is no point in demanding security and entrusting oneself and society to the police or the security services, he wrote in the apostolic exhortation *Evangelii gaudium*. "Evil embedded in the structures of a society" bears within itself a potential for violence, death, and disintegration. "But until exclusion and inequality in society and between peoples are reversed, it will be impossible to eliminate violence. The poor and the poorer peoples are accused of violence, yet without equal opportunities the different forms of aggression and conflict will find a fertile terrain for growth and eventually explode." Not just because "inequality provokes a violent reaction from those excluded from the system, but because the socioeconomic system is unjust at its root."[1]

No one may feel themselves exonerated from concern for the poor and for social justice, Francis affirms in this document, which amounts to a manifesto for his pontificate. "No one can demand that religion should be relegated to the inner sanctum of personal life, without influence on societal and national life. . . . Each individual Christian and every community is called to be an instrument of God for the liberation and promotion of the poor." Everywhere those willing to listen can hear the cry of the poor. The fundamental question is the unacceptability of a complete separation between the economy and the common good.

Rome, he asserted in his homily at the solemn mass in the Vatican on 31 December 2013, is full of tourists but also of impoverished, unhappy, and unemployed persons. "Rome in the new year will be better if people do not observe it as 'from afar,' on a postcard, if they do not only watch life pass by 'from the balcony.'"

The Argentine pope has strong views. There will be no root solution to the problem of the poor unless we renounce the doctrine of "the absolute autonomy of the marketplace and financial speculation." *Evangelii gaudium* expresses a highly critical judgment of ideological optimism about the untrammeled free market, against which Pope Wojtyla had already hurled his thunderbolts. Francis does not mince words: "We can no longer trust in the unseen forces and the invisible hand of the market." To achieve a structural resolution of the problem of unjustifiable inequality "requires [specific] decisions, programs, mechanisms" to integrate the poor into society and go beyond mere welfarism.

Rush Limbaugh, a commentator on conservative talk radio in the United States, has accused the pope of purveying "pure Marxism." It's a sad spectacle, says Limbaugh, "because this pope makes it very clear he doesn't know what he's talking about when it comes to capitalism and socialism and so forth. . . . I have been numerous times to the Vatican. It wouldn't exist without tons of money. But regardless, what this is, somebody has either written this for him or gotten to him. . . . Unfettered capitalism? . . . Unfettered capitalism is a liberal socialist phrase to describe the United States."[2] On Rupert Murdoch's *Fox News*, the pope has been described as the Obama of the Catholic Church. Jonathon Moseley, a member of the Tea Party, which blocked the passage of the U.S. government budget for months starting in 2013, went further. He wrote on *World Net Daily* that "Jesus Christ is weeping in heaven hearing Christians espouse a socialist philosophy. . . . Jesus spoke to the individual, never to government or government policy. Jesus was a capitalist, preaching personal responsibility, not a socialist."[3]

In *Evangelii gaudium*, Bergoglio never uses the word *capitalism* or *socialism*. In this respect, John Paul II employed even more direct language. After the Berlin Wall came down, he began to violently attack untrammeled laissez-faire and "radical capitalist ideology," as he called it during a visit to Paderborn, Germany, in 1996. In the 1991 encyclical *Centesimus annus*, Wojtyla criticized those who think that the problems of social justice can be resolved by "blindly entrust[ing] their solution to the free development of market forces." And he made a clear distinction between the positive phenomenon of a "free economy" and the negative reality of "capitalism" understood as "a system in which freedom in the economic sector is not circumscribed within a strong juridical framework that places it at the service of human freedom in its totality . . . the core of which is ethical and religious."

The stance taken by Pope Francis fits into the church's robust tradition of social doctrine, which has become ever more incisive over the past hundred years, from Leo XIII's first social encyclical, *Rerum novarum* (1891), to John XXIII's encyclical *Pacem in terris* (1963) and Paul VI's *Populorum progressio* (1967). The latter states: "The injustice of certain situations cries out for God's attention. Lacking the bare necessities of life, whole nations are under the thumb of others; they cannot act on their own initiative; they cannot exercise personal responsibility; they cannot work toward a higher degree of cultural refinement or a greater participation in social and public life."[4]

Benedict XVI, too, in the encyclical *Caritas in veritate* (2009) stressed the ethical duties incumbent on the world of the economy and finance and denounced the growing erosion of "the human rights of workers" in both the first and third worlds. The German pope put forward a proposal for the creation of a "world political authority" to guarantee an international economic and juridical order oriented toward the development of peoples in solidarity.

Still, among the documents and speeches of all these popes, one thing about Pope Francis stands out: the timbre of personal experience. Bergoglio has lived where the shantytowns brush up against the skyscrapers. He knows firsthand the difference between the smell of poverty and the brutal egoism of the dominant classes. Experience makes the difference. Karol Wojtyla had known war up close: the clanking of armored vehicles invading a city, the cruelty of foreign occupation, clandestine cultural activity as a form of spiritual resistance, the fear of being caught in a dragnet and taken to a concentration camp, the substitution of one dictatorship for another. Joseph Ratzinger, who spent most of World War II in his native Bavarian village and saw the conflict up close for only a few months as it was winding down, carried different baggage. It was direct experience that explains John Paul II's determined opposition to the invasion of Iraq, with his famous words of 16 March 2003, "No more war, no more, no more," uttered from the window of his study, his face swollen and his movements impeded by Parkinson's disease.

The same thing goes for Pope Francis. When he talks about poverty and exploitation, it is not because he has been given briefing notes to read. He has walked along the open sewers of the shantytowns and has stood at the microphone in Plaza de la Constitución in Buenos Aires to denounce the enslavement of workers in the clandestine factories and the trade in children and young women kidnapped in the Argentine hinterland and forced into prostitution thanks to the silent complicity between gangs of people smugglers and local power holders. Hunger, violence, brutality, repressed rage, the stripping away of dignity, daily uncertainty, drug addicts lying prostrate or dead on the sidewalk. Jorge Mario Bergoglio has seen all that up close, year after year, traveling on foot and by public transport throughout the Argentine capital.

That is why he raises his voice when he speaks of the immigrants who drowned at sea or who reached Italy jammed onto the boats of the merchants of human flesh: "Has any one of us grieved for the death of these brothers and sisters? . . . For the young mothers carrying their babies? For these men who were looking for a means of supporting their families? We are a society which has forgotten how to weep, how to experience compassion—'suffering with' others."[5]

The Catholic Church often mysteriously succeeds in electing the right pontiffs at epochal turning points. John XXIII arrived at the watershed of the thaw between the Western and Soviet blocs; Paul VI coincided with the planetwide movement of decolonization; John Paul II marked the taking down of the Iron Curtain. Francis has become pope at a time of global crisis. It isn't just third-world countries that are suffering from serious economic imbalances, poverty, marginalization, corruption, violence, and the intolerable gap between the hyper-rich and swathes of society living close to the edge.

This crisis, starting with the international financial meltdown of 2008, has also gripped the nations of the first world that thought they were immune, eroding the middle class that constitutes their backbone. In many countries, especially the United States, upward social mobility has halted. The European Union is at serious risk and could shear under stress, a predicament that the German chancellor Angela Merkel fears we may be walking into with the same rash heedlessness displayed by the European "sleepwalkers" of 1914 as they stepped over the brink and plunged into the chasm. Greece has been paralyzed by bankruptcy; Spain is struggling to regain its footing. In Italy, out of a population of 60 million persons, more than 9.5 million are living in poverty, and of them almost 5 million are utterly destitute.[6]

In the United States, there are signs of deep social division. As this decade began, the U.S. Census Bureau registered more than 46 million Americans living below the poverty line, meaning on an annual income of less than $22,314 for a family of four. But around half of these people are living in "extreme poverty" because they live on less than 50 percent of the poverty threshold: four people existing on less than $11,000 annually.[7]

In the United States, the steep rise in gross domestic product (GDP) between 2000 and 2007 has had no positive impact on the average income of American families. Only the one percent has benefited. In 2012, average family income sank to 1995 levels.[8] President Barack Obama himself has voiced his alarm at the fact that half the national income goes to 10 percent of Americans. In 2014, the president of the Federal Reserve, Janet L. Yellen, stated that she was worried by the ceaselessly widening gap between "significant income and wealth gains for those at the very top, and stagnant living standards for the majority." Yellen asked whether this process is compatible with "the high value Americans have traditionally placed on equality of opportunity."[9]

Even in an economic powerhouse like China, where over the past three decades hundreds of millions of persons have escaped from conditions of absolute hunger, the divergence between rich and poor continues to grow. In India, the number of billionaires has increased tenfold over the past decade thanks to a favorable fiscality, while as regards access on the part of the population to a sound nutritional intake the country stands at the bottom of international rankings. The economist Stefano Zamagni comments that "globalization has certainly reduced absolute poverty, the condition of those living on less than two dollars a day, but it has boosted the number of poor to worrying levels, meaning those who obtain less than half the per capita income in the community to which they belong." A significant datum: between 1980 and 2007 "in a large number of countries on the planet, income earned from work as a percentage of GDP has fallen by over nine points on median, and the concentration of wealth has reached peaks never seen before."[10]

The January 2014 Oxfam report *Working for the Few* reveals that the income of eighty-five super-rich individuals is equivalent to that of half of the world's population. Another scourge eroding social cohesion is the precarious employment that has rapidly become prevalent throughout the industrial countries. Even in solid welfare states like Germany, the locomotive of the European Union, millions of persons are underpaid. This is the "500 euros a month generation." An investigation by the magazine *Der Spiegel* in 2012 highlighted the fact that along with the drop in unemployment there has gone an abnormal dilation of the underpaid precariat, people who often don't know how they will get through next week. The research revealed that 1.4

million persons were earning less than 5 euros an hour, and another 8 million were getting by on an income of less than 9.15 euros per hour—a lot less than employees performing the same tasks in stable jobs.[11] This is why the governing coalition of Christian Democrats and Social Democrats decided in December 2013 to raise the minimum hourly wage to 8.50 euros starting in 2015.

When Pope Francis talks about intolerable inequalities, it is not an abstract discourse; he speaks the language of millions and millions of families, and he goes into their homes with the same immediacy as when he wishes the crowd a "good Sunday." The English historian Eric Hobsbawm used to say that John Paul II, with his condemnation of the untrammeled free market, could be seen as the last socialist of the twentieth century. *Neues Deutschland,* formerly the organ of the East German Communist Party, published a cartoon in which the profile of Francis flanks those of Marx and Engels.

In fact, there is nothing ideological about the pontiff's stance. Bergoglio has always been opposed to Marxist-inspired liberation theology. His gaze is trained concretely on the inexorably growing divergence between the carefree minority and the care-laden majority for whom well-being is a receding mirage. He once explained, in a straightforward and realistic manner, the problem with the celebrated free-market theory according to which the free play of economic forces unencumbered by state interference will ultimately generate so much wealth that part of it will trickle down to the masses and everybody will be better off. "We were assured that when the glass was full it would overflow, and the poor would get the benefit. What happens instead is that when it is full, the glass magically expands, and so nothing ever spills out for the poor."[12]

Bergoglio doesn't take offense if others label him a Marxist. (If anything, his political background is more akin to social Peronism.) He is opposed to Marxist ideology but doesn't hide the fact that he has known many Marxists to be "good persons," starting with the woman who ran the chemical laboratory where he worked as a youth: Esther Ballestrino, who was kidnapped and murdered in 1977 after the death squads of the dictatorship had already assassinated one daughter and two sons-in-law. For Francis, the imperative is religious. There exists an indissoluble bond between the good news of Christianity and concrete fraternal love. Jesus always urged justice and mercy toward the poor. Why obscure something as clear as that? A religious community that wants to enjoy tranquility without really giving any thought to the inclusion of the poor will wind up in a "spiritual worldliness camouflaged by religious practices, unproductive meetings and empty talk."[13]

For Lent 2014, Francis prepared a message in which he stressed the close linkage between moral misery and the material misery that "touches all who live in a condition unworthy of the human person: deprived of fundamental rights and the basic necessities like food, water, hygienic conditions, work, the opportunity to develop and grow culturally." Misery is much more than an inadequate economic status, he explained. "It is poverty without trust, without solidarity, without hope." The moral poverty that results amounts to "incipient suicide."

These strong words are accompanied by the exhortation that the Lenten period may bring consciences to undergo a conversion to justice, to equality, to sobriety and sharing, in the knowledge that helping others exacts a personal price. "I distrust alms that cost nothing and don't hurt," the pope has declared severely.[14] The idols of power, luxury, and money, he never tires of repeating, are obstacles to an equitable distribution of wealth. The pope is convinced that a crucial theme of the twenty-first century is the problem of fully integrating the poor into society. For all the imposing successes of scientific and technological development, the economy of exclusion persists. "Such an economy kills."[15]

Francis doesn't like to speak in abstractions. Week after week he has hammered home these notions in the language of daily life. "If a computer breaks," he said one day at a general audience in Saint Peter's Square, "it is a tragedy, but . . . if on a winter's night, here on the Via Ottaviano—for example—someone dies, that is not news. If there are children in so many parts of the world who have nothing to eat, that is not news, it seems normal. . . . In this way people are thrown aside as if they were trash."[16] The pope has even launched these ideas on Twitter: "We cannot sleep soundly while children are dying of hunger and old people lack medical care." His account in nine languages, @Pontifex, now has more than 11 million followers.

On 12 December 2013, the pontiff's biting reflection was mirrored by reality. A sixty-three-year-old street person was found unconscious a few meters from St. Peter's Square, near the parking garage of the Gianicolo, and was taken to a hospital, where he died. The event went unrecorded in the newspapers. Francis says explicitly in *Evangelii gaudium*: "How can it be that it is not a news item when an elderly homeless person dies of exposure, but it is news when the stock market loses two points?" Along Via della Conciliazione, many homeless people make camp at night. Francis often sends the papal almoner, the Pole Konrad Krajewski, to bring them something to help out, discharging an ancient onus that goes back to the Middle Ages. He would like to encounter the street people himself, the way he used to do with the *cartoneros* of Buenos Aires, homeless people who shelter themselves under cardboard boxes. But hitherto he has been restrained by Vatican security. At his wish, Monsignor Krajewski has held funerals for vagrants in the presence of the curial cardinal Fernando Filoni.

Bernini's colonnade has become a symbolic refuge for desperate folk, as though the nearness of the Argentine pope were imparting greater resonance to their extreme cry for help. One day an itinerant set himself on fire at the entrance to St. Peter's Square. "I'm tired and I have no work," he had written on the note they found in his jacket pocket before he was taken to hospital, where he later died.

In his battle against the "throw away" economy that discards human beings, Francis stands in substantial isolation from the economic and political powers. The world economic forum at Davos courteously invited him in January 2014 to send a message because awareness is growing that an excessive social imbalance represents a risk, something of which the International Monetary Fund is also cognizant. Christine Lagarde, director general of the IMF, has qualified the level of youth unemployment reached in several European countries as unsustainable, speaking of the risk of a "lost generation." Yet the change of direction that Francis demands is apparently too radical to be accepted by the economic and financial establishment.

On the Italian political scene, not one of the main parties has planks in its platform like those for which the Argentine pope wishes. The same is true in other Western countries, even if at times concern is voiced about the drastic deterioration of the middle class.

The election of the Democrat Bill De Blasio as mayor of New York is a signal that in certain respects the pope has tapped into deep currents of public opinion. De Blasio won (albeit only 24 percent of the electorate turned out to vote) with a platform that sounds radical against the backdrop of American political culture: taxes on incomes greater than $500,000 to finance public housing and daycare centers, a local minimum wage, paid sick leave.

The urgent warnings sounded in *Evangelii gaudium* have often been greeted with hostility. In the economic section of the authoritative German weekly *Die Zeit*, Francis has been attacked head on for denouncing the "invisible tyranny" of financial speculation and the ideology of limitless market autonomy. The commentator rebuked him for having written a pamphlet a century and a half out of date and inquired mockingly whether, considering that he paints capitalism as the sum of all ills, the pope imagines things are better in Cuba, Venezuela, Saudi Arabia, or kleptocapitalistic Russia.[17] In Britain, the *Financial Times* has accused the pontiff of errors of analysis. Although, the paper admits, the gap between rich and poor has grown wider and conditions for the middle class in the West are worse, it should be acknowledged that globalization and the offshoring of production to the third world have led to the "exit from poverty of hundreds of millions of persons in China and India" and other countries where Western firms have relocated.

Unlike the wolf of Gubbio with Saint Francis, the wolves of egoism have no intention of licking the hand of the Francis from Argentina. Bergoglio won't back off. For him, poverty, exclusion, and modern-day slavery are social sins from which he will not avert his gaze. The modern slaves of forced labor carried out in clandestine and illegal conditions are 20 million in number according to data from the UN, and the number rises every year. Francis would have this slave trade, a low priority for governments, punished as a crime against humanity. From President Obama, visiting the Vatican, he requested a concrete commitment. The modern slaves are to be found here in Italy, too, despite a concerted effort to draw a veil over public awareness of the Chinese factory workers of Prato, the clandestine textile workshops full of Bengalese, the exploited tomato pickers at Rosarno.

Bergoglio insists on reminding contemporary society of uncomfortable truths. The message of Saint Francis of Assisi and Mother Teresa of Calcutta cannot be confined inside the temple precinct. Authentic faith, the pope reminds us, is never undemanding or individualistic. It always implies a desire to change the world and "leave behind something better after our passage on earth."

10

The Self-Critique of a Pope

Defeat either forms a leader or shows him he is not cut out for leadership. In his interview with his fellow Jesuit Antonio Spadaro for *La Civiltà Cattolica*, Pope Francis opened up with a surprising admission: "My style of government as a Jesuit at the beginning had many faults. That was a difficult time for the Society: an entire generation of Jesuits had disappeared. Because of this I found myself provincial superior when I was still very young. I was only 36 years old. That was crazy. I had to deal with difficult situations."[1]

Bergoglio became head of the Jesuits of Argentina and Paraguay in 1973 (and remained so until 1979). Three years later, a coup d'état brought to power a military junta headed by General Jorge Rafael Videla, which inaugurated a repressive regime that conducted a dirty war against the guerrilla resistance mounted by the Peronist and Marxist opposition. The regime ended only in 1983, leaving a balance sheet of thirty thousand persons assassinated, tortured, and "disappeared"—the *desaparecidos*.

It was a time when many Jesuits supported post–Vatican II reformism, a strong social commitment, and liberation theology. "I made my decisions," Pope Francis recalls, "abruptly and by myself. But . . . eventually people get tired of authoritarianism. My authoritarian and quick manner of making decisions led me to have serious problems and to be accused of being ultraconservative." Spadaro took note. Never had a modern pontiff spoken with such frankness of his own errors and setbacks in a position of command. Before the tape recorder, the pope continued: "I lived a time of great interior crisis when I was in Córdoba. To be sure, I have never been like Blessed Imelda [a goody-goody], but I have never been a right-winger. It was my authoritarian way of making decisions that created problems."

The pope was alluding to a raw nerve from his past, the role he played during the Videla dictatorship. It had already been a topic of public debate when he was archbishop, and there was a fresh upsurge of discussion about it after he was elected pope. For some time, the Argentine journalist Horacio Verbitsky has claimed that Bergoglio, as provincial superior, abandoned—indeed, practically handed over—two fellow Jesuits to the mercy of the army. Orlando Yorio and Francisco Jalics were kidnapped on 23 May 1976 and tortured in the infamous Escuela de Mecánica de la Armada, where they were held for more than five months.

After democracy was restored in Argentina and inquiries began into human rights violations under Videla, Bergoglio was interrogated twice under oath as a person with knowledge of the facts and was never found guilty of anything. "There were bishops complicit with the dictatorship, but not Bergoglio," the Nobel Peace Prize winner Adolfo Pérez Esquivel stated in a BBC interview.[2] Alicia Oliveira, a leader of the human rights movement and the first judge to sit on Argentina's criminal law bench, from which she had been expelled by the military junta, bore witness to Bergoglio's initiatives in favor of the persecuted. After she herself went underground, Bergoglio transported her in the trunk of his car to meet her children inside the walls of the Jesuits' Colegio Máximo de San Miguel in Buenos Aires.

It is a matter of record that Bergoglio acted on various occasions to save men and women targeted by the regime.[3] But the story of the two

Jesuits is more intricate. Yorio, under whom Bergoglio had studied theology, and Jalics, his spiritual director, had set up a community in the Rivadavia neighborhood in Bajo Flores, beside one of the most densely populated shantytowns of the Argentine capital: Villa 1-11-14. The two were highly committed to social action and aligned with liberation theology; one of their team, who was later kidnapped and tortured, took part in the guerrilla resistance. Bergoglio, as their superior, ordered them to cease their activity in the shantytown. Yorio and Jalics refused to comply and were subsequently kidnapped by the military. It is on record that Bergoglio took action to have them released, going to see the top men of the regime, Admiral Emilio Massera and General Videla, for that purpose. Once they were released, he helped them to get out of the country. Father Yorio went to Rome, and Jalics went first to his native Hungary and then to Germany.

Right after the election of Pope Francis, Jalics stated publicly (Yorio having died in the meantime) that he had since returned to Buenos Aires, had celebrated mass there with Archbishop Bergoglio, and had publicly embraced him at the conclusion of the rite. Bergoglio, said Jalics, "did not give me and Yorio up." But the pain of past wounds did transpire in the words he added: "I have made my peace with those events, and for me the episode is closed . . . for Pope Francis I wish God's copious blessing."

It is past all doubt that Bergoglio never betrayed his two fellow Jesuits; indeed, he offered to shelter them in Colegio San Miguel. The situation in the second half of the 1970s was multifaceted. Bergoglio, who absolutely did not share the political analysis of liberation theology, formally recalled the two Jesuits, invited them to go somewhere else, and ordered them to dissolve the base community they had created.[4]

Upon their refusal, recalls their friend the Argentine Jesuit Ignacio Pérez del Viso, their provincial superior repeated the order. Yorio and Jalics then made conscientious objection, upon which "Bergoglio turned to the general superior of the Jesuits at Rome, Pedro Arrupe, who responded that the two must obey."[5] Stripped of their pastoral charge by the Society of Jesus, the two were also refused a mandate under canon law by Juan Carlos Aramburu, then the archbishop of Buenos Aires.

With no more ecclesiastical cover, Yorio and Jalics were left on their own to face the repressive apparatus of the dictatorship, which

then felt more free to take action against them. The generally acquies-
cent stance of the Argentine ecclesiastical hierarchy vis-à-vis the military regime in those years should be borne in mind—despite the assassination and "disappearance" of at least sixteen priests. When at the
height of the repression the president of Pax Christi, Monsignor Luigi
Bettazzi, proposed via the nuncio Pio Laghi that at Buenos Aires the
church should organize a "solidarity vicarage" on the Chilean model
to aid the victims of the regime, the Argentine Episcopate refused.[6]
The same bishops, headed by Cardinal Aramburu, uttered not a murmur of protest when the 1976 assassination of Bishop Enrique Ange-
lelli, the principal ecclesiastical opponent of the military regime, was
presented as an automobile accident.

Analysis of the relations between the church and the dictatorship
in those years shows that in this respect the ecclesiastical hierarchy
may be grouped into four categories. There were a few bishops with
foresight who opposed the regime; others not openly in opposition
but active in giving succor to the victims; yet others who backed the
regime in one way or another or who maintained secret contact with
it; and a minority of ecclesiastics who were actively complicit.[7] Bergoglio, who at the time was not a bishop but a provincial superior of
the Jesuit Order, certainly belongs to the second group, those who
discreetly helped the persecuted whenever it was possible.

Only during the Jubilee year of 2000 did the Argentine Episcopal
Conference, under the presidency of Monsignor Estanislao Karlic, seek
pardon because "at different moments of our history we were indulgent
toward totalitarian positions, violating the democratic liberties that
originate in human dignity; because by our actions or omissions we discriminated against many of our brothers, without engaging sufficiently
in the defense of their rights." It was a public mea culpa on behalf of all
who had taken part in "violence against freedom, torture and delation,
political persecution and ideological intransigence."[8]

In 2006, as president of the Argentine Episcopal Conference, Bergoglio put out a second declaration of repentance for "enormous
errors against life and human dignity and disdain for law and the institutions" with the onset of the regime in 1976.

Apart from the question of the church's comportment under the
dictatorship, another topic of some discussion in Argentina has been

Bergoglio's management of the Society of Jesus when he was provincial superior. In Catholic circles, there are those who concede off the record that he was both "loved and hated" by his Jesuit brethren on account of his style of command and several decisions he made while he was in charge.

One of his first biographers, the Argentine journalist Evangelina Himitian, reports explicitly that Bergoglio faced "criticism and opposition." He spoke frankly with her when he was still archbishop: "I made plenty of mistakes, I don't deny it. Mistakes and sins. It would be hypocritical of me to beg pardon today for the sins and offenses I may have committed. Today I beg pardon for the sins and offenses I did in fact commit."[9]

Father Ignacio Pérez del Viso was one of Bergoglio's teachers and has followed his ascent. When we spoke in Buenos Aires, I mentioned the interview the pontiff gave to *La Civiltà Cattolica* and asked Father Ignacio why Bergoglio regarded his own experience as provincial superior of the Jesuits as a failure. "The pope doesn't qualify it as a failure," he cautioned me; readers might get that impression because no pope had ever been so pitilessly self-critical before.

"He was a very demanding provincial," said Father Ignacio, now almost eighty. He gave an account of what was going on in the Society of Jesus during the 1970s and the phenomena that caused Bergoglio to feel he had to intervene. "There was a certain amount of postconciliar [post–Vatican II] disorder, a tendency for mass meetings to act like sovereign assemblies, occasionally radical reversals of established theology." Bergoglio stood firm. He put a stop to the "rage for residing in tiny apartments" that for some Jesuits back then represented a way to immerse themselves more deeply in society. He wanted all students to reside in the San Miguel College, insisted that on certain occasions they should resume wearing their clerical collars, and "removed a few avant-garde professors." The provincial superior stood for order as opposed to what the Vatican, in the wake of the council, perceived as the hasty overthrow of the rules.

Pérez del Viso also recalls that once General Videla, furious at an article about human rights that appeared in a Jesuit periodical published by the Center for Social Research and Action,[10] had all the copies seized. Bergoglio then decided that in future every article ought to cross his desk prior to publication. "It was preventive censorship," commented Father Ignacio, "and I approve certain restrictions in times of emergency; only one has to know when to end them."

Consternation and outcry followed Bergoglio's decision to change the status of the Universidad del Salvador, founded and run by the Jesuits. It was encumbered by debt, and the last thing Bergoglio wanted was for the society to be involved in financial disorders. So he privatized it completely, ceded ownership to a lay association, and for good measure prohibited Jesuit professors from teaching there without his explicit authorization. The affair procured him many internal enemies.

Father Ignacio remembered that before Bergoglio's nomination as provincial superior, the local Jesuits were consulted. "I was opposed to his nomination because he was young and had never been superior of any community; he had dealt only with novices. There's quite a difference: you warn a young fellow once, then a second time, and then you kick him out. Learning to live with difficult people in a religious community is something else." A superior has to know how to handle challenges. For example, Father Ignacio recalled that in his community at that time three of the Jesuits were alcoholics who used to raid the communion wine. Situations like that are tricky to manage.

Nevertheless, it was decided in 1973 that Bergoglio should become provincial superior. "The word was that there were no other high-quality candidates and that he had a clear vision of what needed doing and a strong spirituality." For many, concluded the elderly Jesuit, Bergoglio was a good provincial superior; for a minority, he was not. As our conversation ended, after we had discussed a great many matters concerning the Catholic Church in Argentina, Father Ignacio Pérez del Viso bade me farewell and added: "The fact that he doesn't regard it as a failure doesn't mean that it was a success."

And indeed, after Jorge Mario Bergoglio held the post of provincial superior and participated in 1979 in the gathering of the Latin American Episcopate at Puebla, his career took a fairly drastic dip.

From 1980 to 1986, he was rector of the Colegio Máximo de San Miguel at Buenos Aires, then went to Germany to work on his doctoral thesis, and upon his return became a simple teacher of theology in the Argentine capital. Then in 1990, out of the blue, his superiors sent him to Córdoba as confessor to the local Jesuits and spiritual director of the parish attached to their principal residence. The assignment amounted to outright exile.[11] Bergoglio was fifty-four, and in Córdoba he lived through the season of "great interior crisis" to which he refers in his confession to Father Spadaro in *La Civiltà Cattolica*.

It was the prelude to a dramatic turn. In 1992, Cardinal Antonio Quarracino brought Bergoglio back to Buenos Aires as his auxiliary bishop. In 1993, he became vicar general of the diocese and in 1997 coadjutor bishop with the right of succession. Quarracino died, and on 28 February 1998 Jorge Mario Bergoglio ascended the archiepiscopal throne of the Argentine capital. Three years later John Paul II named him cardinal.

Bergoglio's leadership of the diocese of Buenos Aires and then the presidency of the Argentine Episcopal Conference from 2005 to 2011 were formative: they taught him that governing is not just issuing orders but listening, building consensus, and resolving problems by taking the time to assess them in depth. The exercise of authority, he learned, means fostering the growth of the abilities of one's team rather than waving the staff of command. As archbishop of Buenos Aires, he learned to check the temptation to make choices in haste. Today the new Bergoglio says as much explicitly: "I am always wary of the first decision, that is, the first thing that comes to my mind if I have to make a decision. This is usually the wrong thing. I have to wait and assess, looking deep into myself, taking the necessary time."[12]

Father Ignacio summed it up this way: "As archbishop, his byword was *compañerismo* rather than *authoritarianism*." (The Spanish word suggests a style of closeness to the clergy as opposed to loftiness.) "If a priest was worried about the health of his mother, he would say, 'Go visit her. I'll attend to the parish for three days.'"

In close contact with the priests of the diocese, Archbishop Bergoglio manifested an intense spirituality and systematically encouraged them to practice attentive mercy toward the faithful in their struggle with existence. The great sensitivity to social problems he already had grew more intense.

Thirty years after his experience as provincial superior of the Jesuits, Bergoglio is quick to acknowledge: "God picked me up after my stumbles along my path, he aided me especially during the hardest spells . . . little by little I learned."[13] At Buenos Aires, he developed his sense of self-critique. "Sometimes in facing a problem I err, I behave badly, and then I have to reverse myself and ask for pardon. . . . It does me good because it helps me to understand the errors of others."[14]

In the crucible of a metropolis with millions of inhabitants, he learned what it meant to work with his auxiliary bishops as a team, taking part in meetings of neighborhood priests, listening to teachers in the Catholic schools where 50 percent of children receive their education, coming to terms with politics (often quite conflictual terms, especially vis-à-vis the governments of the two Kirchners), and measuring up to the cultural pluralism of the vast city through engagement with Jews, Muslims, and evangelical Christians.

It is not true that Francis has come from "the ends of the earth," as he said to the faithful with a touch of genial self-deprecation on the evening of his election. He is the first pope to have been born, raised, lived, and worked in a contemporary metropolis, however far from Europe, and the only one to have been nourished by the tumultuous, dramatic, and variegated experience of such a gigantic urban region with its 13 million inhabitants. Joseph Ratzinger, Angelo Roncalli, Karol Wojtyla, and Albino Luciani were born in small provincial towns, and the course of their careers never taught them the true rhythm of the metropolis. The Kraków of the future John Paul II and the Milan of the future Paul VI pale in comparison to the complexity and the violent contrasts of Buenos Aires.

The Rome of the interwar period of the twentieth century, in which Eugenio Pacelli, the future Pius XII, grew, may have resounded with the rhetoric of Mussolini, but it had a provincial air for all that. The Vatican Secretariat of State in which Pius XII and Paul VI matured may have constituted a refined observatory of great intellectual finesse, but the dimensions of a true metropolis are of a different order.

Already at the midpoint of the twentieth century, the true metropolis offered a foretaste of globalization and urban gigantism (and of the gigantic problems lying ahead). The pulsating mixture of races, cultures, faiths, and contrasting lifestyles leaves a different imprint, just as travel by ocean liner leaves a different imprint to travel by rowboat.

As archbishop of Buenos Aires, Bergoglio learned to reckon with a process of secularization identical to that of the great urban areas of the Northern Hemisphere. Father Guillermo Marcó, his spokesman, points out that "in Argentina as a whole 87 percent identify as Catholic as compared to 9 percent evangelical. But in Buenos Aires only 60 percent identify as Catholic, and only 12 percent go to mass." Popular Catholic devotion finds other outlets: millions of pilgrims visit the sanctuary of the Virgin of Luján or take part in the procession for San Cayetano, protector of bread and work. Nevertheless, when it comes to making religious and moral choices, personal autonomy continues to make headway, albeit at a different pace in the urban areas than in the rural ones.

A survey published in 2013 by a major Argentine research center reveals that 91 percent of the population believe in God, but only 23 percent maintain that the mediation of a church institution is indispensable, and 61 percent prefer to relate directly to the divinity. The individualization of religious life manifests itself in the high numbers of those who pray regularly at home: 73 percent in the larger cities and 86 percent in the smaller ones.

In the sample of those who have completed primary schooling, more than 60 percent are in favor of married priests, and more than half maintain that women should be allowed into the priesthood. A litmus test of the radical sociocultural mutation under way is the response to the question of whether sexual relations prior to marriage are a good thing for both men and women. The overwhelming "yes" of the Catholic faithful under forty-four exceeds 87 percent. The notion that homosexuality is a sickness stalls, still among Catholics, at 39 percent.[15] This explains why in 2010 Argentina legalized same-sex marriage—Archbishop Bergoglio's firm opposition notwithstanding.

But when a municipal law regarding de facto couples, including same-sex ones, had been put to the vote in the district of Buenos Aires a few years earlier, Bergoglio did not oppose it, despite pressure from the Vatican and the Catholic Right. His collaborator, Father Marcó, remembers it well: "I said to him, 'Jorge, we are in a pluralistic society, it isn't a sacrament, why oppose it?' And he took no public stance."

In Italy at the same period, the Italian Episcopal Conference, spurred on by Pope Ratzinger, mobilized every Catholic association in the peninsula to block a bill put forward by the government of Romano Prodi to regularize de facto unions. And block it they did.

11

The Program
of the Revolution

At Buenos Aires, in circles both Catholic and not, the assessment of Bergoglio's character as a manager is unanimous. He is a man who takes charge, they say, "a pure politician, with an extraordinary capacity for work and a tendency to centralize, a fine mind with a clear sense of power."

It is the flip side of that dimension, the tenderness and fellowship, that has won the hearts of millions of the faithful. Francis has goodness, the goodness of the shepherd of souls, but he doesn't wear rose-colored glasses. And he knows perfectly well how hard the push back will be against the reforms he is planning for the church.

"I'm cunning," he has warned his adversaries.[1] He knows that there is conflict occurring offstage and that some of it is inevitably going to spill out into public view: it has happened before, with John XXIII and Paul VI.

Right from the start of his pontificate, he has been laying the groundwork for major changes, with the platform hammered together during the preconclave as the point of departure, incorporating points of view and concerns raised by the cardinals during the general congregations that lasted from 4 March to 11 March 2013. The proposals advanced in those meetings boiled down to three: reform the Roman Curia to make it leaner and more efficient; clean up the Vatican Bank; and promote "collegiality" by institutionalizing frequent consultations between the pontiff and the College of Cardinals, on one hand, and the pontiff and the Conferences of Bishops, on the other so as to make the worldwide episcopate into a partner in the formation of papal strategy.

Both in this planning exercise and in his public statements, Francis has gone further than the platform of those who elected him—and in certain respects a lot further than many cardinals could have imagined. Fully aware of this, he spent 2013 bolting into place, in successive strokes, the machinery for the renewal he has in mind. He began in July, addressing himself to the leadership of the Latin American Episcopal Council at its meeting in Brazil and continued more informally in the autumn with the interview granted to *Civiltà Cattolica*. Finally, he put the stamp of the papal magisterium on his program in November, spelling it out in the apostolic exhortation *Evangelii gaudium*.

His announcements are aimed at the whole church, using the full array of modern media channels, and he sets out precise objectives so as to make it harder for the tentacles of curial routine and bureaucratic inertia to tie him down the way they tied Pope Ratzinger down—for Benedict XVI had also planned to make changes but failed to carry them out because of timidity and lack of skill at working the levers of power.

Francis's revolution has a name: the missionary transformation of the church. The Catholic Church is going to have to "abandon the complacent attitude that says: 'We have always done it this way.'"[2] The first step is to remotivate the clergy, to prevent it from becoming just another bureaucracy, seeking solutions in stricter discipline or in "the restoration of outdated manners and forms which, even on the cultural level, are no longer meaningful." Priests should not be spending their time preparing "detailed forecasts" and verifying the results obtained in quantifiable, statistical terms. Francis's desire is for a clergy strong enough to resist the temptation to ideologize the gospel or run their parishes like little dictators.[3] "The phenomenon of clericalism," said the pope to the leaders of the Latin American Episcopate in Rio de Janeiro, "explains, in great part, the lack of maturity and Christian freedom in a good part of the Latin American laity." Not that this is a uniquely South American problem: it applies to many regions of the Catholic empire. In Italy, there has been a decades-long attempt to bring to life an independent instance representing the Catholic laity with the power to express itself freely and exchange views with the hierarchy without reading from a prepared script, and for decades the national Conference of Italian Bishops has blocked the attempt. Francis asks: Do we, bishops and priests, give their just freedom to laypeople? "Do we support them and accompany them, overcoming the temptation to manipulate them or infantilize them?"

Something is amiss, he warns, when the church turns into a "central command," abandoning its mission to serve the faithful and all people of good will. What Francis wants is an open church that looks the world in the face. He criticizes religious institutions that project a forbidding presence and parishes that simply ensure the performance of the sacraments. He gives confessors a shake: "I want to remind priests that the confessional must not be a torture chamber but rather an encounter with the Lord's mercy which spurs us on to do our best." He reminds the faithful that "a small step, in the midst of great human limitations, can be more pleasing to God than a life which appears outwardly in order but moves through the day without confronting great difficulties."[4]

His judgment on "integralism" (roughly speaking, the Catholic counterpart of Protestant fundamentalism) is harsh in the extreme. While still an archbishop, he warned: "Let us not enslave ourselves to a virtually paranoid defense of *our truth* (if *I* have it, *he* doesn't; if *he* possesses it, *I* am robbed of it). Truth is an expansive gift . . . it amplifies and elevates us." The last thing he wishes for is a church that abhors the present and adores the past: "The complaints of today about how 'barbaric' the world is—these complaints sometimes end up giving birth within the church to desires to establish order in the sense of pure conservation, as a defense. No: God is to be encountered in the world of today."[5]

He presses the Catholic hierarchy to reconfigure itself. Bishops must be humble guides rather than imperious leaders, as close to the people as if they were their own fathers and brothers, patient and compassionate. They must have a style of inward and outward poverty, shunning ambition and leading a simple and austere life.[6] Instead of the bishop as commander, Francis points to the figure of the shepherd who knows how to walk before the flock to show them the way, how to walk in their midst to keep them together, and how to trail after them so as to round up the strays, "but also, and primarily, so that the flock itself can sniff out new paths."[7] The image of the faithful flock scenting the breeze in the vanguard and then sending cues back to the bishop trudging in the rear is a jolting one, especially on the lips of a pontiff.

The church that Francis wants is a church not obsessed by the uncoordinated transmission of a hoard of doctrines that it strives "insistently" to impose.[8] Quite the contrary: he wants a church ready to run the risk of measuring up to modern humanity in the real world and ready to respond to humanity's thirst for God. Such a church will need to undergo reform of a structural kind, and Francis does indeed have concrete intentions that will affect the whole ecclesiastical pyramid: the papacy, the curia, the synods, the Episcopal Conferences, the procedures for consultation within dioceses, the role of the faithful, and the responsibilities to be entrusted to women.

The reform of the papacy is at the top of the list. Francis wants to bring it into line with the significance "that Jesus Christ meant it to have" and to get it into shape to cope with the challenge of evangelization in the modern world. Francis makes an analogy with "conversion," but in this case the convert he is striving to save is the papacy itself. The Uruguayan jurist Guzmán Carriquiry, secretary of the Pontifical Commission for Latin America, sums up this reshaping of the papacy with a telling comparison: "Bergoglio is the successor of Peter, not of Constantine."[9]

Pope Francis emphasizes that too much centralization is not a help to the church but a hindrance to its existence and its missionary dynamism.[10] And here the Argentinian pope refers to two important documents that sank into oblivion during the pontificate of Benedict XVI. The first is the encyclical *Ut unum sint* by John Paul II (May 1995), which proposed to search for a new, more participatory model of the papal primacy, in view of an ecumenical reunification, with the heads of the other Christian denominations being consulted. The other document featured is a text drafted at Ravenna in 2007 by a combined Eastern Orthodox and Catholic committee, with the participation of Cardinal Walter Kasper and the metropolitan Joannis Zizioulas of the Ecumenical Patriarchate of Constantinople. In this document, the bishop of Rome is recognized, in black and white for the first time, by the Orthodox party, as "first among patriarchs" and the Roman See as the church that "presides in love" (the same wording used by Francis in his speech to the crowd on the evening he was elected). At the same time, the document underlines the need for the Roman pontiff to play his part in a process of genuine collaboration with all Christian bishops—in "accord" with them." This, in the Orthodox world, is called synodality, and Francis makes explicit reference to the Orthodox pattern, where a patriarch may indeed be the head of a church but cannot govern it without input from his council, the synod. "From our Orthodox brethren we can learn more," he says, "about the meaning of episcopal collegiality and the tradition of synodality."[11]

The counterpart of papal reform is reform of the Roman Curia. And that doesn't mean just pruning the bureaucratic deadwood and running the machine more efficiently. At Buenos Aires, one of Bergoglio's colleagues from the period when he was archbishop mentions that for some time a number of bishoprics have been asking for the "police powers" of the curia to be reduced. It is on the record that at one time or another bishoprics in the United States, France, Germany, and some Latin American countries (at the time when liberation theology was flourishing) have felt the heavy hand of Vatican control and pressure. For centuries, the Roman Curia, presenting itself as an instrument in the service of the papal monarchy, has thought of itself as the church's high command—and has acted like it too.

In the apostolic exhortation *Evangelii gaudium*, Francis confines himself to stating that the "central structures of the universal church also need to hear the call to pastoral conversion." In his conversation with the Jesuit Antonio Spadaro, he was more frank: "The Roman dicasteries are at the service of the pope and the bishops. They must help both the particular churches and the bishops' conferences."[12] Even to state that much is to conjure up the specter of a Copernican revolution, for the apparatus of the curia, hitherto at the sole disposition of its commander in chief, is now supposed to transform itself into an "instrument of help," a transmission belt between the papacy and bishops all over the world. In the September 2013 interview the pope gave to *Spadaro*, which represents the first programmatic manifesto of his pontificate, he boldly foregrounded the numerous criticisms that have been circulating for years about the power of the curia: "In some cases, however, when they [the dicasteries] are not properly understood, they run the risk of becoming institutions of censorship. It is amazing to see the denunciations for lack of orthodoxy that come to Rome." Bergoglio starkly rejects the whole notion of the curia as a power center; it is not his intention that those who run its departments should view themselves as the managers in charge of the universal church. That, at least, is his aim.

It is telling that in both the interview and the apostolic exhortation, Francis never makes use of the word *curia*, as though wishing to eliminate a word so redolent of the exercise of power. The pope prefers more technical terms, such as *central structures* or *dicasteries*, for these departments of government. In the culture of linguistic ritual that has prevailed for millennia in the Catholic Church, the choice to name or to avoid naming something is always fraught with meaning.

Only in the speech of 21 December 2013, in which he offered Christmas greetings to the prelates and functionaries of the Roman dicasteries, did the pope expressly name the curia. He praised the dedication, professionalism, and sanctity of life of so many of his audience but uttered a warning as well: "When the attitude is no longer one of service to the particular churches and their bishops, the structure of the curia turns into a ponderous, bureaucratic customs house, constantly inspecting and questioning, hindering the working of the Holy Spirit and the growth of God's people."[13] These words have already aroused some ill feelings. To change the orientation of the central apparatus of the church will be one of the most difficult challenges of his pontificate.

The privy council of cardinals has faced up to the problem operationally. The decision has been taken, with the pope's blessing, that a new statute will be drafted for the central government of the church. The most recent reform was the one carried out by John Paul II with the apostolic constitution *Pastor bonus* (1988), which reorganized the curial departments and offices, the ecclesiastical tribunals and the pontifical councils, with the secretary of state playing a leading role as coordinator. After only a few meetings of the council of eight cardinals, it became apparent that the constitution of John Paul II could not be changed by tinkering. The whole model of the curia demands to be rethought starting from zero, after centuries of ultracentralization of power.

At the same time, Francis wishes to grant more autonomy to the national Conferences of Bishops. Reversing the position held by Pope Ratzinger, who while still a cardinal had denied that the Episcopal Conferences could take decisions binding on the individual bishops of any country, the Argentine pontiff intends to endow them with a precise statute that will treat them as "subjects of specific attributions, including genuine doctrinal authority."[14]

Previously, in an interview-based book published in 1985 and entitled in English *The Ratzinger Report*, the German cardinal had asserted that "the episcopal conferences have no theological basis, they do not belong to the structure of the church, as willed by Christ, that cannot be eliminated; they have only a practical, concrete function."[15] And again in 1998, Ratzinger, as prefect of the Holy Office, repeated that the Episcopal Conferences "do not constitute per se a doctrinal instance which is binding and superior to the authority of each bishop who comprises them."[16]

This is not an abstract theological question. On one hand, it throws into relief a difference of opinion between the retired pope and the reigning one; on the other, it concerns the model the church will actually follow in the twenty-first century. Will it still be a rigidly centralized imperial church like the one we have known for centuries, especially during the half-millennium since the Council of Trent? Or will it be a more communitarian church, in which the papal primacy is offset by the active collaboration of the bishops in the central government and a degree of autonomous self-management at the national level?

It is not indispensable for a world religion to be highly central-ized. Islam, Judaism, and Buddhism have existed for millennia with-out a "Vatican." The Protestant world and the evangelical movements exist and expand with no central management. But for the Catholic Church, with its history and its sense of itself, Francis's proposal to move toward a more participatory model amounts to a challenge. And indeed, harsh criticism was immediately voiced by the man who holds the position once held by Cardinal Ratzinger: Archbishop Ludwig Müller, the prefect of the Congregation for the Doctrine of the Faith. "It is out of the question," he said, to favor a tendency that allows the local churches to take their distance from Rome. "Particularism, like centralism, is heresy." The presidents of the Episcopal Conferences are mere coordinators, he insisted, not vice popes.[17]

Pope Francis wants to put a stop to the vicious practice of denun-ciations for lack of orthodoxy. These delations arrive at Rome from every corner of the globe, insinuating doctrinal errors that often ruin the careers of those accused. "I think the cases should be investigated by the local bishops' conferences, which can get valuable assistance from Rome."[18] Though the pope doesn't say much about it, he firmly intends to change the methods of the Congregation for the Doctrine of the Faith—historically the watchdog against doctrinal deviation. In a meeting with its members at the beginning of 2014, he insisted that they should work collaboratively with local bishops and the national Episcopal Conferences and should engage in a "constructive, respect-ful, and patient dialogue" with the theologians under investigation.[19]

Francis is convinced above all that it is indispensable for the pope not to reign in solitude but to govern with the help of consultative organs, within which real debate occurs. That is why he has created his privy council of cardinals. And that is how he intends to utilize both the College of Cardinals and the Synod of Bishops, as "impor-tant places to make real and active this consultation."[20] He wants their agendas to be short and concrete so that the pros and cons can be thoroughly assessed.

The synod, where bishops from all over the world are represented and which meets in the Vatican at least every three years, is the body to which Francis has entrusted the debate on the thorniest questions: communion for divorced and remarried Catholics; the problems related to sexuality and fertility; and the role of the laity, who are at present subjected to "an excessive clericalism which keeps them away from decision-making."[21] And that in turn leads to the matter of the functions to be handed over to women—for Francis has made it his goal to insert women into the nerve centers of church decision making.

It is a complex program of reform, and foci of resistance have sprung up all over the map. There are those who object to an excess of democracy that risks diminishing the papal primacy, and there are those who object to the arrival of women at the top level of church government. "There are already more women than men in the church. No to 'pink' quotas" is the opposition line one hears from part of the hierarchy.

What remains unspecified at present in this vision of government is the church's stance in international politics. John XXIII, Paul VI, and especially John Paul II had a precise geopolitical outlook. Francis appears to be driven primarily by pastoral concerns and to meet international occasions as they arise. When he was elected, he was an unknown quantity when it came to directing the foreign policy of the Holy See. John XXIII, Paul VI, and notably John Paul II had had a firm grasp of geopolitics. Benedict XVI, more of a theologian, did not appear to be at ease in exercising political leadership. Bergoglio did not engage in much international travel when he was a cardinal and does not speak English fluently: What would he do as pope?

Within a few months, Francis began to move with assurance on the international scene. He acts from pastoral motives above all, but with a precise vision of international crises and the Catholic Church's political-religious role. The view that the planet is living through "a third world war . . . scattered here and there" accurately captures the need for the heads of nations to undertake a global and collective initiative to extinguish the embers of the endemic crises that have tormented the planet for years.

His intervention in the Syrian crisis was extremely effective and brought the Holy See back onto the international stage after a long absence under Benedict XVI. When a U.S.-led attack on Syria was under consideration in late August and early September 2013, the pope threw the authority of his personality into the balance, giving voice to the opposition to the war in European public opinion and in a large section of American opinion too.

Speaking directly to Vladimir Putin, the president of the Russian Federation, at the time of the G20 meeting in Moscow, the pontiff reminded him that armed conflicts always create "deep divisions and lacerations that take many years to heal." With a realism appreciated by long-term Vatican diplomats, Francis stressed the fact that too many partisan interests had prevailed since the start of the civil war in Syria "and in fact hindered the search for a solution that would have avoided the senseless massacre now unfolding."[22] With its forceful demand for a peaceful solution, the pope's intervention certainly favored the agreement reached at the UN that blocked the invasion and led to the gradual dismantling of the chemical weapons possessed by the Assad regime.

During his first sortie into the international political arena, Bergoglio (who was not known in Buenos Aires as a fan of technology) made daily use of Twitter, holding center stage uninterruptedly. On 4 September: "Let the cry of peace resound strongly throughout the world!" On 5 September: "With all my strength I ask the parties to the conflict not to shut themselves up in their own interests." On 6 September: "Peace is a good that overcomes all barriers, because it is a good for all of humanity." So he continued for days, launching the special hashtag #prayforpeace and meanwhile organizing a prayer vigil attended by one hundred thousand people to stop the fratricidal war in Syria. The day after the vigil, the Argentine pope used his habitual simple and direct language. In his Angelus for 8 September 2013, he said: "And the doubt always remains: is this war or that war—because wars are everywhere—really a war to solve problems or is it a commercial war for selling weapons in illegal trade?"

His voyage to the Holy Land on 24–26 May 2014 was, like those of his predecessors John Paul II and Benedict XVI, characterized by a stance equally empathetic to the claims of the Israelis and the Palestinians and by an impassioned summons to dialogue and the repudiation of violence. Still, there were shadings worthy of the Jesuit tradition, each of which constituted a subtle political signal.

To avoid being caught between conflicting nationalisms, the pope rejected the idea of an interreligious summit with the grand mufti of

Jerusalem and the two grand rabbis of Israel. Instead he brought two friends from Argentina with him on his pilgrimage, Rabbi Abraham Skorka and Omar Aboud, the Muslim president of the Buenos Aires Institute for Interreligious Dialogue, demonstrating that his relations with Judaism and Islam have deep roots.

The photo of the pontiff in silent prayer, his head resting on the wall, standing on Palestinian territory, went round the world as no speech could have done. It was a tacit admonition to the Israeli government that this wall, which does not conform to the territorial division of 1967, cannot stand forever.

On the Middle East question, Francis has taken up the assertive policy of Pope Wojtyla, who on 16 November 2003, the eve of a visit by the Israeli prime minister Ariel Sharon to Rome, had warned that "the Holy Land needs bridges, not walls." At that time, the government of Israel was engaged in constructing what it calls a "barrier" but which the Holy See has always regarded as a wall.

Even more subtle was Pope Francis's gesture of organizing a prayer meeting in the gardens of the Vatican on 8 June 2014, to which he invited the president of Israel Shimon Peres and the Palestinian president Abu Mazen, along with the ecumenical patriarch of Constantinople, Bartholomew I. By inviting the two presidents to this solemn act of commitment to peace, the Argentine pope sent out the implicit message that it is no longer just the Palestinians who must recognize Israel, but also that the Jewish state must recognize the State of Palestine because it is no longer up to Israel to decide whether the Palestinians have the right to organize a state for themselves. As for the Arabs, they must learn to comprehend the "pain of the other," as Francis stated to the grand mufti of Jerusalem.

"Peacemaking calls for courage," said the pope on a limpid evening in Rome, amid the greenery, while a half-moon rose over the cupola of St. Peter's, "much more so than warfare. It calls for the courage to say yes to encounter and no to conflict: yes to dialogue and no to violence; yes to negotiations and no to hostilities; yes to respect for agreements and no to acts of provocation; yes to sincerity and no to duplicity."[23]

Following the bloody new war in Gaza—with more than two thousand Palestinian dead, including around five hundred children, and casualties among the Israelis amounting to sixty-four soldiers and five civilians[24]—Francis returned in August to the topic of that singular meeting in the Vatican, emphasizing that "the door is still open."

Like Wojtyla, who was always careful not to equate the Catholic Church with the West, Francis rejects any crusading ideal, despite the increase in the persecution of Christians in the Middle East in the wake of the civil wars in Syria and Iraq, especially after the wave of violence unleashed by the jihadi militias of the so-called caliphate of the Islamic State of Iraq and Syria (ISIS). We need to be concerned for all the victims, he remarked, not just those on our side. There are men and women who belong to other persecuted religious minorities besides the Christians, he reminded journalists while returning to Rome from his visit to South Korea on 18 August 2014. "And all are equal before God."

In the face of the cruelty of the massacres perpetrated by ISIS, Francis has revived John Paul II's concept of humanitarian intervention. It is, he maintains, licit to resist the "unjust aggressor." Yet, in perfect continuity with the Polish pope's opposition to George W. Bush's invasion of Iraq, Francis specifies that often, under the pretext of halting an aggressor, "the powers have taken over peoples and carried on an actual war of conquest!" Hence, "one nation alone cannot determine how to stop an unjust aggressor." That role falls solely to the United Nations.

Much like his Polish predecessor, Pope Francis has become steadily more active on the international scene as the months have passed. With shrewd timing, he sent a private letter to Barack Obama and Raul Castro in the summer of 2014 to promote an exchange of prisoners between Cuba and the United States (the liberation of the American contractor Alan Gross, incarcerated by the Castro regime since 2009, in exchange for three Cuban agents being held in the United States). In October 2014, the Vatican played host to delegations from the two nations, who met in Canada for secret talks. Thus, with moral backing from Francis, whom Obama thanked explicitly, the president of the United States was able to announce the end of the U.S. embargo on the Caribbean island on 17 December 2014, opening the way to a restoration of diplomatic relations with Havana.

Another world leader who has received a private letter from the Pope is the Chinese president Xi Jinping. Francis entrusted it to the South American trading bloc Mercosur for delivery to two Argentine emissaries, Ricardo Romano, a member of the Partido Justicialista, and José Lujan, the official representative of the Chinese Academy of Sciences. It contained an invitation to President Xi to visit him at the Vatican to discuss world peace. Peking and Moscow are destinations that Pope John Paul II once dreamed of.

12

St. Peter Had
No Bank Account

E ven before he was elected, Jorge Mario Bergoglio was irritated
and disgusted, like most cardinals from outside Italy, by the
ongoing parade of financial scandals in the Vatican. The Vatican leaks scandal brought to light the misappropriations denounced
by the secretary-general of the governorate, Carlo Maria Viganò: fraud
and false billing were draining off funds from the papal administration.
There followed the defenestration of the president of the Vatican Bank,
the IOR (Istituto per le Opere di Religione), Ettore Gotti Tedeschi,
with a communiqué from the board of directors, quite unusual in the
financial world, that aimed to ruin him professionally by accusing him
of "incapacity to carry out the basic duties" of his office.[1]

Benedict XVI, who regarded the president of the IOR with esteem
and friendship, learned the news on television. He was badly shaken,
and according to some he even wept. Gotti's efforts to bring transparency to the IOR were well known, as were his clashes with the director

general Paolo Cipriani, who denied him information about irregular current accounts. The clamor raised by Gotti's removal further degraded the reputation of the Vatican Bank, which had served in the 1990s to transfer funds illegally to Italian political parties (the Enimont scandal) and had been utilized for decades to execute "massive money laundering operations" of Mafia cash, according to a determination by the Rome Court of Appeal.[2]

In the meetings of cardinals prior to the conclave, the IOR was a topic of lively debate, especially at the last meeting on 11 March 2013, following a brief report by Secretary of State Tarcisio Bertone. The Nigerian cardinal John Onaiyekan conveyed the state of mind of many cardinals when he commented: "IOR is not essential to the ministry of the Holy Father. . . . IOR is not fundamental, it is not sacramental, it is not dogmatic."[3] Bergoglio's thoughts were running that way too. The cardinals were unanimous in demanding a cleanup.

After Pope Benedict had already announced his resignation but before it took effect, he appointed a new president of the IOR, Ernst von Freyberg. This appointment provoked consternation. Von Freyberg's installation on 15 February 2013 amounted to forestalling the next pope. Once more criticism rained down on Cardinal Bertone. Still, the choice of von Freyberg was the upshot of a selection process that had lasted several months and had employed the services of the international headhunting agency Spencer Stuart. Freyberg was a German business lawyer, director general of the Frankfurt investment consultancy Daiwa Corporate Advisory, and president of the shipbuilding firm Blohm and Voss of Hamburg. He was picked from a long list of forty candidates.

On the day of the announcement, it was revealed that von Freyberg's firm also builds frigates for the German navy—not exactly a shining qualification to work for the Holy See. But he was a member of the Catholic order of the Knights of Malta and had created a foundation that was active in the field of Catholic education. He was to serve as president of IOR on a part-time basis, spending three days a week in Rome.

This was the climate in which Bergoglio ascended the papal throne. Spread out before him was a deeply rooted and widely ramified network binding together heavyweight players in politics, business, and religion. Shortly before his election, at the end of February 2013, the Italian financial police stopped an IOR consultant, the lawyer Michele Briamonte, at Ciampino Airport as he got off a private airplane accompanied by one of Cardinal Bertone's closest collaborators, Monsignor Roberto Lucchini. Briamonte refused to hand over his luggage for inspection and showed the officers a Vatican passport. It was the police who backed down after Cardinal Bertone intervened.

The papal spokesman Federico Lombardi did issue a statement to the effect that Briamonte's Vatican passport was valid when he was traveling abroad on behalf of the Holy See "but not valid for an Italian citizen in Italy."[4] Nevertheless, it was the Italian authorities who had caved in. Briamonte was dismissive, asserting that a police dog had sniffed his bags without lunging.[5]

For Pope Francis, the IOR was like a dripping faucet of displeasing news. An investigation of the IOR for money laundering, launched by prosecutors in Rome, turned up numerous embarrassing episodes. The Bank of Italy's Financial Intelligence Unit, which targets suspect transactions, reported that a nun belonging to the Suore Francescane Angeline had showed up one day at a branch of the Banca Prossima and had paid into the account of her order's school the sum of $150,000 in bundles of $100 notes wrapped in bands stamped "IOR." The Financial Intelligence Unit characterized the amount and the source of the money as "without adequate justification."[6]

In 2010, the Roman prosecutors sequestered 23 million euros held in IOR accounts with the Credito Artigiano and the Banca del Fucino for failure to adhere to the guidelines against money laundering. The judicial investigation revealed intense activity by IOR through the Milan and Frankfurt branches of the American bank J. P. Morgan. At the request of the financial intelligence unit, J. P. Morgan asked the Vatican Bank for clarification. The answers they got were sketchy, and a follow-up request for details on eleven specific cases elicited evasive replies from IOR once again.[7]

The investigation brought to the surface some bizarre facts. The archbishop emeritus of Urbino, Monsignor Francesco Marinelli, had executed six transfers totaling 1.1 million euros in the space of three weeks from his own IOR account with J. P. Morgan. The beneficiaries were four of his relatives. J. P. Morgan asked the Vatican Bank for information about "the source of the funds[,] . . . their congruity with the activities [of the author of the transfers,] . . . the eventual origin of third parties," and the reason given for the transfers. The Vatican Bank did not even deign to respond. Given that a bishop receives a gross monthly stipend of between 1,300 and, at most, 1,800 euros, it was hard to see where Marinelli had gotten more than a million euros. Asked for comment by a journalist, Monsignor Marinelli answered, "I know nothing about all this."[8]

The magistrates responsible for the investigation—Nello Rossi, the assistant chief prosecutor of Rome, and prosecutors Stefano Fava and Stefano Pesci—wrote that the IOR's books were in a state of total confusion: "Sums deposited in an IOR account could be withdrawn from any other current account held with the same institution, and there was no standard procedure for executing such operations. Thus, we see not just uncertainty about where the sums end up—in itself an alarm signal for money laundering—but above all the existence of a mechanism that also blinds the regulator to the intermediate transfers."[9] From 2009 to 2012, 1.36 billion euros transited through the IOR account with J. P. Morgan, but to evade regulatory controls the account was emptied every evening.[10] J. P. Morgan decided to break off its relationship with the Vatican Bank and closed the account in 2012.

All these details were cascading into the media while Francis was already in office and painting a picture of tangled and opaque business dealings in strident contrast with the image of "a poor church for the poor" desired by the pope.

A mass of emails from Gotti Tedeschi made public in the context of an investigation of the industrial group Finmeccanica must have left the pontiff even more depressed. They reveal political and economic intrigues light-years removed from the church's ostensible mission. One email from Gotti addressed to Cardinal Bertone's assistant, Don Lech Piechota, concerned the position of chief executive of Sogin, a subsidiary of Finmeccanica that operates in the nuclear industry. On behalf of someone in the Berlusconi government (probably Minister of Economy and Finance Giulio Tremonti), Gotti wanted to know in confidence if a certain candidate was indeed "welcome" to the Vatican secretary of state and "close" to the bishop of Trieste, Monsignor Crepaldi. Gotti was awaiting "guidance."[11]

Another email Gotti sent to Bertone's right-hand man was about the candidacy of Lorenza Lei for the post of director general of the Italian public broadcaster RAI. There would seem to be obstacles, wrote Gotti, both on account of Lei's imprudence and the Lega Nord party, which wanted more appointees beholden to it in the RAI. "It seems that Dr. Lei 'whispered' on a couple of occasions that 'cardinal Bertone has received assurances from Berlusconi concerning her [Lei's] nomination' . . . and these utterances have generated a certain amount of internal and external opposition." Lorenza Lei, who also had strong ties to the president of the Italian Episcopal Conference, Angelo Bagnasco, did in fact succeed in becoming director general of the RAI for a year.[12]

The emails showed that the financial irregularities in the Vatican denounced by Monsignor Viganò were not imaginary. Gotti Tedeschi communicated to Cardinal Giuseppe Bertello, president of the Vatican governorate, the results of a confidential investigation. Random audits "have revealed that prices charged to the governorate exceed market prices by fifty to one hundred and fifty percent." There were also cases of conflict of interest.[13] Further details came to light of Vatican collusion with Minister Tremonti to avoid the payment of property tax arrears—going back to 2005—on ecclesiastical properties that also house private enterprises.

Whichever way Pope Francis looked, he saw a Vatican bogged down in operations and negotiations having little to do with religious commitment or charitable concerns. A church that prioritizes organization in the worldly sense loses meaning, he admonished several weeks after taking office, during a morning mass attended by employees of the Vatican Bank: "But there are those from the IOR . . . excuse me, eh! . . . some things are necessary, offices are required . . . OK! but they are necessary up to a certain point: as an aid to this love story. But when organization takes first place, love falls down and the church, poor thing, becomes an NGO. And this is not the way forward."[14]

Francis appraised the situation for a couple of months, during which he did not even meet the president of the bank, von Freyberg, despite crossing his path frequently at the Santa Marta residence, where the German manager stays when in Rome. Four months after his election, in June 2013, he repeated: "St. Peter had no bank account and when he had to pay taxes, the Lord sent him to fish in the sea to find money in the fish to pay them."[15] Alarmed, the IOR director general, Cipriani, responded in an interview a few days later that ownership of a financial institution is a guarantee of independence for the Holy See. To possess an instrument such as the IOR is "a matter of duty."[16]

The pope was making his plans. Twenty-four hours after the interview with Cipriani appeared—by coincidence—Francis appointed a curial "prelate" for the IOR. It was Monsignor Battista Ricca, director of the Santa Marta residence and other ecclesiastical residences, including the Casa Internationale del Clero in Via della Scrofa, where Bergoglio had made his acquaintance. The pope had made up his mind: for now the IOR would remain, but it was to be profoundly transformed and brought into line once and for all with international standards of transparency. Monsignor Ricca would be the pope's "eyes and ears" on the bank's board of directors.

Francis proceeded quickly to set up an investigative committee to examine the IOR on 26 June, and then on 10 July he finally held a formal meeting jointly with the president of the Vatican Bank and the new committee. Von Freyberg breathed a sigh of relief. "It's a pleasure," he asserted, "to receive observations written in the pope's own hand."[17] The machinery to radically transform the bank was set decisively in motion, and in a climate of austerity the five cardinals who sat on the bank's supervisory committee were stripped of their special indemnity of 25,000 euros annually.

The fact is that Francis would have preferred not to deal with the Vatican finances until the second year of his pontificate, but the cascade of negative headlines forced him to move faster. "The agenda changed," he confessed to reporters on the flight home from Brazil. Using the metaphor of a goalkeeper on a soccer pitch, he added: "But these things happen when running a government, right? One moves this way, but they kick a goal shot at him from over there instead, and he has to block it, isn't that right?" The pope concluded: "I don't know how the IOR will end up. . . . But the hallmarks of the IOR—whether it be a bank, an aid fund, or whatever else—have to be transparency and honesty."[18]

Ernst von Freyberg is fifty-five years old; his manner is discreet; his outlook is that of an "average entrepreneur" (his own words). He recalled the moment when Cardinal Bertone rang him on the telephone to let him know about his nomination: "I drew a deep breath and said to myself, good God, help me." A businessman, he did not believe that this bank could operate to a uniquely high ethical standard, but he did have a precise goal: "My commitment is to change the bad reputation of the IOR and make it a modern, efficient, and discreet financial institution: full transparency and total compliance with international regulatory standards." That included strict adherence to anti-money-laundering norms.

As the Ratzinger papacy drew to a close, the IOR had 5,200 institutional clients (religious orders, foundations, and so on) and 13,700 individual clients.[19] The second category comprises 5,000 employees of the Vatican; around 8,000 priests, friars, and nuns; and 700 diplomats and "miscellaneous" account holders. The sum held in individual current accounts was 1.1 billion euros.

Beginning in mid-May 2013, von Freyberg brought into the bank a team of experts from the international agency Promontory, twenty to twenty-five persons whom he installed in the presidential salon in the tower of Nicholas V in the Vatican with instructions to sift through the files on all the clients and their current accounts. At the end of thirteen months of work, all 18,900 positions had been analyzed. Von Freyberg closed 396 accounts in the name of persons who did not qualify to be IOR clients. Also closed were 2,600 potentially perilous "dormant accounts." Henceforth, accounts will be opened only for "Catholic institutions, ecclesiastics, employees, or ex-employees of the Vatican holding accounts for the payment of salaries and pensions, as well as diplomats accredited to the Holy See."

The closure of these accounts was done by the book. The holders, von Freyberg assured, "could not simply disappear with the cash, or transfer it to the Cayman Islands. No cash withdrawals were permitted. They could only transfer the funds to countries conforming to international norms. If necessary, we forwarded a 'report of a suspect transaction' to the Financial Information Authority."[20]

Upon taking office, von Freyberg had obtained a list of the so-called external accounts opened in the past on behalf of persons who did not meet the statutory requirements, and he had made a commitment to eliminate them completely. The Italian politician Giulio

Andreotti, for example, had an account,[21] as did the shady intermediary Angelo Balducci, a man convicted of corruption who had been honored in his time with the title "Gentleman of His Holiness." The inspection by Promontory brought to light positions of "clients we didn't like," confessed the IOR president. With the undesirables, he said, "we broke off the relationship." There seem to have been less than one hundred of them. Von Freyberg spoke of a number in two figures but would not identify these holders of suspect accounts. In any case, more than a year later 359 accounts remained to be closed — a sign that they require more thorough investigation.

As the months passed, new procedures were put in place to flag up suspect transactions and transmit them automatically to the bank's director general, Rolando Marranci, and simultaneously to a risk manager, Antonio Montaresi. Autorità di Informazione Finanziaria (AIF), the Vatican regulator, receives a daily record of cash deposits in excess of 10,000 euros and a list of the transactions carried out by IOR.

The vulnerabilities in the IOR system have always been the "external" accounts and the accounts held by individual clerics, through which funds were moved in amounts often not all that large, but, as sources inside the IOR admit, often in highly irregular ways. Then there was the problem of delegated signing powers. The possibility of using priests as "fronts" for murky transactions was one of the reasons those engaged in money laundering sought out IOR.

Von Freyberg had a manual drafted prescribing in detail the procedures the bank personnel must follow to monitor clients, delegated signing powers, deposits, donations, and every other type of operation.

On 28 June 2013, a Vatican prelate was arrested: Nunzio Scarano, head of the accounting department of the Amministrazione del Patrimonio della Sede Apostolica (APSA), the agency administering the patrimony of the Holy See. In his home city of Salerno, he was known as "Monsignor 500" on account of his practice of proposing an exchange to his entrepreneur friends: bundles of 500 euro banknotes in exchange for cashier's checks (a.k.a. bank drafts) for sums of 5,000 to 10,000 euros. The Salerno public prosecutor's offices was investigating the cleric for money laundering. He was arrested after the discovery of a shambolic plan to smuggle 20 million euros in cash into Italy illegally from Switzerland. In collaboration with a financial broker, Giovanni Carenzio, Monsignor Scarano had commissioned a former member of the Italian security service, Giovanni Maria Zito, to fly to Lugano in a private plane, withdraw the money, and bring it back to Italy. Zito did go to Switzerland, but the plan fell through. He demanded his fee nonetheless and received an initial check from Monsignor Scarano of 400,000 euros. When he demanded a further 200,000 euros, Scarano gave him a check for that amount as well but then blocked it and reported it stolen. This report alerted the authorities, and the whole story came to light. Scarano had IOR accounts and in 2009 withdrew 560,000 euros in cash.[22]

The particulars of Scarano's web of crooked dealings under the cover of a prelate's religious habit dragged the Vatican into the glare of publicity. Age sixty-one at the time the scandal broke, Scarano had come to the priesthood late after a career as a banker; the court handling his case has called him a "consummate delinquent." Every month Scarano was receiving a "charitable" transfer to his bank account to the tune of 20,000 euros from the shipping magnate Cesare D'Amico. In a tapped telephone conversation, he boasted of having received a commission of 2.5 million euros for smuggling capital back into Italy on behalf of the D'Amico family.

In 1999, Monsignor Scarano bought a two-story mansion in the heart of Salerno from an order of nuns for scarcely 300 million lire (a low figure). He subsequently bought a parking garage, a six-room apartment, and, as reported by *Il Mattino*, became part owner of three property agencies. When the carabinieri came to his house after he reported a theft, they found an art collection that included works by De Chirico and Guttuso as well as a crucifix by Gian Lorenzo Bernini from the altar of St. Peter's.[23]

Telephone taps revealed that Scarano had close ties to senior management at IOR. "I wanted to let you know that I've had permission from the management [of the IOR], so that when you want, I'll let you know about . . . that endorsed transfer," the monsignor told one of his callers. When IOR received requests from other banks about his transactions, Scarano is heard explaining on the telephone: "I asked the director [of IOR, Paolo Cipriani,] and he said, 'Nunzio, no, look . . . we get hundreds of these letters, and we reply to all of them, and yours will get a reply more or less like the others, it's normal that we don't go around revealing how much is in your current account.'"[24] At IOR, Nunzio Scarano was a top-level client.

The affair rattled the Vatican Bank. "We were up the creek," admitted von Freyberg, "but we had a team to face the problem. In a six-hour meeting we put five members of staff to work going through ten years of operations by Scarano. The result was an eighty-nine-page report sent to the Financial Information Authority."

They had the pope's backing for a total cleanup. Federico Lombardi, the papal spokesman, said in a communiqué that Scarano had already been suspended from APSA a month earlier, as soon as it became known that he was under investigation in Salerno for money laundering. The Holy See, Lombardi said, "confirms its readiness to collaborate fully" with the Italian judicial authorities. The tangible sensation that the Vatican had changed course with respect to the wall of silence of the past came from the pope himself. To journalists' questions he replied: "We have this monsignor in prison, I think he is still in prison. He didn't exactly go to prison because he was like Blessed Imelda."[25] That is an Argentine way of saying that Scarano was no angel. Rejecting evasive turns of phrase, Pope Francis used frank and colorful language to communicate that the prelate was in prison because he deserved it.

He knew what he was talking about because both the IOR and the Financial Information Authority immediately forwarded detailed reports on Scarano's dealings to him. Over the past decade, the monsignor had held ten current accounts, of which five were empty at the moment of his arrest, three were active, and two invested in securities. Scarano operated in different currencies. Over the decade, he had moved 7 million euros, 4.7 incoming and 2.3 outgoing. Never before had IOR gone through its own books the way it did after the Scarano scandal. His accounts were frozen, and the Vatican prosecutor (whose formal title is "promoter of justice") opened an investigation parallel to the Italian one already under way.

On 1 July 2013, Paolo Cipriani, director general of the IOR, was forced to resign along with his deputy Massimo Tulli, and the Vatican prosecutor also put both of them under investigation. The Scarano affair was in a way a piece of luck for Pope Francis because the decapitation of the compromised former management accelerated the task of reforming the bank.

On 1 October 2013, von Freyberg published the IOR balance sheet online. Net profit as of 31 December 2012 was 86.6 million euros, a fourfold increase compared to the preceding year. The assets entrusted to the bank amounted to 6.3 billion euros. Von Freyberg subsequently concentrated on elaborating an information system to help personnel pinpoint abuses and risks. Client categories with specific risk profiles were defined and digitized—for example, a Swiss guard, a Vatican employee, a priest, a bishop, or a cardinal. For each, a normal volume of transactions was set as a baseline, taking into consideration the length of time the person in question had been a client, whether he or she had delegated signing powers, the quality and frequency of his or her transactions, the amounts, and the geographical area concerned. In the sanitized IOR, declared von Freyberg, "the deposits must serve exclusively for works of religion in the service of the church."

For Francis, it was the first concrete result of his pontificate. The cleanup of the bank was real, although not yet complete. The AIF, set up by Benedict XVI in 2010 to exercise general control over movements of money in all the Vatican administrations—and rendered toothless by Cardinal Bertone in 2011—regained full powers of vigilance and prevention with Francis. He has dedicated no less than three papal documents to the topic: a decree of 8 August 2013; law XVIII of 8 October 2013; and the reform of the statute of the AIF on 15 November 2013.

The AIF has joined the Egmont Group of Financial Intelligence Units, the international coordinating group of such regulatory bodies, and signed memorandums of understanding with a number of countries, including the United States, Italy, and Germany. For the first time, the Vatican has begun to respond seriously to formal requests for information from the Italian judicial authorities. The onset of a regime of real controls is evident in the upturn in alerts to suspect transactions: there were only 6 alerts in 2012, but 105 in the first ten months of 2013.

The pontiff has moved on another front, authorizing the Ernst and Young professional services firm to carry out an inspection of the economic activities and the management of the Vatican governorate.[26]

The goal is to attain greater efficiency at lower cost. For the first time, the inner economic sanctuaries of the pontifical state have been subjected to close scrutiny by outside agencies. The move has generated much disgruntlement among inside players in the Vatican, for whom the prospect of indiscreet eyes from outside peering into the secrets of power of the Catholic Church's central government is a fearful one. "We have to be careful to safeguard the sovereignty of the Holy See," notes a cardinal in the know, "because its finances are part of the sovereignty of a state that is the base of the church's mission."

His Argentine experience has aided Pope Francis. No sooner had he become archbishop of Buenos Aires than he had to deal with a financial scandal in connection with a bank on the verge of collapse, the Banco de Crédito Provincial. A prelate who had worked closely with Bergoglio's predecessor, Cardinal Antonio Quarracino, had involved the diocese in a shady financial operation to the tune of $10 million. Bergoglio brought in the international consultancy Arthur Andersen, had them go through the archbishopric's books, and was able to show that not one dirty dollar had gone into the diocesan treasury, and, moreover, that Cardinal Quarracino's signature on a purported financial guarantee was false.

In the Vatican, the pope regards financial questions as matters requiring strict surveillance. On 9 December 2013, MONEYVAL (the acronym for the Council of Europe's Committee of Experts on the Evaluation of Anti–Money Laundering Measures and the Financing of Terrorism) approved a report certifying that at the Holy See "much work has been done in a short time to meet most of the MONEYVAL technical recommendations," especially by enhancing the legal framework for the "tracing, freezing and seizure and confiscation of the proceeds of money laundering."[27] MONEYVAL does, however, ask for more: random inspections of the IOR and APSA and, above all, concrete punishment of those found guilty by the Vatican and confiscation of the illegal sums. This report is an acknowledgment of the determination behind the policy measures of the new pontificate. In 2012, the operations of the Holy See had obtained no more than a grudging pass mark from MONEYVAL, being found in regulatory compliance on only nine of sixteen fundamental points.

Pope Francis has realized that to clean out the stables is a Herculean task that it seems will never end. In January 2014, he completely changed the membership of the cardinalatial committee of vigilance over the IOR, appointing among others the secretary of state Monsignor Pietro Parolin and the archbishop of Vienna Christoph Schönborn, one of the best known reform-minded personalities in the German-speaking world.

At the same time, the pope nominated a curial monsignor, Giorgio Corbellini, as interim president of AIF, sending into retirement Cardinal Attilio Nicora, one of the major champions of transparency during the difficult years of Benedict XVI's stumbling reforms.

The cleanup in the economic field has gone on relentlessly. At the end of the first year of his pontificate, Francis set up a Council for the Economy comprising eight bishops and seven lay professionals to maintain permanent surveillance over the economic management and the administrative and financial activities of all the branches of the Holy See. At its head, he placed the cardinal of Munich, Reinhard Marx, also a member of the privy council of cardinals. Simultaneously a new Vatican department was created—a species of treasury, budget, and finance ministry all in one. It is entitled Secretariat for the Economy, and George Pell, cardinal of Sydney and likewise a member of the privy council, became its prefect, and the pope chose his own personal secretary, Monsignor Alfred Xuereb, as prelate and secretary-general. This dicastery answers directly to the pontiff and will exert operational control over the management of the Vatican bureaucracy, especially in the area of purchasing, in order to root out the crookedness in the tendering and provisioning process that has always tainted the reputation of the Vatican. There will be a general auditor to go over the books of the individual offices, and a detailed annual budget for the Holy See and Vatican City will be published, as provided for by the motu proprio *Fidelis dispensator et prudens*. The APSA has for the first time been officially declared the Vatican's "central bank." Meanwhile, the pope is still reflecting on the ultimate form the IOR will take. In any case, it is his intention that the church's entire portfolio of assets should henceforth be oriented toward meeting the needs not just of evangelization but also of charity for the needy.

Subsequently, in July 2014, von Freyberg returned to his business career in Germany, and his place was taken by a fifty-one-year-old French financier, Jean-Baptiste de Franssu—formerly executive director of Ivesco Europe and president of Efama, the European association of investment fund managers. For the first time, a woman was also seated on the IOR board of directors: the American Mary Ann Glendon.

With de Franssu, the second, technocratic phase of IOR reform began, following the initial housecleaning phase. The Istituto per le Opere di Religione will increasingly be less of a bank and more of an institute specializing in financial consultancy and payment services for religious congregations, dioceses, and clergy (including the lay employees of the Vatican). The new president has also announced plans to create a "Vatican Asset Management" corporation to manage the IOR patrimony.

De Franssu is facing an unexpected downturn in IOR's economic position. The balance for 2013 showed a net profit of 2.9 million euros, but the corresponding figure for 2012 was 86.6 million. The beam of light cast by von Freyberg into dark corners has not only led to the closure of current accounts but also revealed the existence of unwise investment decisions taken by top-level Vatican management in the past. Still, the bottom line for 2013 did put a sum of 54 million euros at the pontiff's personal disposition for charitable works.

The fact is that in the space of a year the Italian grip on the financial ganglia of the Vatican was pried loose. A Frenchman (de Franssu) is now in charge of the IOR; a Spaniard (Abril y Castelló) heads the cardinalatial committee of vigilance over the bank; an American (Wells) heads the anti-money-laundering committee; a German (Marx) heads the economic council; an Australian (Pell) heads the new finance ministry; and a Swiss (René Bruelhart) is director of the AIF. Nor have the inner sanctums of the Vatican ever been thrown open to so many non-Italian agencies as they are now: Promontory, Ernst and Young, KPMG, and McKinsey (tasked with rationalizing the Vatican structures for news and public relations).

Much remains to be done. APSA still awaits an in-depth inspection. During the interrogation of Monsignor Scarano by the Roman prosecutors, he revealed there exist numbered accounts at the APSA held by "outside laymen."[28] Another unfinished chapter is the management of the assets of the Congregation for the Propagation of the Faith, which has generated a number of scandals in recent years. With backing from Pope Francis, the Brazilian cardinal João Braz de Aviz, prefect of the Congregation for Institutes of Consecrated Life and Societies of Apostolic Life, has set out guidelines to encourage the religious orders to practice maximum transparency in their financial dealings, to watch their accounts closely and document their transactions rigorously, and to take action against waste in the management of their assets and their charitable works.

There is a submerged network of ramified interests that regard the Argentine pope's reforms with mistrust and irritation. A shadow is still cast over relations between the Holy See and Italy by the fact that the Vatican AIF possesses the names of those who transport large sums of cash across the border between the two states but withholds this information from the Italian authorities. In 2012, the AIF registered 598 declarations of significant sums brought into the Vatican and 1,782 declarations of money carried out. Over the same period, however, just 13 declarations of movements of money into the city-state and a mere 4 declarations of outbound movements were registered at the Italian customs office in Rome. The discrepancy gave rise to suspicion that large-scale tax evasion was occurring.[29] As this book was being written, the lack of full disclosure on the part of the IOR leaves little room for control of charitable donations—potentially the easiest channel of all for moving dirty money. In January 2014, Monsignor Scarano was arrested again on charges of laundering money by means of fictitious donations to the tune of 6 million euros. The case involves a notary and fifty or so other persons.

Pope Francis feels disgust at the corruption of hearts. "We are all sinners, but not all of us are corrupt," he said to a meeting of heads of religious orders. "Sinners we accept, but not corrupt individuals," who should be expelled from seminaries and other institutions, said the pope. Those who manage the church's "works" (opere, all ecclesiastical entities engaged in economic transactions of any kind) should do so with poverty of heart; priests should not "annul themselves" by thinking like entrepreneurs.

The words seem to resound in a desert. "For me, Francis [of Assisi] is . . . the poor man," the pope told journalists soon after his election.

Austerity is the only fitting style for those who labor in the service of the church because a "rich church" turns into a lifeless church. This is the most complicated of Francis's battles—and the most lonely. On every side he meets a great deal of courteous inertia.

In wartime, the pope said during an audience at Caritas Internationalis, one needs to care for the wounded. "We should even sell churches to feed the poor." "That was a quip" meant to "stimulate and provoke," commented Cardinal Bagnasco, president of the Italian Episcopal Conference. End of story. "Who is going to buy churches? To do what?" declared Bagnasco. "Outside Italy it happens with disused churches, but I don't know if they made much money out of it."[30]

At the Astalli Center, set up by Jesuits to help immigrants, Francis was provocative once more. "The church isn't served if empty convents are converted into hotels to make money." He proceeded to make his meaning clear: "Closed convents? They ought to serve for the flesh of Christ, and refugees are Christ's flesh."[31] Rome is full of convents and headquarters of religious orders that have been turned into hotels; they were often sold through middlemen in transactions that would scarcely stand the light of day. The trend shows no signs of going into reverse. As Pope Bergoglio's seventy-seventh birthday loomed, the former headquarters of a religious order, transformed into the luxurious Grand Hotel del Gianicolo (four stars and a swimming pool), was seized in an operation against the 'ndrangheta, a Calabria-based criminal organization.

The affair was a classic of its kind. In the 1990s, a small hotel on the outskirts of Palmi in the province of Reggio Calabria became a well-capitalized property firm that acquired the religious building in Rome for 15 billion lire on the eve of the Jubilee of 2000. At the signing of the contract, the buyers put around 11 billion lire on the table in cash, but then—to mask the operation—they requested a loan of 13 billion.[32] The joint investigation by prosecutors in Rome and Reggio Calabria led to the seizure of assets worth 150 million euros: fifty-three properties in Rome, the province of Bologna, and Calabria. The investigators suspected that the proprietors of the hotel in Palmi, Giuseppe and Pasquale Mattiani, were a front for the Gallico crime family.[33] It is no coincidence that the guidelines devised by Cardinal Braz de Aviz on the management of the assets of religious orders demand "prudent decisions about the selling off of assets." It is an area in which too many deals that would not pass the smell test have been done in recent years.

In his first twelve months as pontiff, Francis confronted an abyss of embezzlement and shady dealings. In Germany, a scandal erupted around the Catholic bishop of Limburg, Franz-Peter van Elst, who had spent 31 million euros for the construction of a palatial new residence, where the bathtub cost 15,000 euros, the walk-in closets cost 350,000 euros, and a "Marian garden" was created at a cost of 783,000 euros. The *Frankfurter Allgemeine Sonntagszeitung* reported that in the summer of 2011 the estimates for the new residence—amounting to 17 million euros—were broken up into ten different construction projects so that none would exceed the threshold of 5 million euros, above which authorization from the Vatican would have been obligatory. The Catholic faithful in the diocese were furious, the German Episcopal Conference set up an investigative committee, and Francis sent van Elst into exile to await the results.[34] Ultimately he removed him from office.

Since entering office, the pope has already forced the Slovene bishops of Maribor (Marjan Turnsek) and Ljubljana (Anton Stres) to resign because of a financial crash of 800 million euros. Francis applied canon 401, paragraph 2, of the Code of Canon Law, which provides for the removal of a bishop who "through infirmity or other grave cause proves to be unfit to discharge his office." In Cameroon, the archbishop of Yaoundé, Simon-Victor Tonyé Bakot, was forced out after the laity protested at the way he administered church property. Vatican Radio reported on the numerous property deals in which he was involved. The diocese of Yaoundé holds the largest property portfolio in Cameroon.[35]

But it was Italy that caused the greatest headaches for the pope because of the money-making ambitions of many members of the Italian clergy. Francis looked around him and saw rapacious and untrustworthy wolves. After the Scarano case, there came the arrest in November 2013 of the head of Order of Camilliani, Renato Salvatore, after a power struggle over contracts worth millions of euros in public funds spent on the management of two hundred hospitals around the world. Salvatore's associate, the Roman tax lawyer Paolo Oliverio, was also arrested on a charge of money laundering on behalf of members of the 'ndrangheta and other organized crime groups.

On the day the Camilliani were to vote on renewing the mandate of their leadership, Father Salvatore used Oliverio to have two of his fellow religious detained in order to keep them from voting against his reelection. Oliverio got two crooked members of the Guardia di Finanza (the financial police) to detain and question the two religious, Rosario Messina and Antonio Puca, at the Guardia offices in Rome. The scheme came to light thanks to tapped telephone conversations, in which Oliverio is heard saying to one of the police officers: "So Monday you go and pick up this prick of a priest and take him to the Guardia di Finanza . . . and we'll keep him there for three or four hours." The judge of the preliminary investigation noted that Father Salvatore was reelected by "a margin of just two votes, thanks to the absence of the two prelates." On the day of the vote, he was "in constant contact with Paolo Oliverio."[36]

Oliverio is typical of the kind of wheeler-dealers who make a specialty of linking up with businessmen, politicians, and ecclesiastics. On his computer hard drive, investigators found evidence of his contacts with important churchmen, members of the Italian intelligence services, entrepreneurs, and politicians. The pope is surrounded by thickets and swamps where the wolves prowl. He never had any illusions about human weakness in the face of the temptations of power and money, but in the end it is the Vatican that is left tarnished.

In 2013, another major scandal reached its final phase: the bankruptcy of the Istituto Dermatologico Italiano (IDI, Italian Dermatological Institute), managed by the order of the Figli dell'Immacolata Concezione (Sons of the Immaculate Conception, or "Conceptionists"), together with the Saint-Charles Hospital in Nancy, France. Like other religious "works," this one originated with a disinterested charitable impulse on the part of a leading Catholic personality: in the late nineteenth century, Luigi Maria Monti led the Conceptionists to specialize in the education of needy orphaned children. Thus were created institutions and hospitals in various parts of Italy.

A century later the enterprise was under strain and creaking. In 2003, IDI's financial position worsened, but the management kept quiet about it. Eight years later the collapse became public knowledge: the 1,500 employees were no longer being paid regularly, and the deficit was said to be somewhere between 450 and 600 million euros. On 18 February 2013, a few days after the resignation of Benedict XVI, Cardinal Bertone entrusted the emergency management of the IDI to Cardinal Giuseppe Versaldi, who was responsible for the Prefecture of Economic Affairs in the Vatican. On 30 March 2013, the Italian government named three commissioners to run the IDI.

On 4 April 2013, Father Franco Decaminada, IDI's managing director until 2011, was arrested along with the former administrative director of the institute, Domenico Temperini, and a consultant to the Conceptionists, Antonio Nicolella, a former agent of the Italian military intelligence agency. Decaminada denied all responsibility and claimed to be totally in the dark. The investigation uncovered a "spoliation" of IDI assets to the tune of 14 million euros, of which 4 million were in the hands of Father Decaminada.[37]

The previous year, while executing a search warrant on the Conceptionists' offices in Via della Conciliazione, the investigators had noted that the daily intake of 60,000 to 70,000 euros was no longer being deposited in IDI accounts and that on one occasion Decaminada had effected a withdrawal of 6.8 million euros at one stroke. It also emerged that "many individuals are being paid monthly by IDI as employees, even though they had never worked in a hospital and the work they were performing for the organization was undetermined."[38]

Oddities abounded. From 2006 to 2009, Decaminada had practically handed the economic management of the IDI over to an unknown entrepreneur from Campania, Giovanni Rusciano. In 2011, the local health agency Roma3 had reported to the Corte de Conti (Court of Accounts) that IDI had been billing repeatedly for the same medical services.[39]

It was discovered that companies, some of them fictitious, were being utilized as communicating vessels to drain money out of the IDI and out of the Conceptionists' Italian province: "Elea F. P.," "Elea spa," "G.I.Esse Service" (sole proprietor Decaminada), "Punto immobiliare srl" (headed by Decaminada). The manager of IDI had also set up an oil industry firm called "Ibos II" in the Democratic Republic of Congo.[40] The investigative television program *Report*, anchored by

Milena Gabanelli, has even documented cases of shoeboxes full of cash being carried out of Decaminada's office.[41]

All those under investigation are suspected of criminal conspiracy, "improper appropriation" (i.e., theft), and billing for nonexistent transactions. Under the pope's eyes, what had once been a jewel of ecclesiastically sponsored medical excellence at Rome in the fields of dermatology and oncology was set to be sold at auction. The accumulated debt came to 750 million euros.

Francis has often spoken out against the culture of theft and *tangenti* (the "cuts" paid to those who facilitate illegal ventures) as well as against those who evade taxes and then try to get off by posing as church benefactors. In September 2013, in one of his morning meditations at mass in Santa Marta, he spoke in a particularly heartfelt manner against the "idolization" of money. Attachment to money, he said, takes us away from God. "Money sickens our thought, sickens our faith." It happens in the church too, he added. Love of money causes bishops and priests to commit sins. If avidity gains the upper hand, men grow "corrupt of mind [and risk] seeing religion as a source of gain." May the Lord, Francis concluded, "aid all of us not to fall into the trap of idolatry of money."[42] He uttered an equally harsh admonition against those who are corrupt and "remote from the people" in a mass for Italian parliamentarians.

Pope Francis is fighting against daunting opposition. In Italy and especially at Rome, the culture of money making has intertwined with that of the church to form a dense undergrowth ever since the Vatican was recognized as a sovereign city-state on 11 February 1929. To tear it out by the roots is a challenge beyond the strength of one man alone.

13

The Enemies of Francis

The enemies of Francis act and speak behind the scenes. They blend into the atmosphere of general applause and display submissiveness to the pope. Indeed, they do not even allow themselves to be defined as his adversaries: they say they want to keep him from making mistakes. But in private they can be cutting, in the style of Cardinal Siri, archbishop of Genoa from right after World War II until 1987, who considered John XXIII incapable and labeled the Vatican II council a "disaster."

In some curial circles, it is fashionable to deride Francis's simple eloquence and claim that his doctrine is scarcely consistent. "He talks like a country priest," one cardinal said to Andrea Riccardi.[1] "If all the country priests had spoken that way, the history of the church would have been different," replied the head of the Sant'Egidio community. There are also cardinals from outside Italy who fling darts about the need to "help the pope out with his theology" and openly praise Benedict XVI.

The ill will in the corridors of the Roman Curia began on the evening of the election. Along with the chorus of enthusiasm for the toned-down style of his appearance before the crowd, there were slighting remarks about his refusal to wear the stole or the red slippers and what was considered his ostentatious avoidance of the word *pope*. Bergoglio upset too many conventional expectations. The elderly cardinal Cormac Murphy-O'Connor, former archbishop of Westminster, commented humorously: "They wanted change, a new style, but the cardinals did not expect a breeze *that* fresh. A man like that gave them a surprise."

It was an unpleasant surprise for those drawn to the Ratzinger style—a cerebral defense of identity and tradition conveyed through refined theological, philosophical, and cultural discourse. "Francis is more attentive to pastoral positions than to doctrinal ones, the exact reversal of before," explained the head of one Vatican dicastery. When the pope said to *La Civiltà Cattolica* that the church must drop its obsessive focus on abortion, contraception, and gay marriage, the discontent of the conservatives reverberated around the web. Immediately there came demands that the pope should issue a "clarification." And "dismay" was voiced because he didn't publicly oppose a law against homophobia under discussion in the Italian Parliament or the UN guidelines on sexual education for young people, which his critics feared would produce confusion between what is natural and what is "against nature."[2]

Francis's language is irritating and scary to the ultratraditionalist sectors of the curia. He scares them when he evokes the specter of the "little monsters" that may emerge from a bad seminary education.[3] He irritates them when he scourges "unctuous priests" imprisoned in vanity, the kind recognizable by "an affected attitude and way of speaking . . . a butterfly . . . always fluttering about vanities . . . a devotee of the god Narcissus."[4] He unsettles them deeply because rather than stay within the bounds of pious exhortation, he points in direct language straight to where the rot is.

The pope, who bent over during a general audience to pick up a lady's purse for her, disgusts the extreme advocates of papal sacrality. "His style of great simplicity doesn't please those who like to imagine the pope always on his throne with a miter on his head," observed the vice dean of the College of Cardinals, Giovanni Battista Re.

Within the curia, there are nests of criticism and dislike. Francis's tendency to make papal ceremonies simpler is disquieting to the lovers of ceremonial protocol. Even the fact that he chose to celebrate the washing of the feet on Holy Thursday at a different location than usual, exchanging the Lateran basilica for the prison at Casal di Marmo, was upsetting to them.

Many cardinals haven't come to terms with Francis's decision not to move into the papal apartment. "The head of the church ought to install himself there, in his apartment," a curial cardinal stated; "it's not proper that some people can encounter him casually and others not." Another longtime wearer of the purple put it more strongly: "To abandon the residence of so many popes amounts to criticizing them . . . . [I]t makes no sense to live elsewhere and visit the apostolic palace for official business." There has been an ongoing vein of subtly poisonous remarks about how in the papal study "the lights have gone out," no longer casting a reassuring glow late in the evening to let passersby in St. Peter's Square know that the pope is busy at his desk.

What the cardinals and monsignors who balk at the new course cannot say openly does burst out into the open on conservative websites. In this turbulent phase, sites and blogs at the margins of the mainstream no longer represent their own small coteries; they act as megaphones for the resistance to and criticism of Pope Francis widespread in sectors of the Vatican hierarchy and bureaucracy. One curial insider, the secretary of the Pontifical Commission for Latin America, Guzmán Carriquiry, detected an "irrepressible nostalgia for Ratzinger that is used to denigrate his successor."[5]

The drumbeat of criticism is inexorable. This pope, who takes on and puts off his white skullcap in the course of his general audiences and sometimes gives it away and accepts another from the public, is compared to "an old grandfather playing with his grandchild. . . . [It tends to] desacralize the symbols of the papacy in order to cheapen and abolish them."[6] From the start, the website Pontifex has accused Francis of "populism, pauperism, and demagogy." The blog Messa in Latino (Mass in Latin) called him "a pope who is out to please" and condemns his style as an "implicit criticism of the pontificate of Benedict XVI."

In the United States, the website Tradition in Action fumes with rage, drawing up a list of forty-eight infractions of traditional protocol by Francis under the title "Bergoglio's Devastation of Papal Symbols." The take-no-prisoners attitude is characteristic of contemporary American political culture. The list is a catch-all, ranging from the placement of the candles on the altar to the rejection of the luxurious papal Mercedes, from his refusal to wear lace-trimmed vestments to the fact that during mass the deacon does not kneel before the pope as he imparts his blessing. Francis's "improper" way of distributing the communion wafer is as bad as his refusal to remain seated on his throne. These reactionaries are obsessed with the symbolism of the throne. Tradition in Action published photos of Francis and Benedict XVI in the basilica of San Giovanni in Laterano to illustrate and deplore how the Argentine pope has sent Ratzinger's heavy gilded throne into storage and contents himself with a sober white chair. Readers are constantly invited not to idolize Pope Francis—in other words, to decry him.

Then there are the accusations of "unwillingness to take up the mantle of Christ's authority" and of holding the belief "that Catholic teaching must be adapted to humankind, not vice versa."[7] The tempestuous attackers will even sink to mockery: "The world applauds Bergoglio the pauperist . . . because he speaks to people's bellies . . . telling them what they want to hear: God always pardons everybody . . . long live love . . . let's all be fond of each other . . . solidarity, miserablism, third-worldism, ecologism—and of course a dash of feminism never hurts either."[8]

Similar points of view expressed in more cautious, sophisticated, and allusive terms may be heard in certain rooms in the Vatican. The pope drives the worshippers of papal sacrality crazy by going down the hall in the Santa Marta residence to get coffee at the coin-operated espresso machine and chatting informally with the employees at the reception desk. To tarnish the icon of an authority so closely bound to heaven is intolerable for part of the ecclesiastical world and pregnant with future woes for Catholicism: a ruinous drift toward Protestantism.

It is possible to spend an hour in conversation with a cardinal and not hear a word of criticism about the pope, and then just as you are leaving, out it comes: "It's not a good thing for the pope to give interviews to newspapers . . . he is creating too many committees . . . there's too much criticism of the priesthood; it's not as if they do no good at all!"

Monsignor Georg Gänswein gave this muted dissatisfaction a voice in speaking to the German weekly *Die Zeit*. The paper wrote (without attributing it as a direct quote) that Benedict XVI's right-hand man took Francis's decision not to reside in the papal apartment as an affront. But Gänswein is quoted as saying disconsolately, "Every day I wait afresh [to see] what novelty the day will bring."[9] When his words caused a stir, Monsignor Gänswein asserted that he had never granted an interview to *Die Zeit*.

Conservative U.S. bishops have sent signals of dissent on their own behalf and that of others. The bishop of Providence, Rhode Island, Thomas Joseph Tobin, said in the diocesan newspaper that he was "disappointed" that in the pope's interview with *La Civiltà Cattolica* he had not adequately addressed the question of abortion and the "unborn children." The pontiff, he said, ought to give more backing to the pro-life movement. At the website of the diocese of Philadelphia, Archbishop Charles Chaput insisted on the official stance of the American Episcopate: "All direct attacks on innocent human life, such as abortion and euthanasia, strike at the foundation of the house of God." Chaput also gave voice to the dissatisfaction of part of the American clergy, relating the views of one priest: "The problem is that the Holy Father makes all of the wrong people happy, people who will never believe in the Gospel and who will continue to persecute the church."

In Italy, those hostile to change—and especially to the participatory model of the church Francis has in mind—find their views echoed in Giuliano Ferrara's newspaper *Il Foglio*. Clergymen nostalgic for the days when Cardinal Camillo Ruini was leading the effort to maintain the influence of the Catholic Church on Italian public policy, those nostalgic for Ratzinger's strict conservatism, can read in this sheet, under the bylines of lay reporters, the words they dare not utter themselves.

In its pages, the historian Roberto de Mattei, a supporter of creationism and the author of harsh polemics against Vatican II, has combated the notion of reforming the papal monarchy. De Mattei, with the silent backing of part of the ecclesiastical hierarchy, finds it unacceptable to speak of the primacy of the bishop of Rome as a matter of honor or love, as Francis did the evening of his election. The mark of the Roman pontiff, de Mattei contends, is the "full and absolute" power of supreme jurisdiction that elevates him above all other bishops. His is the power of supreme government, and any change in that, de Mattei warns, "would alter not the historical form but the divine essence of the papacy."[10]

These words are signals directed at the Argentine pope on behalf of third parties to nip in the bud his project of promoting "collegial" leadership of the Catholic Church.

Admonitions originating in the same circles reach print in the writings of an alert and meticulous observer of ecclesiastical affairs, Sandro Magister. Some of Francis's gestures from the earliest days of his pontificate, Magister noted, "have awakened bad urges in public opinion, inside and outside Catholicism: from doing away with the central government of the church to dropping the title of 'pope,' from inaugurating a spiritual 'new church' to abasing . . . the symbolism of sacred rites, habits, furniture, and buildings."[11]

As the pontificate has gone forward, opposition to the Bergoglio line has grown more clear-cut. Two representatives of the traditionalist reaction, the journalist Alessandro Gnocchi and the late canonist and lecturer in bioethics Mario Palmaro, both contributors to Radio Maria, published an article in *Il Foglio* that reads like a manifesto under the title "We Don't Like This Pope." They direct a barrage of criticism at his "display of poverty," condemn his refusal to encourage proselytism, accuse him of subjectivism (for having said to Eugenio Scalfari that "everyone has his own idea of good and evil and must choose to follow the good and fight evil as he conceives them"), and stoutly oppose the concept of the church as a "field hospital."

The most disquieting aspect of Bergoglio's thought, Gnocchi and Palmaro conclude, to the discreet applause of the pope's opponents, lies in "the idea that there is an unbridgeable gap between doctrinal rigor and mercifulness: if there is one, the other is supposedly negated. . . . What we are seeing is the phenomenon of a leader telling the crowd exactly what the crowd wants to hear." The two mount an outright challenge to Bergoglio: there are "laws that not even the vicar of Christ can alter," they assert. "Christ cannot be just one option among the rest. Not for his vicar anyway."[12] The day after the article was published, Radio Maria fired the two contributors, but Bergoglio, for his part, knowing that Palmaro was ill, rang him on the telephone to offer personal consolation and assure him that the radio station had not been pressured to take this action.

In America, too, Catholic spokesmen from beyond the pale of the priesthood have opened fire on the pope. Michael Novak, a conservative essayist, hurled this stone: "A friend asked me if the Pope is aware of the damage he causes with these extemporaneous comments. Using the word 'obsession' about those who have always worked to defend life is certainly something that wounds." Novak, a supporter of John Paul II and Benedict XVI and an outspoken Catholic traditionalist, claimed that the positions staked out by the pope "encourage criticism against the church on the part of its declared adversaries, who hoped for nothing better."[13]

In the United States, as the historian of Christianity Massimo Faggioli has noted, there exists a robust network of Catholic universities, colleges, and lobbies that, in parallel to conservative American Protestantism, consider a traditionalist outlook on faith essential to the moral health of the United States. It is a sector that looks with suspicion, if not open hostility, upon Pope Francis's pastoral innovations.

His opponents are recognizable, whatever their longitude, by the stance they adopt of not wanting to join the chorus of applause. Another telltale sign is that they dress up their criticism as advice. "The absence of control [of the papal texts] destined for publication by trusted persons, wise, cultivated, and Italian ones," is detrimental, wrote the philosopher and sociologist of religion Pietro De Marco. He perceives in Francis "a certain authoritarian inclination . . . typical of democratic 'revolutionaries,' creating the risk of imprudent collisions with millennia-old traditions." The philosopher delivered a stringent assessment of Bergoglio, claiming that the pope clung to the public-relations dimension of his job as though "he feared not knowing what to do once he was left alone, as pope, in the apartment of the popes."[14]

Passive resistance is an age-old way of expressing criticism without sticking one's neck out. "Let him talk" is the reaction from the pope's silent opposition, which is growing more stubborn, confident in the knowledge that popes come and go, but the Roman Curia remains.

The curia is a complex world, a melting pot of nationalities, a mosaic of persons of great and diminutive stature, in large measure animated by a marked sense of mission and a strong attachment to the institution. Many of them, although not all, are motivated by the pride that comes from working in a command center of international dimensions. The mentality of the high curial dignitaries is complex and not easily classifiable into pigeonholes. It is possible to encounter prelates who are quite prepared to give communion to divorced and remarried Catholics but who will balk at the idea of seeing women in positions of leadership. There are those who are nonjudgmental about homosexuality but intransigent on the pope's duty to stick to traditional protocol and those tolerant on social questions but at the same time resistant to the prospect of a democratization of the ecclesiastical institution. Both the traditionalist and the reforming camps contain shades of opinion—everyone has his own reasons, and there are areas of convergence.

"We are influential because we are different," maintain the enlightened conservatives, citing many examples of statesmen and political leaders on whom the ancient stability of the Roman institution has left a deep impression. "We are authoritative because we move with the times" is the stance of the balanced reformers, who applaud the flexibility of the Holy See over its millennial history. The unexpected brevity of the recent conclaves reveals a capacity for dialogue and understanding among different points of view within the cardinals as a class—to the greater glory of the Church of Rome.

The Vatican is not monolithic. There does exist a nucleus of monsignors in favor of the new direction, who are thankful to the conclave for the choice it made. For that matter, the curia was already split prior to the conclave among different currents: there were the backers of Angelo Scola, the backers of the Brazilian cardinal Odilo Scherer; there were and are supporters of the pope from Argentina.

As a cardinal, Bergoglio was never particularly enamored of the Vatican. During his time as archbishop of Buenos Aires, relations were cool between him and the nunzio Adriano Bernardini, who had close ties to the secretary of state at the time, Cardinal Angelo Sodano. Conservative Argentine bishops would appeal directly to Rome to accuse their chief of not being intransigent enough on ethical questions. As president of the Argentine Episcopal Conference,

Bergoglio was in disagreement with a number of episcopal nomina-
tions imposed on him by the Vatican. Rome returned the antipathy.

In 2009, Cardinal Bergoglio nominated the biblicist and writer Victor Manuel Fernández, a former president of the Argentine Theological Society, as rector of the Catholic University of Buenos Aires. He
was forced to mark time as the Vatican engaged in delaying tactics
on the pretext of verifying the theologian's orthodoxy. It was not until
May 2011, after being made to wait irksome amounts of time in outer
offices in the Vatican, that Fernández was able to swear his oath as
rector of the university.

Bergoglio was always repelled by the practice of forwarding denunciations to the Vatican concerning someone else's supposed doctrinal
deviations, just as he never shared the obsessive insistence on the so-
called nonnegotiable principles. "At Rome they want to sheath the
world in a condom" is a phrase attributed to him during the period
when he was a cardinal.

The fact is that at Buenos Aires he was already showing himself
increasingly alarmed at the deteriorating state of affairs in the church.
He once confessed to a priest who was a friend of his: "If my mother
and your mother were resuscitated today, they would beg the Lord
to send them back underground so that they wouldn't have to witness the degradation of this church."[15] Gianni Valente, a Roman
journalist friend at whose home Bergoglio was often a dinner guest,
recalled that Bergoglio went to the Vatican as little as possible. "He
disliked the court atmosphere and the lack of attention to the needs
of local churches."[16] Bergoglio was particularly displeased by the sort
of bishop who is always calculating how to move up to another and
bigger diocese, like anyone else scrambling up the greasy pole in any
walk of life. Nor was he at ease with the self-referentiality of the curia
or with the compulsive careerism of some of the curial fauna.

That a few baited traps and improvised explosive devices would be
waiting for Francis as he made his way through the curial maze was
probably inevitable. In July 2013, when he created the committee for
the economic reform of the Vatican administration, observers noted
with interest that among the eight members (all of them laymen with
the exception of Monsignor Vallejo Balda, the APSA secretary) there
was a woman: Francesca Immacolata Chaouqui, an Italian Egyptian.

Her presence looked like further proof of Francis's will to involve female professionals in his plans for renewal, as he had done several weeks earlier when he appointed Professor Mary Ann Glendon to the committee investigating the IOR.

But this time he had taken poisoned bait. Chaouqui, who was just thirty-one years old and came from Ernst and Young, proclaimed herself a devotee of Saint Josemaría Escrivá de Balaguer, the founder of Opus Dei, and a fervent admirer of Pope Francis. She was active in the field of public relations and a frenetic user of Twitter. Her tweets were reckless. "The pope [Benedict XVI] has had leukemia for over a year," she tweeted in February 2012. And it kept getting worse: "I believe in the one, holy, Catholic, apostolic church. Maybe somebody ought to remind Bertone what this means." "Bertone corrupt. It seems that the papal archive and a Venetian firm are involved." "[Benedict XVI] has given up. As a believer I am simply disappointed." The former minister of the economy in the Berlusconi government got spattered with mud as well: "Tremonti had an IOR account. Once it was on the record that he was gay, they closed it on him."[17]

Dogged by scandal and threatened with lawsuits, Chaouqui closed her Twitter account and declared that it had been hacked by unknown parties and that the tweets were not hers. The young public-relations specialist was an adept social climber, and her address book included such names as Giulio Andreotti; Countess Marisa Pinto Olori del Poggio; the lawyer Patrizio Messina, with whom she worked in the Orrick law firm; Stefano Lucchini of the giant energy firm ENI; and Gianluca Comin of the power company ENEL.[18] But the most striking thing about her is that she possessed none of the qualifications needed to assume a position as demanding as the one to which the pope had appointed her. In the midst of individuals of the caliber of the president, Joseph Zahra, former director of the central bank of Malta; the Frenchman Jean-Baptiste de Franssu, former CEO of the investment firm Invesco Europe (and now the head of the IOR); the Spaniard Enrique Llano, a financier who had worked with the international accounting firms Deloitte and KPMG; the German Jochen Messemer, president of the investment firm Ergo International; the French businessman Jean Videlain-Sevestre; and George Yeo, the former foreign minister of Singapore,

Francesca Immacolata Chaouqui looked like someone who had stumbled into the wrong room.

In the wake of her appointment, people in the Vatican were wondering who had slipped her name onto the short list submitted to the pontiff. Several clues pointed to the secretary of the committee, the Spaniard and member of Opus Dei Vallejo Balda, who had drafted her flattering CV.[19] Pope Francis, who had been kept in the dark about her real reputation, was furious that he had been tricked into opening up the Holy See's most confidential financial files to a person regarded as the "deep throat" of the journalist Gianluigi Nuzzi and the website Dagospia. As the buzz about the matter grew, a prelate who knew Bergoglio well commented: "It was an inopportune choice, and the person who recommended it will have some explaining to do." But the pontiff knows how to wait. Eight months later, when the new Council for the Economy was created, Vallejo Balda was left off it. As for Francesca Immacolata Chaouqui, once the committee completed its activity, she received no further assignments from the Vatican.

Francis was also kept in the dark when he decided to appoint Monsignor Battista Ricca to watch over the IOR. Ricca, who had a background in the Holy See's diplomatic service, was the object of detailed accusations inside the apostolic palace. When he was posted to Montevideo in 1999, he had brought with him a companion, Patrick Haari, a captain in the Swiss army, and their ménage had caused a scandal. Following repeated incidents, the nunzio Janusz Bolonek was able to convince the secretary of state to have Ricca removed from his post in 2001.[20]

Before Ricca was appointed to keep tabs on IOR, the Secretariat of State, still headed by Cardinal Bertone, submitted an immaculate dossier about him to the pope. The scandal burst subsequently, and Francis had to ride it out. To journalists he said, "About Monsignor Ricca: I did what canon law calls for, that is a preliminary investigation. And from this investigation, there was nothing of what had been alleged. We did not find anything of that."[21]

It amounted to confirmation that the Argentine pope had not been given a complete picture of the situation. He went on, though, to give the media and the personnel of the Vatican, who were taking turns in the game of leaking compromising news, a little lesson in classy behavior: "I see that many times in the church, over and above this case, but including this case, people search for 'sins from youth,' for example, and then publish them. They are not crimes, right? Crimes are something different: the abuse of minors is a crime. No, sins. But if a person, whether it be a lay person, a priest or a religious sister, commits a sin and then converts, the Lord forgives, and when the Lord forgives, the Lord forgets . . . and so we have no right not to forget, because otherwise we would run the risk of the Lord not forgetting our sins."[22]

In comparison to the Buenos Aires years, Francis is at a disadvantage; back home he knew every one of the eight hundred priests in his diocese. In Rome, he doesn't possess the same acquaintance with the denizens of the Vatican, and until he has built up a sufficiently ramified team of his own, he risks finding his path beset with further baited traps and improvised explosive devices.

For its part, the curial world lives in an atmosphere of uncertainty, unable to foresee the direction that Francis's revolution will take. "The old guidelines aren't there anymore," noted Cardinal Renato Martino, with his long-term experience as a diplomat.

The feeling of not knowing exactly where the new era is going to take them is shared by both supporters and adversaries. "I pray for the pope because one of these days, when the honeymoon is over and decision time arrives, they'll try to back him up against the wall," sighs Cardinal Roger Etchegaray, formerly John Paul II's roving ambassador in crisis zones and a supporter of Bergoglio's transformation. "It is easy to change the occupants of positions; the difficulty lies in changing the mentality and the habits of Christians with a backward-looking vision," Etchegaray concludes.

A pontiff who innovates day after day is disorienting. The most cunning enemies of Francis's reform policies are nestled in the Vatican undergrowth among those accustomed to traffic with wheeler-dealers of various kinds. In economic terms, the Vatican yields material well-being for those who, as the pope likes to put it, have turned away from Christ and devoted themselves to the world. The head of an office who earns 2,800 euros monthly can add 2,000 euros to his earnings by winning an appointment as papal master of ceremonies. A position as a canon of the chapter of St. Peter's will add 1,500 more euros per month, and membership on a committee brings in another 600 to 800 euros. All of this is tax free, and that's on top of the apartments available at below-market rents.[23]

But there are those who hunger for more, and some of them are rapacious wolves. The scandals that periodically explode in the media wreak incalculable harm on the Holy See. "Starting with the last years of John Paul II, the absence of a governing pope has led to bad practices," says a diplomat who has followed the Vatican closely. "An unhealthy system of power has formed that needs to be dismantled." He is talking about a network of personal relationships and interests binding together unscrupulous people from both sides of the Tiber and covered by *omertà*, the code of silence. The repeated explosion of economic scandals is proof of this. One cardinal from northern Europe confides that he was once contacted by a bishop who had learned of shady dealings to the tune of millions of euros in one Vatican dicastery. The cardinal sent a letter about it to the secretary of state, invoking what the canon law calls "a case of conscience." He never received a response and did not dare to raise the matter in public.

For this milieu of crooked operators, a pope who aims at a total cleanup is worse than annoying. According to the adjunct prosecutor of Reggio Calabria, Nicola Gratteri, the financial mafia finds a pontiff who "takes a stand against luxury, who is coherent and credible," a thorn in its side. Gratteri explained that Francis had sent a significant message right from the start and that "those who have hitherto fed off sources of power and wealth directly linked to the church are nervous and agitated. Pope Bergoglio is taking down hubs of economic power in the Vatican. If the bosses could trip him up somehow, they wouldn't hesitate." Asked whether the pontiff is at risk, the magistrate answered: "I don't know if organized crime is in a position to pull something off, but they are certainly pondering the question. There could be danger."[24]

Francis has moved against the Mafia with great determination. Celebrating mass at Sibari in the heart of Calabria on 21 June 2014, the pope launched an excommunication against the Mafia and the 'ndrangheta. The 'ndrangheta, he said, is the adoration of evil. "This

evil must be fought, it must be cast out! One must say 'no' to it! . . .
Those who follow this evil path in life, such as members of the mafia,
are not in communion with God: they are excommunicated!"[25]

Never had such a definitive statement been uttered from the top
level of the Catholic Church. Twenty-one years earlier, in the Valle
dei Templi of Agrigento, John Paul II had addressed this cry to Mafia
assassins: "Convert! One day the justice of God will come!" Benedict
XVI had also condemned the crimes of the Camorra during a visit to
Naples. But only Bergoglio has flung the church's solemn anathema
against organized crime by whatever name: "Mafia," "'ndrangheta,"
"Camorra." He alone has declared that they will be barred from the
sacraments until they repent their crimes.

By excommunicating mafiosi, Francis has committed bishops,
clergy, religious orders, and practicing Catholics to break off all ties
with the underworld, for the Argentine pope knows that not everyone
in ecclesiastical circles is eager to take a stand in defense of legality.
Not all of them are heroes like Pino Puglisi, a priest of Palermo killed
by the Mafia in front of his home in 1993 and elevated to the ranks
of the blessed by Francis. The pope knows that there exists a vast gray
area of fearful priests who look the other way, preferring to take no
notice of criminal behavior on the grounds that they are not magistrates. In this gray area, favors are requested or granted, a blind eye is
turned to subtle forms of intimidation, the pastoral care of erring souls
shades off into complicit silence.

The Mafia bosses didn't wait long to react. In southern Italy,
ancient tradition dictates that during religious processions the statue
of the Virgin or the patron saint is brought to halt before the residences of powerful citizens—often Mafia chieftains. It is called the
ceremony of the "bow." On 2 July 2014, in the city of Oppido Mamertina, in the same region of Calabria where the pope had just spoken
out, the procession of the Virgin of the Graces halted before the
house of the eighty-two-year-old boss Giuseppe Mazzagatti, who had
received a life sentence for homicide and Mafia involvement and
who was regarded as a protagonist of the wave of violence between
criminal gangs that rocked the area in the 1990s. The local commander of the carabinieri left the procession in disgust, while the
parish priest and the mayor pretended to notice nothing. Two years

earlier in the same territory, another boss of the 'ndrangheta, Francesco Raccosta, an opponent of the Polimeni-Mazzagatti-Bonarrigo criminal alliance, had been the victim of a revenge killing, beaten half to death and thrown to a herd of pigs to be devoured while still alive. The killer, whose phone was tapped by the carabinieri, told the tale to an acquaintance this way: "He was squealing and squealing. . . . I said, look how those pigs eat!"[26]

The local bishop's response to the "bow" in Oppido Mamertina was immediate: all the processions in the diocese were suspended. The president of the bishops of Calabria, Salvatore Nunnari, stated that the clergy should also have shunned the rite of the "bow." The secretary of the Italian Episcopal Conference, monsignor Nunzio Galantino, also reacted harshly, urging that such a deplorable attitude on the part of political and religious authorities "should be uprooted completely." "It was not a bow (of the statue) but an act of submission," he stated indignantly.

Yet the Mafia continues to push back, attempting to counteract Francis's excommunication. A few days after the scandal at Oppido Mamertina, in the maximum-security wing of the prison at Larino in southern Italy, two hundred prisoners convicted of Mafia offences threatened a strike against attendance at mass. A delegation of around thirty prisoners went to see the chaplain, Marco Colonna, requesting "clarification" in typical Mafia language. They threatened that "if they could no longer take the sacraments, they would stop coming to mass." The chaplain gave in. "After days of reflection, I assured them that they could continue to take the sacraments."[27]

At the end of July 2014, the Mafia sent a third signal to Pope Francis. In the city of Palermo, during the procession of the Vergine del Carmine in the old quarter of Ballarò, a middle-aged man wearing the cassock of a religious fraternity uttered the loud command "Halt!" Those bearing the statue of the Virgin obeyed and stopped in front of a funeral home where the Mafia chieftain Alessandro D'Ambrogio used to organize his secret meetings. D'Ambrogio is serving time in prison at Novara, but the funeral home belongs to his family and is a symbol of his power. Two children ran out from the building and were allowed to climb onto the statue and kiss it in a public challenge to the church of Pope Francis. The protest of the prisoners at Larino was an attack aimed precisely at him. The mafiosi "demand to continue killing, stealing, and trafficking drugs without being condemned as 'sinners.' They identify Pope Francis as the enemy and they defy him," commented the former prosecutor of Palermo, Gian Carlo Caselli, who achieved major victories in the battle against organized crime from 1993 to 1999.

The curia is an interweave of individual lives, a scene of refined speculation and deadly quicksand. The bond that has always held the whole thing together, overriding the tensions, oppositions, and conflicts, has been the idea of the papacy as an absolute power. It can be summed up in a snapshot: Bernini's colonnade embracing the whole world, Michelangelo's cupola reflecting a church perfect in its structure, and on its summit the cross, in memory of Christ and his vicar, who stands over and above the kings and presidents of all the earth.

This is the setting into which Francis is driving a wedge. On one hand are those unwilling to let go of the old imagery and the old way of wielding power. On the other are those prepared to face the hazards of reshaping the church to render it capable of speaking to the men and women of the third millennium.

The curia is also a microcosm of jealousies, abnegation, lethal rumor mongering, careerism, and the spirit of sacrifice. "There are saints in the Roman Curia," the pope has said more than once, referring to the exemplary monsignors who perform their work with professionalism but are also men of prayer who dedicate their free time to the work of charity. But Francis knows what is amiss. "I think that the curia has fallen somewhat from the level it once had," he said a few months after taking office, speaking regretfully of "the profile of the old curialist, faithful, doing his work."[28] There is a sociological explanation for the dimmed luster of the curial class: the overall decline in vocations. In epochs past, with candidates vying in droves to enter the priesthood, a bishop could send his best priests to the Vatican and still have first-class clerical staff at home in his diocese. In the current season of dearth, if a bishop finds a young priest of particularly high quality, he tends to retain him in the diocese and employ him there.

It wasn't by chance that in his first Christmas speech to the curia Francis stressed "professionalism, by which I mean competence, study, keeping abreast of things . . . this is a basic requisite for working in the curia." And he added a second requisite: "conscientious objection. Yes, conscientious objection to gossip! . . . For gossip is harmful to people, harmful to our work and our surroundings."[29] And in this case, gossip is a pale euphemism.

The ecclesiastical historian Alberto Melloni uses very severe terms to describe the arena that Francis has entered. The personnel of the curia "have inherited the notion of being the center and the whole at the same time." In this environment, careerism prospers, with its sorry train of adulation and backbiting, thanks to "inflated egos that disdain the very institutional setting they exploit."[30] The degradation worsened, according to Melloni, in the third of a century that ran from the election of Wojtyla to the resignation of Ratzinger.

Pope Francis realizes that he remains fairly isolated within the structure of the curia and that in Rome and beyond Rome many midlevel ecclesiastics applaud him while hesitating to walk in his footsteps. "He risks not having many imitators," observes Bishop Giancarlo Bregantini. "The risk is that, despite everyone calling him 'holy, good, and gifted,' in the end the pontiff will be left all alone."[31] But as his Argentine friends will tell you, Francis can be a ramrod.

14

The War of the Cardinals

Pope Bergoglio needs opposition that he can face out in the open. And he needs a lineup of reformers able to make its voice heard. It is part of the Argentine pope's strategy that the changes not be decided on in solitude and then announced to the church from the window of the papal study.

He is convinced that the fundamental decisions of his program can be realized only as part of a broad movement within the church. That means, in the first place, involving the worldwide episcopate in the crucial decisions while at the same time stimulating the Catholic laity, the people of God. The flock, as he puts it, is sometimes out ahead of its shepherd. The course correction he strove to achieve with a series of moves during his first year at the helm of the mighty vessel of Catholicism demanded that the conciliar atmosphere be revived.

Vatican II was a great school of liberty for Catholicism: the bishops learned to speak their minds without constantly awaiting guidance from their superiors. And it was also a school of participation: the bishops learned to compare their experiences, debate one another, draft a text, vote, make emendations, reach agreement so as to arrive at documents that passed with large majorities, and set a course for the church in modern society. The results achieved in the council hall were the fruits of consensus sought and won. It was a time of extraordinary growth for the ecclesiastical hierarchy.

As the protagonists of Vatican II left the stage one by one during the 1990s, the quality of public debate within the Catholic Church declined. At the conclave of 2005, only two of the cardinal electors present had attended the council in person: Joseph Ratzinger and William Wakefield Baum, who had been young consultants to the conciliar fathers.

The era of the council was also a bloom time for theologians, stimulating their research, and for the Catholic laity, which was involved in the debates and in the execution of the directives encapsulated in the council texts.

Pope Bergoglio belongs to the generation of postconciliar bishops for whom Vatican II is a given, and the debate (dear to Ratzinger) over whether the council signified a sharp break or an instance of smooth continuity is not of much interest. His assessment is lapidary: "The fruits [of Vatican II] are enormous. . . . [T]he dynamic of reading the Gospel, actualizing its message for today—which was typical of Vatican II—is absolutely irreversible."[1] Celebrating mass in Santa Marta on 16 April 2013, Benedict XVI's eighty-sixth birthday, Francis stressed that the council had been "a beautiful work of the Holy Spirit. . . . Pope John XXIII was obedient to the Holy Spirit . . . . [W]e hear the voices of those who want to reverse its accomplishments. That is called 'being stubborn,' that is called wishing 'to tame the Holy Spirit,' that is called becoming 'stolid and sluggish of heart.'"[2]

The difference from the approach dominant during the time of Benedict XVI is dramatic. In October 2012, at the commencement of the Year of Faith and the Synod of Bishops on the new evangelization, the report by Cardinal Donald Wuerl lamented the negative effects of the postcouncil decades, with their "aberrational liturgical practice" and the abandonment of traditional methods of transmitting the faith. In apocalyptic tones, the American cardinal stated that "it is as if a tsunami of secular influence has swept across the cultural landscape, taking with it such societal markers as marriage, family, the concept of the common good and objective right and wrong."[3]

Just a few days before leaving the throne, Benedict XVI addressed the Roman clergy and spoke of the damage done by what he called "the media's council," which supposedly had overlaid the real council that had unfolded in the Vatican basilica. Journalists had portrayed the council, said Ratzinger, in a manner that had nothing to do with the faith, thus causing disasters, problems, and suffering: "seminaries closed, convents closed, banal liturgy."[4] It was a deeply pessimistic public statement, among the most infelicitous of all those delivered by Pope Ratzinger on account of its failure to comprehend the invisible link between the action of the church—or that of any other social actor—and mass communication.

Francis has no wish to remain fettered to the diatribes of the past; he wants to push ahead. And if, as the old saying goes, *ecclesia semper reformanda* (the church is always in need of reform), then it is indispensable that the whole ecclesiastical body be mobilized to push ahead. Advancing along the way and working constructively are two of the pope's guiding notions, to which he has given voice ever since his first mass with the cardinals in the Sistine Chapel.

During the first year of his pontificate, the national episcopates remained rather subdued and passive with respect to the revolution under way. Hence, for the second year, Francis topped his agenda with a concrete and controversial topic on which the laity are demanding a decision. He chose the family as the main theme of the Extraordinary Synod of Bishops held in autumn 2014, and in the year that preceded the synod Catholic public opinion translated that theme into one overriding practical question: Should divorced and remarried believers be admitted to communion?

Right away the fuse was lit. Ratzinger's successor at the Congregation for the Doctrine of the Faith (a.k.a. the Holy Office), Gerhard Ludwig Müller, published a document in seven languages that confirms again that divorced individuals are barred from communion. Between a baptized man and woman, he stiffly asserted, the "unconditional indissolubility" of marriage applies. This is church doctrine, based on the words of Jesus and repeated by John Paul II and Benedict

XVI in two separate documents. Those who remarry are barred from communion and "may not present themselves for holy communion on the basis of their own conscience." The Holy Office had promulgated its own dictate about this in 1994.[5]

The prefect of the Holy Office did not stop short at a historical reconstruction of the debate on the matter. He touched with polemical emphasis on one of the key principles of Francis's pontificate: mercy. To invoke mercy for those divorced and remarried on the grounds that Jesus showed solidarity with the suffering "is correct, but it misses the mark when adopted as an argument in the field of sacramental theology. The entire sacramental economy is a work of divine mercy." Hence, the veto stands.[6]

Pope Francis remained impassive. "That is his opinion," he commented in private. In February 2014, he made Müller a cardinal in line with his strategy of bringing all camps into his movement for reform. But Cardinal Marx, archbishop of Munich and Müller's fellow German, did intervene. "The prefect of the Congregation for the Doctrine of the Faith cannot impose closure on debate" about a matter to be discussed at the synod, he replied.[7] Marx is a member of the privy council of cardinals the pope created as a permanent consultative organ. A few days after that, Müller struck back at Marx, maintaining that the teaching of Christ and the church cannot be the object of debate because faith is not "a party platform that can be modified according to the wishes of the members."

At this point, Cardinal Oscar Rodríguez Maradiaga, coordinator of the pope's privy council, stepped in. With a touch of humor, the Honduran cardinal stated that Müller "is German—yes, I have to say this, on top of this he is a professor, a German professor of theology. In his mind there is only right or wrong, that's it. But I am saying: 'My brother, the world is not like this. You should be more flexible dealing with other voices. Don't just listen and say no, this is the wall.'"[8]

Maradiaga said that he had asked the pope face to face why he wanted to hold another synod on the family when there had already been one in 1980 and had received this reply. "That was thirty years ago. For most people today the type of family we had then does not exist anymore." Maradiaga added his own comment: "And it is true: There are divorces, patchwork families, single parents, things like surrogate mothers, marriages without children and same sex couples. These things were not even on the horizon in 1980. All of this demands answers for today's world. It is not good enough to say: We have the traditional teaching. Of course, the traditional teaching will continue to be there. But the pastoral challenges require answers for today. And these answers do not come from authoritarianism and moralism."[9]

Thus, Francis set the stage for a dramatic confrontation at the synod—exactly as he desired. Meanwhile, another authoritative curial cardinal staked out a position, the American Raymond Leo Burke, prefect of the Tribunal of the Apostolic Segnatura. "To spread the idea that there will be a radical change, and that the church will cease to respect the indissolubility of marriage," he said, "is mistaken and damaging."[10] Contradicting Burke's statement, Cardinal Walter Kasper, formerly in charge of the Council for the Union of Christians, maintained that the possibility of making exceptions is envisageable. For those whose first matrimony has failed and who recognize their own mistakes and repent, emphasized Kasper, "there ought to be some way to take part once more in the full life of the church"— communion included.[11] Cardinal Angelo Bagnasco, president of the Italian Episcopal Conference, in contrast, stated coldly: "To rethink the problems of the family doesn't mean to change; it means thinking in light of the historical situation in which we are living."[12]

There exists a hard core in the curia that defends the barriers erected by John Paul II and Benedict XVI with respect to a series of problems that have emerged in the relation between the church and contemporary culture, problems having to do with the way life in a relationship is understood, the role of women, and the function of the priesthood.

Raymond Burke, whom Pope Ratzinger brought to the curia in 2008, belongs to this group. As archbishop of Saint Louis, he insisted in 2000 that there was a duty to deny communion to the U.S. Democratic presidential candidate, John Kerry, who supported the law legalizing abortion. Burke had also criticized the cardinal of Boston, Sean Patrick O'Malley, for allowing the funeral of Ted Kennedy to be celebrated in church. "Neither funerals nor communion should be administered to abortionist politicians" was his position. Cardinal

O'Malley's stance is radically opposed: "We won't change hearts by abandoning people in their time of need and grief."[13]

In May 2013, Burke chose to take part in person in the march for life staged in Rome by the most integrist Catholic groups. The American cardinal opposes what he calls the "multi-million-dollar lobby" committed to spreading the culture of contraception, abortion, and the denaturing of the family. The "homosexual agenda," he has said, is the fruit of "lies that come from Satan." (And for that matter, when Cardinal Bergoglio was opposing the law on same-sex marriage at Buenos Aires, he too brought the devil into the debate.)

In December 2013, Burke openly challenged Pope Francis, who not long before had asserted in his interview with *La Civiltà Cattolica* that the church "cannot insist only on issues related to abortion, gay marriage and the use of contraceptive methods."[14] Interviewed for the American Catholic broadcaster EWTN, Burke repeated that there could be nothing "more essential" than the natural moral law. "We can never talk enough about that as long as in our society innocent and defenseless human life is being attacked in the most savage way."[15]

Another member of this entrenched platoon of defenders of the Ratzinger doctrine is Cardinal Mauro Piacenza, whom the pope has moved from his position as head of the Congregation for the Clergy to the Apostolic Penitentiary. Piacenza is a hard-liner, molded by Cardinal Giuseppe Siri, the tenacious opponent of conciliar reformism. Piacenza cites as an example for the clergy the curate of the French village of Ars-sur-Formans, Jean-Marie Vianney, who lived in the first half of the nineteenth century in an environment totally remote from the problems of modern society. Piacenza has uttered a firm "no" to any review of the problem of priestly celibacy and women priests, although he did concede prior to the arrival of Francis that a "leading economist" might become "head of the administration of the Holy See or Vatican press spokesman." Regarding collegiality in the government of the church, Piacenza keeps to the empyrean of abstractions. The church hierarchy is of "direct divine institution," and the substance of collegiality is not sociopolitical but consists of "feeding on the sole bread [of the Eucharist] and living the sole faith."[16]

Cardinal Müller also belongs to the group of defenders of inherited doctrine. Known for authoritarianism in his diocese when he was bishop of Regensburg, he arrived in the Vatican in 2007 at the invitation of Benedict XVI to head the Holy Office. In December 2013, he delivered a lecture to reassert the principles of bioethics as formulated during the season of Wojtyla and Ratzinger, disregarding the direction in which Pope Francis had been trying to steer the church for almost a year. The outlook is the assertive one that Benedict XVI repeatedly expressed: "Bioethics formulates and verifies moral rules for technical and scientific comportment regarding life in general, and human life in particular." The church's teaching is not a defense of particular Catholic interests but protects the dignity of persons in general and the "conditions of human life and coexistence."[17]

In other areas, showing greater openness, Müller confirms the rule that curial personalities are often many sided. A student of the liberation theologian Gustavo Gutiérrez, the German cardinal wrote a book with him to promote a theology "on the side of the poor." As a theologian, he asserts in a volume of dogmatics that Mary's retention of her virginity "even while giving birth" (as the dogma proclaimed at the Second Council of Constantinople in 553 c.e. puts it) should not be understood "as an anomalous physiological peculiarity in the natural process of childbirth"—in other words, as if her hymen had remained intact—but in the context of the salvific influence.[18] In a book on the mass, the German theologian rejects any materialistic conception of the real presence of the body and blood of Christ in the Eucharist.[19] And for that matter, if further confirmation were needed of the fact that factions are not rigidly divided but fluid within the curia, Pope Francis himself wrote the preface to Müller's recent essay on poverty and the church's mission.

Within the conservative lineup that identifies with the theological rigidification of the past thirty years, Rino Fisichella—president of the Pontifical Academy for Life from 2008 to 2010 and then appointed by Benedict XVI to head the Council for Promoting the New Evangelization—stands out as one of the firmest supporters of the nonnegotiable principles sanctioned by Joseph Ratzinger. He has defended these principles not just theologically but also politically through intense lobbying focused primarily on Silvio Berlusconi's center–right political grouping.

During the years of Cardinal Camillo Ruini's presidency of the Conference of Italian Bishops (1991–2007), Fisichella busied himself organizing a campaign of abstention to make the referendum on assisted procreation fail (2005), promoting "family day" to impede the approval in Parliament of the law on de facto couples backed by the Prodi government in 2007, and battling against any law that would permit individuals to make living wills.

This group of personalities is characterized by their relative youth in ecclesiastical terms (Burke is sixty-six, Piacenza seventy, Fisichella sixty-three) and the fact that they were brought into the curia under Ratzinger. While for some of them the future might still hold a career as archbishop of some important diocese, they remain the focal point of a block of traditionalist opinion inside the curia and beyond—for the fact is that the national episcopates are just as divided internally as the Roman Curia.

Tarcisio Bertone, former secretary of state and already a close collaborator of Ratzinger at the Congregation for the Doctrine of the Faith from 1995 to 2002, belongs with the traditionalists, although the onset of his ninth decade has gradually reduced his influence.

Pope Francis did not choose the focus on the family for the 2014 episcopal synod at random. Contraception, divorce, and the interruption of pregnancy together constitute the arena in which the sentiments and the behavior of the Catholic laity have shown the strongest divergence from the dictates of the ecclesiastical hierarchy for almost half a century. Francis doesn't want to alter the doctrine, but he does regard it as imperative to change the pastoral approach radically. Notably, there have been repeated attempts over the decades to somehow get around the refusal of communion to those divorced and remarried. In 1993, while Karl Lehmann and Walter Kasper were still bishops, they had requested—in vain—the head of the Holy Office, Cardinal Ratzinger, to consent to a clause of conscience that in certain cases would at least allow the wronged partner who had been abandoned and had then remarried to receive the communion wafer. The German chancellor Helmut Kohl raised the problem—in vain—in a personal letter to John Paul II. The federal president Christian Wulff had even felt compelled to raise the matter—in vain—before Benedict XVI during the pope's visit to Berlin in 2011, while welcoming him to Germany.

There is a certain flavor of historical justice in entrusting a fresh debate on family life to a Synod of Bishops. It was in fact at the synod of 1980 that an overwhelming majority of bishops approved a proposal to study the system in place in the Orthodox churches, where it is possible to remarry (albeit with a more subdued rite, for penitential reasons) and continue to receive communion. It amounted to a request by the bishops to adopt that or a similar solution. Pope Wojtyla ignored the views of the world's bishops and a year later put out a document that affirmed the contrary: "The church reaffirms her practice . . . of not admitting to eucharistic communion divorced persons who have remarried." And on top of that, it "forbids any pastor, for whatever reason or pretext even of a pastoral nature, to perform ceremonies of any kind for divorced people who remarry."[20]

More than thirty years later, Pope Francis intends to give the episcopate the opportunity to work out a concrete pastoral solution. Bergoglio has his own method of preparing the ground for innovation with small verbal nudges. "I also consider the situation of a woman with a failed marriage in her past and who also had an abortion. Then this woman remarries, and she is now happy and has five children. That abortion in her past weighs heavily on her conscience and she sincerely regrets it. She would like to move forward in her Christian life. What is the confessor to do?"[21] "If someone is gay and is searching for the Lord and has good will, then who am I to judge him?"[22] "I remember the case of a very sad little girl who finally confided to her teacher the reason for her state of mind: 'my mother's fiancée doesn't like me.' The percentage of children studying in schools who have separated parents is very high. The situation in which we live now provides us with new challenges which sometimes are difficult for us to understand. How can we proclaim Christ to these boys and girls?"[23]

In every case, the query is left hanging, but the message is that the church's old doctrinal posture has become unsustainable. "Francis throws open the windows and leaves them that way, without immediately supplying an answer," comments Antonio Spadaro of La Civiltà Cattolica, to whom the first and third of these queries were posed. It is the bishops who will have to give the answer under the sign of collegiality.

But Francis knows that the ecclesiastical apparatus needs to be jolted awake. So without warning and without even involving the Pontifical Council for the Family, he launched a survey prior to the

2014 synod to find out what the lay faithful think about all the problems that everyone deals with in their daily lives. It was unheard of: to pose these thirty-nine questions is already revolutionary, and even more so is the fact that the person who wants to know the answers is the pope. They are questions that during the previous pontificates were never clearly formulated because it was always taken for granted that the views of the faithful were irrelevant and their agreement or disagreement even less so. Their job was to obey the instructions they were given.

The questions, which were set out in the "Preparatory Document" for the synod, lift the lid on a range of problems.[24]

Is the idea of the natural law in the union between a man and a woman commonly accepted as such by the baptized in general?

Is cohabitation *ad experimentum* a pastoral reality in your particular church? Can you approximate a percentage?

Do unions which are not recognized either religiously or civilly exist? Are reliable statistics available?

Are separated couples and those divorced and remarried a pastoral reality in your particular church? Can you approximate a percentage?

In all the above cases, how do the baptized live in this irregular situation? Are they aware of it? Are they simply indifferent? Do they feel marginalized or suffer from the impossibility of receiving the sacraments?

What questions do divorced and remarried people pose to the church concerning the Sacraments of the Eucharist and Reconciliation? Among those persons who find themselves in these situations, how many ask for these sacraments?

What pastoral attention can be given to people who have chosen to live in these types of union [i.e., same-sex unions]?

In the case of unions of persons of the same sex who have adopted children, what can be done pastorally in light of transmitting the faith?

[And finally the question that has refused to go away for half a century, ever since Paul VI prohibited the use of contraceptives by Catholics in the encyclical *Humanae vitae*:] Is this moral teaching [prohibiting contraception] accepted? What aspects pose the most difficulties in a large majority of couples accepting this teaching?

This preparatory document was dispatched to the national Episcopal Conferences in October 2013 with an invitation to supply responses by January 2014. If Pope Francis wanted to see how the episcopates would react, he didn't have long to wait. The Episcopal Conference in the United Kingdom put the questions online; its Italian counterpart did not. The British sought answers from individual church members; the Italians sent the questionnaire to bishops so they could consult Catholic lay movements and parishes, but of what they learned when they did so, if they did so, little is known. Episcopates around the world tended to follow one model or the other. Many dioceses treated the survey as an executive matter for discussion between bishops and the leadership of pastoral bodies and lay associations. Others did as the British and put the questionnaire online, requesting the laity to submit their views. At Vienna, Lyon, Malta, Baltimore, and Chicago, to give some examples, the bishops sought direct input from individual Catholics. The same was true in a number of dioceses in Germany, France, and the United States.

In Italy, *Avvenire*, the newspaper of the episcopate, did not put the questions on its website even as the January deadline approached, despite the fact that the secretary-general of the Synod of Bishops, Monsignor Lorenzo Baldisseri, had stated in a press conference on 5 November 2013 that any Catholic could send his or her answers to the Vatican. The lay movement We Are Church accused the Italian ecclesiastical hierarchy of "obvious foot-dragging."

With the questionnaire in existence, initiatives multiplied. Catholic newspapers printed it and gave it a boost; groups at the base mobilized the faithful to get them to send their answers to their bishops. In Switzerland, the Episcopal Conference reworded the questions in the survey to make them more accessible to the public and received around twenty-five thousand sets of answers. In Germany, a group of seventeen theology instructors launched an appeal for the church "to abandon a tradition of moral theology fixated on the sexual act and the wish to regulate every aspect of sexuality."[25] A survey of the Catholic Youth Association in Germany (Bund der Deutschen Katholischen Jugend) revealed that 90 percent of young German Catholics do not care about the church's sexual doctrine. Such attitudes broadly prevail, with some variation, throughout the Western world.

The initiative of the questionnaire roused the enthusiasm of many Catholics. "The church is going into the street," said the Spanish movement Redes Cristianas. "Many people say they are positively surprised to see the pontiff take an interest in their specific life situations," commented Arnd Bünker, director of the Swiss Pastoral-Sociological Institute of St. Gallen. In London, the BBC gathered plenty of comments. Clare from Luton wrote: "I am very much Catholic but I am also very much gay. The fact that the Catholic Church has now a leader who is willing to accept these two identities as not mutually exclusive fills me with hope. Pope Francis has the power to change the world—certainly my world—and I am proud to be part of his movement of acceptance and understanding within the Catholic Church." Sam from Leeds wrote: "This is the kind of action I've been hoping for as a young Catholic." Arthur Croker from Cheddar wrote, "The Catholic Church does not need reforming," while Paula Thompson from Reading said that "I filled in the questionnaire when it first came out and I think it is a very good idea."[26]

The Catholic Church is setting off down a new path. The varied reactions of the cardinals are evidence of that. "It is neither a referendum nor the application of democratic methods to the internal life of the church. It is a survey meant to yield well thought out and operational answers," said the prudent secretary-general of the synod, Cardinal Baldisseri.[27] "We need to work on these questions as artisans of peace, without fear of the truth that makes us free," the French cardinal Philippe Barbarin exhorted the faithful.[28]

"We perceive a range of situations where we can find concrete solutions, in the sense of the doctrine and the message of Jesus Christ . . . . [I]t is not a question of public opinion," asserted the Hungarian cardinal Péter Erdö, rapporteur for the synod. The Italian bishop Bruno Forte, appointed by the pope to the position of special secretary of the synod, added that while it was not a case of making choices based on society's mood, it was impossible "to ignore what the bulk of public opinion is thinking and [impossible not to] reflect on it."[29] The archbishop of Westminster, Vincent Nichols, president of the Episcopal Conference of England and Wales, summed it up in a phrase of which Bergoglio would approve: "God gave us one mouth and two ears. The fact that we may hear things that make us uncomfortable—that's fine."[30]

The first evaluations of the answers received by several German dioceses bore witness to the enormous distance separating the doctrine of the church and the lived experience of people. In a communiqué, the diocese of Mainz—the see of Cardinal Lehmann, who served four terms as president of the German Episcopal Conference—referred to it as a "deep fissure." Lehmann himself added: "The results of the survey produce and reinforce, even if they are not representative, the impression of an awkward situation. Actually we have known this for a long time. Much has been repressed. Now Pope Francis is offering us in many ways the chance of a clear acknowledgment and a resolute healing of the shortcomings indicated."[31]

Lehmann's successor as president of the German bishops, Robert Zollitsch, seventy-six years old, took a decision at the end of his mandate that raised a clamor. The pastoral office of his diocese at Freiburg im Breisgau jumped the gun and published a guide allowing communion to be granted to the divorced and remarried after a series of meetings with their parish priest, a searching examination of conscience, and the manifestation of sincere repentance. From Rome there immediately arrived a warning from Cardinal Müller, the prefect of the Congregation for the Doctrine of the Faith.

But in the face of the results of the survey promoted by Pope Francis, one gets the impression that the age of the imperious veto from Rome is drawing to a close. The Swiss Episcopate was the first to present the results it had obtained, and they amount to a snapshot that holds good for large swathes of the Western world. Swiss Catholics reject by a huge majority the doctrine that bars the divorced and remarried from receiving the Eucharist. Around 60 percent of the answers endorse recognition and an ecclesiastical blessing for same-sex couples (without reference to marriage). The ban on the contraceptive pill is totally ignored. The official summary, drafted by the Swiss Pastoral-Sociological Institute of St. Gallen, to which the Swiss bishops entrusted the task of analyzing the answers to the survey, states that "the ban on artificial methods of contraception is very remote from the practice and the thinking of the great majority of Catholics."[32]

This general comment from the St. Gallen institute was lapidary and it resonated in the hall of the Extraordinary Synod in one form or another. "It is necessary that the church cease to attribute absolute value to certain norms and directives in the face of the concrete experiences and life situations of the people. When the church demands that Catholic women and men submit, unconditionally and acritically, to concrete norms and given directives for behavior, the church ultimately harms its own aspiration to transmit to people the most central and essential aspects of its message."[33]

A worldwide survey undertaken on behalf of Univision, a Spanish-language broadcaster in the United States, by the polling firm Bendixen and Amandi International among Catholics in the United States, Argentina, Brazil, Colombia, Mexico, France, Italy, Poland, Spain, the Democratic Republic of the Congo, Uganda, and the Philippines reveals that 58 percent of those queried reject the veto on offering communion to the divorced and remarried. Fifty-seven percent would allow abortion in certain cases; 78 percent are in favor of contraceptives. But there is a geographical and cultural fault line between regions, with Catholics in Africa and Asia more solidly behind the traditional doctrine.

At the time of writing, in the wake of the 2014 synod, everything is in movement on this front, and both sides are fighting hard. Like the political strategist he is, Pope Francis has arranged his timetable so that the final decisions were not taken at the Extraordinary Synod of October 2014; there the situation was assessed. The church has now been granted a year so that participation in the discussion can widen internally, the reforming bishops can have a chance to strengthen themselves, and the laity can be properly heard. It will fall to a second synod in 2015 to pass the definitive resolutions.

The issues of family life constitute a decisive test in which Francis is putting at stake his credibility as a reformer and his authority within the church.

15

The Italian Knot

The Italian Episcopate has been left dazed by the revolution of the pope from Argentina. The vision he has sketched out of a poor church, not overburdened with doctrine and not forever intruding (on spiritual grounds) into people's private lives and in the nation's politics, a church that makes room for women, heeds the laity, and rejects the temptation to manipulate them — all this has convulsed the framework within which the Italian Episcopal Conference (CEI, Conferenza Episcopale Italiana) has operated for decades.

Many sectors of the Italian Catholic Church may be motivated by a strong sense of social engagement, but it has always been accustomed to regard itself primarily as an institution meant to exert sway over the consciences of Italian men and women, and over Italian politics and society in general

The CEI has never enjoyed much liberty itself (unlike the other national Episcopal Conferences, it never had the right to elect its own president) and in turn has accorded even less to the Italian laity. It has always smothered any attempt to create a forum in which organs representing the faithful could express themselves freely on ecclesiastical questions and on the relation between faith and the socioeconomic challenges of the Italian nation.

In Germany, the homeland of Benedict XVI, the Central Committee of German Catholics (ZDK, Zentralkomitee der Deutschen Katholiken) has been a vital voice for the laity, intervening in the most controversial areas of ecclesiastical life. In Italy, the National Consultative Organ of Laic Aggregations (Consulta Nazionale delle Aggregazioni Laicali, formerly the Consulta per l'Apostolato dei Laici) reveals, in the tortuous wording of the first article of its own statute, the bishops' fear of having to reckon with an autonomous instance representing the laity. It says that the Consulta is the place where Italian Catholic associations and movements "live in unitary form their relation with the Italian Episcopate, offering the richness of their apostolic capacities, and accepting from it operationally programs and pastoral guidance."[1]

In the course of recent decades, at crucial moments involving the relation between faith and society in Italy—from the referendums on divorce, abortion, and assisted procreation to the proposed parliamentary bills on de facto couples and living wills—the Consulta has never taken a concrete part in public debate or carried out the function its own statute assigns it of supplying "proposals in view of the elaboration of the overall orientation and the pastoral guidelines of the CEI."[2]

On the contrary, the hierarchy has systematically instructed the Italian laity how they should think and act in the context of national debates and expected to receive obedient compliance. At the most recent national convention of the Italian church, held at Verona in 2006, the fear that voices moderately out of tune with the choir might make themselves heard led the presidency of the CEI to order the working groups not to pass any resolutions.

Among the bishops themselves, bounds on their liberty are set from above. The practice of submitting the introductory report of the president of the CEI to the pope prior to its delivery at the annual assembly in May has permanently muzzled general debate. What is there left to

debate if a report has been approved in advance by the pontiff, sometimes with authoritative last-minute corrections? The CEI is marked
by this top-down style. "The speech is given, everyone intervenes to
say 'OK, not OK,' and in the end the president of the CEI responds
on the basis of his own viewpoint," Monsignor Alesandro Plotti, vice
president of the CEI from 2000 to 2005, once remarked. No rules
are bent, he added, "but it is a personal opinion that doesn't reflect
whatever input he may have received. It appears to be the voice of the
Italian bishops, when the bishops have been sidelined."[3]

The scant autonomy of a national episcopate overridden by the
pope and the pope's confidants reached the point of maximum impo-
tence in 2007, when Cardinal Angelo Bagnasco assumed the presidency of the CEI. The Vatican secretary of state at the time, Cardinal
Tarsicio Bertone, sent him an official letter stating that he (Bertone)
alone would conduct all dealings with the state authorities. "As
regards relations with the political institutions, I assure your excel-
lency straightaway of the cordial collaboration and respectful guidance of the Holy See and myself personally."[4]

Italians have stood by as the Vatican and the CEI have systematically woven themselves into the fabric of the nation's political system.
From the end of World War II until the 1990s, they worked with and
through the country's major political party on the right, the Democra-
zia Cristiana (Christian Democracy). That party collapsed in 1994,
and since the turn of the millennium the church has had a less open
but certainly privileged relationship with Silvio Berlusconi's center–
right faction, first while Cardinal Ruini was president of the CEI and
subsequently while Cardinal Bertone was pulling the strings as secretary of state. The proffered reason was the need to defend the so-
called nonnegotiable principles in the areas of life, matrimony, and
freedom of education. The political substance was an agreement to
guarantee the financing of Catholic schools and opposition to legisla-
tive innovation with respect to de facto couples, same-sex unions, living wills, more rapid divorce procedures, and artificial insemination.

Though there were intermittent moments of tension, especially
over the Boffo affair, the de facto alliance between the CEI and Berlusconi's center–right political formation was dissolved only when the
Monti government came into being in 2011. (Dino Boffo, the director

of *Avvenire*, had criticized Berlusconi's lurid lifestyle and had con-
sequently been forced to resign in the summer of 2009 after a campaign of defamation against him by *Il Giornale*, a paper owned by
the Berlusconi family, based on a false document alleging homosexual transgressions.)

In 2011 and 2012, in two successive gatherings entitled "social
weeks" at Todi, there was an attempt by Catholic associations and
movements to create a new political force, but it failed to get off the
ground. Sectors of the Vatican close to Cardinal Bertone propounded
the idea of ending the "diaspora ideology" and inaugurating a new
"protagonism" on the part of the Catholic laity. "Bishops, politicians,
economists, jurists, movements, and civil society" were meant to
converge and advance a program of political action inspired by the
social doctrine of the church—something closely resembling a political movement.[5] Cardinal Bagnasco, president of the CEI, was more
reserved, hoping merely for a "cultural and social" force. None of
these projects came to fruition in any case, and with the electoral flop
of the Monti list in the 2013 elections, organized Italian Catholicism
was left essentially adrift, no longer a vital political player.

A feature of this sociopolitical eclipse was the incomprehensible
aphasia of the Catholic intelligentsia, except for a few outliers. It
seemed as though Catholic thought had become irrelevant to Italian
society, despite the high-quality analyses and positions put forward
during the "social weeks."

A few months before the abdication of Benedict XVI, one voice
was raised in the Italian church demanding a radical change of
course. "The church has remained two hundred years behind. Why
on earth does it not shake itself awake? Has fear replaced courage?"
These words were uttered on the point of death by Cardinal Carlo
Maria Martini, a Jesuit and former archbishop of Milan. In an interview (and testament) published on 1 September 2012, shortly after
his death, the cardinal lamented the existence of a "tired church"
in Europe and America. "Our culture has aged, our churches are
huge, our religious houses are empty while the bureaucratic apparatus of the church swells, our rites and our habits are pompous." Carlo
Maria Martini expressed hope for a church able to shed the weight of
material well-being and to unite men close to the poorest with young

people capable of trying out new things. "I advise the pope and the bishops," he said, "to seek out twelve persons outside the norm for the leading positions."[6]

Martini showed himself a precursor of Pope Francis. His first recommendation was a conversion of the church, which "ought to acknowledge its own errors and pursue a radical path of change, starting with the pope and the bishops." The cardinal stressed the need to confront the themes of sexuality and the body, alluding to the questions that, a year after his death, Francis would raise with the questionnaire prepared in advance of the synod of 2014. "We must ask ourselves if people still heed the counsels of the church in sexual matters. Is the church still an authority of reference in this field, or just a media caricature?"

Martini was much more than a great personality of Italian Catholicism. He was a point of reference in the Catholic Church worldwide, listened to in both the Protestant and the Orthodox worlds. In the conclave of 2005, at which Ratzinger was elected, the former archbishop of Milan was considered the symbolic antagonist of the prefect of the Congregation for the Doctrine of the Faith. Even some of his parables overlap with the things Pope Francis says. "A woman has been abandoned by her husband and finds a new companion who takes care of her and her three children. Her second love is a success. If this family is discriminated against, then it is not just the mother who is frozen out, but her children too." The sacraments, Martini insisted, are not "an instrument of discipline, but an aid for men and women in the weak moments of life."[7]

During his time as archbishop of Milan, Martini had launched a "chair for nonbelievers," an initiative that contrasted the believer's reasoning and the nonbeliever's reasoning on a wide range of topics. The fundamental point of this dialogue, he explained, is to be found in the interior of every person. "I maintain that each of us has inside himself a nonbeliever and a believer that converse inside him, that query each other . . . the unbeliever in me unsettles the believer, and vice versa."[8] The world is not divided between believers and nonbelievers, he maintained, but between those who think and those who don't.

Martini's trajectory is telling with respect to what, over the past thirty years, has been considered acceptable or not acceptable at the top levels of the Italian Catholic Church. Discovered, so to speak, by Pope Wojtyla, who made him archbishop of Milan in 1979, the Jesuit scholar had hitherto been known solely as rector of the Pontifical Biblical Institute and then of the Gregorian University. But the archbishop of Milan was gradually pushed to the sidelines when he began to express opinions at variance with the CEI's dedication to meddling in Italian politics under the aegis of Cardinal Ruini, and to advance propositions that did not chime with John Paul II's design for a reevangelization of contemporary society. Martini was chosen to serve as president of the Council of European Episcopal Conferences from 1986 to 1993 because of his prestige and his openness to dialogue with Judaism and Islam as well as with the other Christian denominations. But he was removed from that post at the behest of Pope Wojtyla, who changed the organization's statute to ensure that only a sitting president of one of the national Episcopal Conferences could be elected president of this pan-European council.

In 1999, during the Synod of Bishops that John Paul II focused on the European situation after the fall of the Berlin Wall, the archbishop of Milan surprised his brother bishops by speaking of his "dream"—a vision of a new council with the courage to face up to the most pressing problems: collegiality in church government, the desperate shortage of priests, the position of women in the ecclesiastical community, the participation of laymen, the theme of sexuality, Catholic discipline of matrimony, ecumenism. The top levels of the hierarchy greeted the proposal with irritated silence. Neither John Paul II nor Benedict XVI had any wish to confront that set of questions.

In 2002, when Martini reached the age of seventy-five, he was sent into retirement for reasons of health, to the notable relief of some in the Vatican. He retired to Jerusalem for a few years and then returned to Gallarate in Lombardy. He was far from inactive, and in long conversations with his fellow Jesuit Georg Sporschill, later assembled in a book, he spoke his mind.

Churches in the West, he said, could not continue to import priests from abroad; there needed to be a conversation about employing what in ecclesiastical Latin are called *viri probati*—in other words, the eventuality of ordaining as priests married men of proven faith and moral probity. Martini also considered female priests a possibility worth exploring. He recounted a conversation he had had with the archbishop of Canterbury, George Carey, the Anglican primate from 1991 to 2002, precisely the years in which the Anglican Church was experiencing tension on account of the first ordinations of women priests, a step the Vatican firmly opposed. "To encourage him, I said to him that this audacity might be of help to us in valorizing women more, and understanding the way ahead."[9]

Settled in Jerusalem, Martini began to write a column for *Corriere della Sera*, a weekly contribution to public debate on sensitive topics that the CEI either repressed altogether or dealt with by condemnation: living wills, homosexual relations, the situation of de facto couples, artificial insemination. In the Vatican, the column was frowned on. "It caused displeasure at Rome," wrote the newspaper's director, Ferruccio De Bortoli, in an editorial commemorating Martini's death: "A prophet has died. I note with regret a certain coldness on the part of certain ecclesiastical sectors. . . . Why was Cardinal Martini seen almost as an eccentric figure, virtually a heretic, the next thing to a Protestant?" De Bortoli expressed the hope that Benedict XVI would come to Milan for Martini's funeral; his hope was not fulfilled.[10] At Martini's obsequies on 3 September 2012, three cardinals spoke: Angelo Comastri, who conveyed a message from Benedict XVI; Angelo Scola, the current archbishop; and Dionigi Tettamanzi, who had followed Martini and preceded Scola in that position. The only really enthusiastic applause was reserved for Tettamanzi, who said, "We loved you for your far-seeing gaze."[11]

Seven months later the first Jesuit pope in history ascended the throne of St. Peter. Though not a disciple of Martini in the strict sense, Bergoglio has put back into circulation many elements of Martini's thought. On becoming pope, he found himself faced with a disoriented Italian Catholic Church, in which the only pole star guiding the leaders of the CEI were the nonnegotiable principles, and the episcopate was fragmented, with some bishops in the regions still apparently in cahoots with small-time local political players, while others were striving to build a church community free of political compromises and capable of addressing society as a whole. It is a church unaccustomed to financial transparency. The "eight per thousand" monies it spends are on the public record,[12] but the ledgers of the dioceses are kept secret, especially as regards real estate holdings. According to *Il Sole 24 Ore*, around 20 percent of Italian real estate belongs to the church, with an approximate value of 1,000 billion euros. That doesn't include the property holdings of the Vatican. Just one Vatican dicastery, the Congregation for the Propagation of the Faith, possesses property in Rome to the tune of 9 billion euros.[13]

The new pontiff, who was accustomed as archbishop of Buenos Aires and president of the Argentine Episcopate to criticize the nation's political leadership with a freedom unthinkable for an Italian bishop, has made no secret, right from the start, of his wish to set the CEI on a different course. He confirmed Cardinal Bagnasco as president and made it clear that the era when the Vatican meddled in Italian political affairs was over. He said in a brief address to the Italian bishops two months after taking office: "You have so many duties. Firstly: the church in Italy—all of you—dialogue with the cultural, social and political institutions, which is one of your tasks and is far from easy. . . . [M]ay the Episcopal Conference carry ahead this dialogue, as I said, with the cultural, social and political institutions. It is your duty."[14]

At his first meeting in the Vatican with the president of the Republic of Italy, Giorgio Napolitano, the pope ignored the nonnegotiable principles and stressed instead: "It is also urgent that believers and non-believers alike collaborate in promoting a society in which injustice in all its forms may be surmounted and individuals, each and every one, be accepted and permitted to contribute to the common good."[15] Visiting the Quirinale (the presidential palace) in turn, the pontiff put a definitive end to the emphasis on nonnegotiable principles, renouncing any insistence on specifically Christian roots and expressing the hope that Italy would draw for its recovery on its "rich heritage of civil and spiritual values. . . . The church's primary task is to bear witness to the mercy of God and to encourage generous reactions of solidarity in order to open a future of hope."[16] (Bergoglio would later say to Ferruccio De Bortoli, director of *Corriere della Sera*, "I have never understood the expression 'non-negotiable values.' Values are values, period.")

Symptomatic of the new climate was President Napolitano's affirmation that in the pontificate of Francis he detected "the absence of all dogmatism, a moving away from 'positions untroubled by any degree of uncertainty,' a summons to that 'leaving room for doubt' proper to the great leaders of the people of God." The head of state stressed the pope's desire to begin a "dialogue with all, even those most distant from him and his adversaries."[17]

Meanwhile, the pope pressed ahead for the drafting of a new statute for the CEI, including a marked reduction of its bureaucracy and its operating costs, a strengthening of the role of the regional Episcopal Conferences, a reduction in the number of dioceses, and a revision of the procedure for electing the president to bring it in line with that of the other Episcopal Conferences around the world.

For years, the Catholic laity have been waiting and hoping for change in the Italian church. Several books, virtual cries of pain, that appeared at around the start of the final year of Ratzinger's reign bear witness to this hope. In *Manca il respiro* (Gasping for breath), the historian Giorgio Campanini and the priest Saverio Xeres, a professor at the Faculty of Theology of northern Italy, wrote of the enormous concern among many laymen on account of the self-referential and domineering hierarchy, the increasing ineffectuality of the conciliar documents, and what the theologian Enzo Bianchi defines as a "preconceived reading of events and circumstances that is then imposed from above on the individual realities of specific regions and dioceses."[18]

The assessment by the former vice director of *L'Osservatore Romano*, Gian Franco Svidercoschi, who had been present as a young journalist at Vatican II and had collaborated with John Paul II on the book *Dono e magistero* (Gift and magisterium), was even harsher: "The number of baptisms, vocations to the priesthood, and church weddings is dropping; the number of the unbaptized is rising, moral life is decaying, and Christians are incapable of playing a public role. And the response [of the clergy] is to withdraw into its own structures, to clutch tightly to clerical privilege, and to take refuge in corporatism, careerism, and Roman centralism." The author of *Mal di chiesa* (Church sickness) and the essay *Il Ritorno dei chierici* (Return of the clerics), Svidercoschi was criticizing the church right up until a few weeks before the election of Pope Francis for shielding itself against modernity behind its identity and for incapacity to face up to the free-

dom of contemporary society. A part of the clergy clings to an excessively sacralized vision of its own role, while "many young priests are
extremely fragile and struggling." Conformism spreads. "The priest
keeps his mouth shut because he wants to become a bishop, the
bishop has his eyes fixed on a bigger diocese, ambition keeps the cardinal quiet. Not all, of course." The result, according to Svidercoschi,
is stagnation, marked by a fear of debate, while "the laity are mere
onlookers of a self-referential system that stifles contradiction."[19]

One sees why, in his first encounter at the Quirinale with the president of the Italian Republic, Giorgio Napolitano, Francis included
one of those rapid emphases that seem to have been penciled in at the
last minute: "[T]he church in Italy—everyone."[20] He meant that the
church is not just the ecclesiastical hierarchy, but the whole people
of God.

The problem of poverty, so important to Francis, has also been
raised for years by sections of the clergy closest to the common folk.
"The church is not for the poor; it is with the poor," the Genoese
street priest Andrea Gallo, who died scarcely two months after Pope
Bergoglio was elected, used to say. "The church is poor, and it is with
all those who are suffering. It is an open door."

The Argentine pope has moved gradually but with determination.
He initially confirmed Monsignor Mariano Crociata as secretary-
general of the CEI, but only ad interim, and on 19 November 2013
replaced him. In early October, however, *Avvenire* had printed the
news that Crociata had been confirmed permanently. The pontiff was
exceedingly angry and forced the editors of the paper to print a revised
notice to the effect that Crociata was staying on only temporarily.

Crociata was not appointed to a major see of cardinalatial status,
like such former secretary-generals of the CEI as Giuseppe Betori
(appointed to Florence) or Tettamanzi (Genoa and then Milan) had
been. He was simply made bishop of Latina. In his place, Francis
summoned a bishop from the far reaches of Italy, Monsignor Nunzio Galantino, bishop of Cassano allo Ionio, the smallest diocese in
Calabria. The new secretary-general of the CEI was a simple yet cultivated personality, close to the activist priest Luigi Ciotti of Turin.
Galantino had taught anthropology at the theological faculty of
southern Italy and upon becoming bishop of Cassano had refused to

install himself in the episcopal palace, choosing instead to reside in the local seminary to stay close to the priests and seminarians.

Galantino had stood last on the short list of three names for the post of secretary-general submitted to Francis by Cardinal Bagnasco. Upon being appointed, he asked the pope if he could continue to care for his diocese, and Francis took pen and paper in hand and wrote directly to the faithful of Cassano allo Ionio asking their permission to employ their bishop part-time on other matters: "I know how much you love your bishop, and I know you won't like having him taken away, and I understand you. . . . I will ask him, for a while at least, while remaining in Rome, to travel regularly for a few days so as to continue to accompany you on the road of faith. I ask you please to understand me and pardon me."[21]

In December 2013, altering the makeup of the curial Congregation for Bishops, Pope Francis excluded Cardinal Bagnasco from the plenary session, installing the vice president of the CEI Gualterio Bassetti, bishop of Perugia. Two months later he made Bassetti a cardinal, advancing him to center stage; indeed, many observers regard him as a candidate for the presidency of the CEI, thinking it not unlikely that Cardinal Bagnasco may resign in 2015. As part of the reorganization of the structures of the Italian church, Dino Boffo, the director of the CEI television station TV 2000 and one of the last remnants of the Ruini era, was also removed.

Relations between Pope Francis and the Italian Episcopal Conference followed a paradoxical course during the first year of his pontificate. The pope was quite prepared to give the CEI the power to elect its own president, but a solid block of bishops refused to assume the responsibility of an open confrontation about the leadership of the episcopate and the consequent duty to vote for the platform of one candidate or another. At a meeting of the permanent council of the episcopate in January 2014, the resistance of the conservatives was manifested in a tortuous proposal: all the bishops would indicate the names of their preferred candidates, and then the general assembly would be asked to express its own preference out of a short list of fifteen names, corresponding to the candidates most frequently signaled.[22]

Finally, at the general assembly in May 2014, following a dramatic split in which no policy proposal reached the two-thirds majority required (104 bishops preferred direct election, and 102 preferred that a short list of three be sent to the pope), it was decided to vote on three names and leave the choice of president of the CEI to the pope. Those who balk at giving the episcopal base the direct power to choose its own leadership justify their reluctance by the "special relationship" between the Italian Catholic Church and the Roman pontiff. For them, "the nomination of the president of the CEI ought to continue to be reserved to the pope, from a list of names" signaled by the bishops.[23]

This is not the only knotty problem in the CEI that needs solving. In the fight against clerical pedophilia, the Italian Episcopal Conference lags behind other Episcopal Conferences in Europe and America, which have organized national agencies to monitor the problem, intervene, and compensate victims. The Bagnasco presidency has tenaciously refused to take responsibility at the national level. The cardinal has always sheltered behind the stance that "the CEI has no authority to constitute anything. . . . [I]t is not our business to create structures; every individual bishop will operate on the basis of his own assessment."[24] The episcopate also refuses to shoulder the obligation to report guilty priests to the police or prosecutors on the grounds that a bishop is not a public official. This stance was reaffirmed in the guidelines published by the CEI in March 2014 after the Holy See judged inadequate a document drafted in 2012 to deal with the phenomenon of clerical abuse of minors.

The CEI rejects any national supervision and any duty to set up agencies to hear complaints from victims and inform the authorities, stating explicitly: "No responsibility, direct or indirect, for eventual abuses rests with the leadership . . . of the Italian Episcopal Conference."[25] The only novelty with respect to the 2012 document is an italicized aside: "Under the Italian constitution, the bishop, not being qualified either as a public official or as one charged with public service, has no juridical obligation—*except for the moral duty to contribute to the common good*—to denounce to the judicial authorities of the state any information he may have received about the illicit deeds that are the object of the present guidelines." About this moral duty the CEI furnishes no specifics, leaving the future interpretation of it to individual bishops.

And yet from a victim, Marie Collins, an Irish Catholic who was raped at age thirteen and has been summoned by Pope Francis to join the international antiabuse commission created in the Vatican, comes a firm stipulation: "Let us establish that if cases of abuse are ascertained and the victim agrees, they should be reported to the civil authorities." As Collins stresses, "This step is decisive."[26]

The CEI document warns Italian bishops that, on the basis of the reform of the Concordat in 1984 and the Code of Penal Procedure, "bishops are exempt from the obligation to depose or submit documents relating to knowledge they may have or dispose of by reason of their proper ministry." The emphasis is aimed at keeping the judicial authorities from gaining the power to compel ecclesiastics to hand over documentation that might implicate them in a cover-up or show a failure of due diligence—as has happened in the United States.

The guidelines do indeed assert that when the civil authorities have launched an investigation or a judicial process, a bishop's cooperation with them "will be important" ("risulterà importante"). Yet the absence of any national monitoring by the CEI robs of its force the exhortation to be active in uncovering crimes and collaborating with the authorities. Even the canonical obligation on bishops who have been made aware of a report of abuse to launch a preventive investigation immediately and remove the suspect from pastoral duties in the meantime has often been violated in Italy.

The most clamorous example of episcopal failure to intervene at the diocesan level and complete lack of interest on the part of the national hierarchy is the case of Don Ruggero Conti, convicted on appeal and sentenced to fourteen years and two months of incarceration for having abused underage boys in a parish in the Rome area between 1998 and 2008. The affair hit the headlines in 2008: the responsible bishop, Monsignor Gino Reali (suburbicarian diocese of Porto-Santa Ruffino), was informed of allegations but did not launch a canonical investigation, and to date, despite two convictions in civil court, no ecclesiastical procedure against Conti has been announced.

The greatest challenge facing the Italian Catholic Church, however, is the steep falloff in participation by young people in institutional Catholicism. Its self-image as the "church of the people" is wearing thin. A survey carried out early in the present century in the

diocese of Venice monitored participation in the mass by young people during one November weekend. "Fewer than 6 out of every 100
persons present in church were young people between ages 18 and
29," said Alessandro Castegnaro, director of the socioreligious observatory of the Triveneto region. On Sunday evening, when young people
attend mass most frequently, they were still less than 10 percent of
the congregation.[27]

The Veneto is traditionally very Catholic, so these figures are telling. Comparison of the parental generation (ages forty-eight to fifty-
six) with their offspring (ages eighteen to twenty-six) shows striking
gaps. Among the latter, only 27 percent state that they belong to
the church with few or no reservations. Whereas 51 percent of the
elders feel that the church is "distant," 73 percent of the young hold
that view.

Another relevant aspect is the uniformity of attitude across youth
of both sexes. Gone is the time when girls were automatically more
likely to attend mass than boys. "Today girls born around 1990 who
assign high importance to religion are 14%; the corresponding figure
for males is 12%." Among women with postsecondary education, the
drift away from the church is even more palpable. Fifty-eight percent
of them express disapproving opinions of it, and only 10 percent have
a clearly positive opinion.

In light of the fact that the intergenerational transmission of religion has always been a female appanage, Castegnaro and his colleagues foresee that the change of attitude among young women will
have strong negative effects—from the perspective of bonds to the
church—on future generations. We are witnessing a rising tide of
exits from traditional Christianity, a heightened freedom of choice
within the religion professed, and heightened subjectivity in deciding
on values, rules, and even the physiognomy of the divinity, to which
the characteristics assigned are often quite indeterminate. Still, only
one young person in four maintains that they do not believe at all.

Setting off to Rome for the conclave in March 2013, Jorge Mario
Bergoglio reminded a group of religious that the church must realize
its error in continuing to believe "there are ninety-nine sheep in the
flock, and just one lost sheep. It is exactly the opposite: just one sheep
is still in the flock, and ninety-nine have gone missing."[28]

The exodus from the traditional church, not just in Italy but also throughout the Western world, is a gigantic phenomenon, and the challenge for the Bergoglio pontificate is enormous. After his advent, it was said, the forecourts of the churches may have been filled with enthusiastic people, but the pews did not suddenly fill up. In the forty-something age group, which had rather drifted away from religious practice, some were coming back. Among those practicing more zealously—as measured by their links to the Pauline periodicals *Credere* and *Famiglia Cristiana*—a survey conducted in March 2014 revealed a notable strengthening of faith, a greater frequency in taking the sacraments, and a greater disposition to engage in prayer. The base of these samples is narrow. At the Caritas organization in Rome, they have seen a greater influx of volunteers, but in society at large no trend of young people "returning" to the pews is perceptible.

To reverse this tendency, converting the ecclesiastical apparatus to a new mode of being a church is the wager of the Argentine pontificate.

16

A Resignable Papacy

wo popes in the Vatican and a resignable papacy on the horizon. The year 2013 set in motion a transformation of Catholicism the outcome of which is unpredictable. It altered the profile of the papacy, and Francis is changing the shape of the church.
His successor will probably go back to residing in the papal apartment,
but never again will he be able to present himself in the imperial rai-
ment of the past. Never again will he succeed in exerting unbounded
sway. The imperial absolutism of the pontiffs has been subverted once
and for all. Pope Francis has stood before the world as a disciple of
Jesus; after him, it will be difficult for any pope to ascend the throne
in the guise of Christ's plenipotentiary.

Pope Francis doesn't have a lot of time for his revolution. In Argentina, where many people addressed him informally as "tu" and he is
held in less reverential awe, quite a few churchmen assume that he
has a short window of opportunity. The church is a body that moves

slowly and undergoes mutation even more slowly. Bergoglio has a limited span of time in which to carry out his program.

Father Ignacio Pérez del Visto, his former professor, says that the pontiff "knows he doesn't have a two-decade papacy ahead of him. He feels the urgency of the reforms he must accomplish within three or four years." He cannot allow himself to be thwarted. "He must act for as long as he feels he has the backing of the people."[1] In Catholic circles in Buenos Aires, many would agree. Bergoglio's former spokesman, Father Marcó, said so openly on the radio: "After Benedict's gesture, it wouldn't seem odd if Francis were to resign, should he feel that he had done what he had to do, and if he felt his strength ebbing."[2]

Ratzinger's abdication utterly changed the anatomy of the papacy. It is no longer a perpetual office; a pope reigns for as long as he feels confident that he controls the levers of government. The summer before Benedict XVI resigned, his biographer Peter Seewald asked him what the faithful had yet to expect from his papacy, and the answer was: "Not much. I am an elderly man; my strength is waning."[3]

In the wake of Benedict's renunciation, the former Vatican foreign minister Cardinal Giovanni Lajolo noted: "Benedict XVI's decision establishes a precedent for his successors." The Nigerian cardinal John Olorunfemi Onaiyekan regards it as unlikely that a pope would remain on the throne past the age of ninety and doesn't exclude that a future pontiff might "set an age limit for popes" by decree.[4] Joseph Ratzinger stepped aside as he was about to turn eighty-six, and Catholics have adjusted with remarkable speed to the end of the papacy for life.

The rumor in the Vatican is that Pope Francis confided to a bishop that he did not exclude resigning. It is hard to imagine him wanting to stay in charge without having full control. To vegetate on the throne at an advanced age would be alien to the intellectual temperament of a Jesuit pontiff, trained to "discern" situations. His stated wish to keep, and indeed renew, his Argentine passport and identity card shows a glimpse of a future existence not necessarily terminated inside the walls of the Vatican. It is likely that he regards retirement as an option just as open to him as to anyone else, something suggested by his insistence, in an interview with the director of *Corriere della Sera*, that people had better get used to the presence of an emeritus pope as a permanent "institution," just as, after the conciliar reforms, they got used to bishops living on in retirement. "The emeritus pope is not a statue in a museum," nor is he compelled to retire to an abbey far from the Vatican; it is a good thing if he continues to meet people and participate in the life of the church. In a press conference during his return flight from South Korea to Rome, Francis addressed the possibility that he might do as Benedict XVI had done. Forestalling a journalist's question, he stated: "You can ask me: 'What if one day you don't feel prepared to go on?' I would do the same, I would do the same!"[5]

On the second anniversary of his election, the pope went even further, stating out of the blue: "I have the sensation that my pontificate will be short. Four or five years . . . I don't know . . . or two or three." And he specified that two or three years had already passed.[6]

Bergoglio is doing all he can to accustom Catholics to the reality of retired popes and to suggest to public opinion that the coexistence of two pontiffs, the emeritus one and the reigning one, should be accepted as normal, not something to gape at.

On Saturday, 22 February 2014, the faithful who gathered in St. Peter's Square for the creation of nine cardinals witnessed a hitherto unthinkable spectacle. At the foot of the Altar of the Confession, surrounded by the purple-clad throng of the College of Cardinals, Pope Francis and Joseph Ratzinger met and embraced. It was Francis's express wish that his predecessor should take part in this solemn ritual in the basilica that symbolizes Catholicism and that the world should see the reigning pope — wearing his vestments, with the miter on his head and his pastoral staff in his left hand — face to face with another man dressed in white, his head uncovered. When Francis went to visit Ratzinger at Castel Gandolfo after his election, he kept the German at his side so that they kneeled in tandem in the chapel of the papal residence: an imposing image of fraternal closeness, without friction.

With political acumen, Francis emphasized continuity by publishing Benedict XVI's unfinished encyclical *Lumen fidei*. Symbolically embracing the text and presenting it as the work of four hands, the Argentine pope nipped in the bud any narrative of a divided magisterium, any notion that the former pope's thinking was at odds with that of the reigning one. It has been calculated that out of eighty pages, only eight were drafted by Bergoglio.[7] The few insertions do, however, bear progammatic significance, including the central affirmation that "one who believes may not be presumptuous. . . . Far from making us inflexible, the security of faith sets us on a journey; it enables witness and dialogue with all."[8]

Benedict XVI has facilitated this set of circumstances, unprecedented for the Catholic Church. On the day of his farewell, saluting the College of Cardinals for the last time, he had promised "unconditional reverence and obedience" to the successor whom they would choose.[9] Since then he has lived in seclusion in the former convent of Mater Ecclesiae in the southwest corner of Vatican City, going out on rare occasions to stay at Castel Gandolfo or to visit his brother at the Gemelli clinic. Friends such as Cardinal Gianfranco Ravasi, head of the Pontifical Council for Culture, call on Benedict in total discretion. His first venture onto the public stage since retirement was a letter of courteous criticism to the scientist Piergiorgio Odifreddi regarding the latter's views on Jesus.

Bergoglio considers Ratzinger a "fantastic old fellow." He said to an Argentine friend, "You can't imagine this man's humility and wisdom,"[10] and to reporters he has said that "it's like having a wise grandfather in the house." Benedict XVI responds similarly. "I am glad to be connected to Pope Francis by strongly coinciding views and cordial friendship," he confided in a letter to the theologian Hans Küng. "Today I see it as my sole and final task to support the new pontificate in prayer."[11]

The two confer, telephone one another, meet and take lunch together with absolute naturalness. Francis, who addresses his predecessor with the traditional papal honorific "Santità" ("Holiness" or, more formally, "Your Holiness"), even sent Ratzinger the first draft of his interview with La Civiltà Cattolica, requesting suggestions. He got back four pages of them. The Argentine pontiff has often said to his predecessor, "Holiness, receive guests, lead your own life."[12]

There is a water clock running on Francis's pontificate. The cardinals backing him know this well. "Basically it took John XXIII just five years to make the turn he imposed on the church irreversible," says one of them. The example supplies food for thought about the conditions necessary for a reform to start yielding fruit. Pope John's project—the Vatican II council—was brought safely into harbor because after him came the fifteen years of the Montini pontificate, during which Paul VI succeeding in implanting the conciliar message in the Catholic Church. But at Paul VI's back there was an active majority of bishops who had voted with conviction for the conciliar documents, there was a robust movement of reform-minded theologians, and there was a Catholic laity that had been aroused and mobilized by the event of the council.

Pope Francis, now in the third year of his pontificate, is still fairly isolated within the ecclesiastical structure. This explains his extraordinary determination. He enjoys ample backing among the laity and in agnostic and nonreligious sectors of public opinion, but a strong pro-Bergoglio party is not evident in the Roman Curia as this book is being written. Indeed, some denizens of those corridors hope that the Argentine pope will be a transitory exception.

There is not, in the universal church, an organized movement of supporters of his revolution. Waves of fervent applause are heard on all sides, and meanwhile one observes an extreme inertia within the church. The associations of Catholic laity have scarcely budged, as if his innovations have left them in a state of shock and they are still trying to digest them, whereas in John Paul II's time the presence and pressure of movements such as Opus Dei and Comunione e Liberazione, actively aligned with the Polish pope's program, were manifest. The Jesuits understandably support the pope discreetly, but certainly not in the combative and unyielding manner in which their nineteenth-century forebears promoted the dogma of infallibility and the absolutism of Pius IX and subsequently opposed modernism.

Satirical wit often intuits the underlying sense of a situation. The comedian Maurizio Crozza is a hit on YouTube with a skit featuring Francis plodding slowly along the Via Salaria at 7:00 a.m. carrying a refrigerator on his shoulders to give to a widow. "It's a good thing we got up at dawn," says the pope, staggering under the weight of his seventy-six-kilogram load, "it's beautiful. . . . What door do we deliver it to?" "Number 1321, Holiness," answers one of two splendidly dressed secretaries who don't lift a finger to help him. "And where are we now?" "Number 23, Holiness." A prostitute, groups of *ciellini* (members of Comunione e Liberazione), Roma football supporters, and two cardinals come along and ask him for photos and blessings. Nobody lends him a hand. The widow refuses the present because it is the wrong color. "It could have been worse," murmurs Francis as he sets off homeward.

To take action within a stratified and ponderous structure such as the Catholic Church is extremely complicated. A pope obtains virtually absolute obedience when he moves along the rails of tradition. But if he wants to effect change and reform, the number of ways large and small to place obstacles in his path is infinite. John XXIII encountered open and hidden resistance to his design for reform. The theologian-monk Enzo Bianchi regards the pontificate of Francis as a "second spring" but doesn't conceal his fear that high summer might never arrive. "The Lord preserve me from the vision of an unseasonable cold spell."[13] As the months pass, Bianchi has become convinced that the pope's adversaries will be counterattacking more and more.

As the months have passed, notes Professor Guzmán Carriquiry, a strong supporter of the pope, the tone of Francis's attackers has become more aggressive. There is a "systematic refusal" to heed him. "It is surprising how much they resemble the Pharisees and the doctors of the Law who followed Jesus, full of ill will, always prepared to put him to the test, always interpreting things in a bad light, hoping to catch him in the slightest deviation from the Law, in order to judge and condemn him."[14] Francis knows this full well. "They are making war on me," he confided during his third Easter in the Vatican.

The conservative forces are counting on the Argentine pope getting worn out and on people getting tired of hearing his repeated exhortations. They spread the fear that Francis is constructing "a different church," veering off the rails of tradition, doctrine, and the right interpretation of the word of God. "You are disconcerting us, and we no longer know where our own headquarters are and where the enemy front is," wrote Lucrecia Rego de Planas, the former director of the Spanish edition of *Catholic.net* in Mexico, to Francis. "I don't want shepherds that smell like the sheep," she continued, revealing the traditionalists' aggressiveness, "but sheep that don't smell of manure because their shepherd watches over them and keeps them clean all the time."

His critics inside the curia blame Francis for creating too many organs and committees, for operating too much on his own, for not concentrating on a handful of goals, for not voicing a coherent theological vision, for speaking too much, for pandering to the taste of the crowd by letting himself be photographed with a trained parrot or a child dressed up in a pope costume for carnival. There are those who are affronted, a curial cardinal confided, by the way Francis has diminished the "sacrality of the papal person." There is an ongoing drizzle of such taunts and pokes, and when Francis criticizes the culture of chatter and calumny in the curia, he is thinking of the saboteurs who murmur them under their breath. It is they who are hoping that this pontificate will be over quickly. "I want to die a Catholic, and I hope Bergoglio leaves his successor the chance to be a pope!" was the exasperated outburst from an anonymous monsignor hostile to the reforms. A handful of cardinals seized the occasion of a meeting with Benedict XVI to complain about "the confusion that now prevails in the Vatican."

Nor should one underestimate the inert opposition of all in the curia who can sense that stable expectations are wobbling and who worry about their own futures and their own roles. There are so many pockets of silent resistance. Along with priests and prelates who admire Francis, there are others who sardonically dismiss his words, especially when he talks about poverty. "At a time of economic crisis," admitted a Roman priest who works with the CEI, "we count as a sheltered category, and that poses a hard question to clerics. To what extent is every priest prepared to be coherent, to model his life on poverty, to go to the outskirts?"

The same question could be put to the bishops of the world: To what extent are they ready to change their profile as the aspect of the Roman papacy changes? The Vatican ecosystem will be the first to feel these shocks. A restructured and slimmed-down curia will mean a loss of power, influence, career prospects, and income for a certain class of ecclesiastical bureaucrats who have lived off it for centuries. It is no accident that the overall reform of the curia is taking a long time. Even reforming cardinals fear the destabilization of the "state" machinery that Paul VI created and John Paul II updated.

What the conservatives tend to hide from themselves is that the change of direction at the conclave of 2013 springs from a deep crisis of credibility into which the Catholic Church has sunk: the crisis of its communication with society, the long-standing crisis of the declining number of men willing to become priests and more recently of women willing to become nuns, the crisis in the church's relation to women and young people. Things are at an impasse. Francis emerged out of the increasing tension provoked, in the frank description of the geopolitical analyst Lucio Caracciolo, by a closed church "very romano-curial and hardly at all universal . . . governed by an introverted hierarchy stubbornly resistant to the signs of the times."[15] That is the reason for what Professor Guzmán Carriquiry, secretary of the Pontifical Committee for Latin America, called "the explosion of expectancy, joy, and hope" triggered by the Bergoglio pontificate.

Francis knows that he is traversing a terrain strewn with baited traps and improvised explosive devices. "Resistance is growing in the curia," admits one insider. Hostility to his vision of the church is also growing. "At times it is possible to detect genuine disdain for his public statements and for the ideas he expressed in his apostolic exhortation *Evangelii gaudium*," admits one highly placed Vatican theologian. The traditionalist hawks are becoming more aggressive, spreading poison against the pope's "incomprehensible, inopportune, aberrant" words. His public interventions have, in their eyes, "stripped sacrality, authority, and reverence" from the function of the vicar of Christ, bringing him down to the level of "the president of a religious multinational."[16] The Argentine pontiff sometimes reacts to such comments with humor, sometimes with brooding concern. "They scored a goal on me from center field," he commented when presented with a rigged shortlist of nominees for an appointment. Usually he is serene in the face of subterranean tension: "The demon is busy . . . we are on the right road."

He doesn't pretend not to see that the throng of those voicing approval includes many who do not in the least share some or most of his positions and whose transformation from Ratzingerians into Bergoglians is only skin deep. At mass with the new cardinals created in the consistory of February 2014, he warned them the Vatican was "not a royal court. May all of us avoid, and help others to avoid, habits and ways of acting typical of a court: intrigue, gossip, cliques, favoritism and partiality." He invited them to use the language of the Gospels as a disinfectant against simulated deferentiality: "Yes when we mean yes; no when we mean no."[17] At the conclusion of the ceremony, the pope addressed the crowd in St. Peter's Square, exhorting them to work for the "unity" of the church, uttering the word four times in a row. It was a signal of alarm.

The complexity of Francis's character contributes in a way to his isolation. The pope who encourages participation in the church, who was so *compañero* with his priests at Buenos Aires, and is so approachable by the laity guards his solitude in private. A Vatican personality who has known him for many years says: "It was written of Saint Ignatius that he maintained a 'cordial distance' vis-à-vis others. Jorge Mario Bergoglio is like that in a way. And it makes it hard for him to build a team around him."

Yet there exists in the vast universe of Catholicism a deposit of human resources favorable to Bergoglio's great reform, consisting of those bishops who in the twilight of the Ratzinger pontificate were anxiously awaiting a change of direction. The hints were there in the debate at the synod on the new evangelization that took place in October 2012, where courageous voices demanded that the church should "in all honesty undertake an examination of conscience on the way of living the faith," in the words of the president of the Latin American Episcopate, Carlos Aguiar Retes. The Filipino bishop José Palma urged that light be shed on "dark areas or failures," and his compatriot Socrates Villegas requested the hierarchy to avoid "arrogance, hypocrisy, and sectarianism," ceasing to cover up mistakes and punishing those who erred.

A diffuse need to change course was manifest across all geographical and cultural areas. Bishop Diarmuid Martin of Dublin recommended that the church not show contemporary society a countenance of "ideological aggression," and Cardinal Gianfranco Ravasi, the Vatican minister of culture, expressed hope for a "dialogue without arrogance" with science. The French bishop Dominique Rey expressed hope for a style of evangelism "not smothered by inertia, bureaucracy, or clericalism." The archbishop of Manila, Luis Antonio Tagle, admonished that among contemporaries witness should be borne to the face of Jesus "with humility, respect, and silence on the part of the church." Others stressed the need to regain credibility.[18]

Under the blanket of the Ratzinger pontificate, then, some bishops were showing their colors as precursors of the approach that the new pope would adopt, including a more "pastoral" lifestyle for priests and bishops and the importance of a new mode of communicating. The world of today and especially young people, remarked the Nigerian bishop Emmanuel Badejo, will no longer accept one-sided communication, and it falls to the church to overcome "the antiquated model of teacher and disciple or orator and listener."[19]

At the 2012 synod, energetic speeches on the theme of justice pointed to the church's primary task as that of fighting for human dignity and committing itself to the fight against "social inequality, violence, and injustice." On the role of women in the church, too, anticipatory voices were heard. One Canadian bishop demanded "the deliberate and systematic involvement of women in leadership positions at every level of church life," and the German bishop Franz-Joseph Bode went a step further, proposing that women be admitted to the diaconate.[20]

These men are allies of the pope, scattered throughout the dioceses of the universal church. The enterprise to which he has dedicated himself demands the awakening and mobilization of these energies. As he began the second year of his pontificate, Francis initiated the construction of a governing team. In the curia, he relied primarily on recruits from the Vatican diplomatic service. The career diplomats include the secretary of state, Pietro Parolin; the prefect of the Congregation for the Clergy, Beniamino Stella; the general secretary of the synod, Lorenzo Baldisseri (all three of whom he has made cardinals); Cardinal Santos Abril y Castelló, who was placed on the cardinalatial Committee of Vigilance over IOR; and the former foreign minister Jean-Louis Tauran, a member of the same body and of the committee investigating the IOR.

These are personalities who came up under Paul VI and his foreign minister Agostino Casaroli, later secretary of state under John Paul II. As a class, they are characterized by a nonsectarian religiosity, firmness on essential principles, and ductility in dealing with problems because they realize full well how pluralistic modern society is. Francis picked them out in the curia as best suited to carry out this phase of his plans for reform.

Before 2013 came to an end, the pope renewed the membership of the key Congregation for Bishops, whose task it is to select new bishops, follow the activities of the Episcopal Conferences, and in the last instance to check on the senior management of the Catholic Church around the world.[21] His exclusions raised eyebrows. The president of the CEI, Cardinal Bagnasco, is no longer a member of this important congregation, nor are three other cardinals of strongly conservative bent: the former prefect of the Congregation for the Clergy, Mauro Piacenza; the American Raymond Burke; and the Spaniard Antonio María Rouco Varela, former president of the Spanish Episcopal Conference and the man behind fervent mass demonstrations against the family legislation of the socialist prime minister José Luis Zapatero. The prefect of the Holy Office has also been excluded from the plenary session of the Congregation for Bishops—the first time this has happened.

The pope has instead placed his three new cardinals—Parolin, Stella, and Baldisseri—in the Congregation for Bishops, along with personalities open to reform, such as the Brazilian cardinal João Braz de Aviz, one of the most vocal critics of the curia during the preconclave debates; Gualterio Bassetti, the vice president of the CEI; the Englishman Vincent Nichols; and the Colombian Rubén Salazar Gómez, known for stating his readiness to recognize same-sex civil unions.[22]

Francis's goal is a new generation of bishops no longer chosen mainly because they are pliant or to balance the interests of competing factions but marked by their freedom of expression and their capacity to speak to humanity "adrift." He has asked the Congregation of Bishops to select bishops with authority and "broadness of horizons." In an address to the congregation's plenary session in February 2014, he said that the church "does not need apologists for her causes nor crusaders for her battles but rather humble and confident sowers of the truth."[23]

Thus, step by step Pope Francis has gone about placing his pawns on the chessboard. For the first meeting of the College of Cardinals in 2014 (20–21 February), with the question of the family and its corollary, the denial of communion for the divorced and remarried, on the agenda, the pope chose Cardinal Walter Kasper as rapporteur. The pope's position—"Every sin can be pardoned . . . it is unthinkable that someone falls into a black hole from which God cannot extract him"[24]—indicates the objective he has in mind: to set the church free of its inquisitorial obsession with sexual matters and personal relationships. "We need to accompany those persons who have failed in their love. We don't need to condemn but to walk with them," said the pope, looking ahead to the synod on the family.[25]

In creating sixteen new cardinals in February 2014 (three of them older than eighty, including Loris Capovilla, secretary of John XXIII), Francis intensified the process of globalization of the church. One is from Haiti, four from Latin America, two from Asia, and one from Canada. It has been calculated that within five or six years Francis will have renewed more than half of the conclave, leaving an electoral college even more globalized, in which the weight of Europe and Italy is destined to shrink. The future of Catholicism no longer lies in the old continent but among the masses of the third world. The pontiff has particularly strengthened the component from Latin America, where almost half the world's Catholics live. The bishops of Buenos Aires, Rio de Janeiro, Santiago de Chile, and Managua have been made cardinals.

Equally significant is the list of those who were not elevated to the purple, among them Rino Fisichella, president of the Pontifical Council for Promoting the New Evangelization created by Benedict XVI. His exclusion strikes at the ideological and doctrinaire Ratzinger line, the opposite of the conception of the church as a "field hospital" taking in the wounded of our time promoted by Francis. The overall reform of the curia places a question mark over the future existence of Fisichella's congregation. Pope Francis is now carrying out the new evangelization in person with his daily interventions. For example, in the Sistine Chapel, the heart of papal symbolism, he baptized the child of a Catholic couple whose marriage is only civil.

Observers marveled that the archbishop of Turin, Cesare Nosiglia (backed by Ruini), and the patriarch of Venice Francesco Moraglia (backed by Bertone) were not made cardinals. This decision signals a change of direction. Turin and Venice are well known as cardinalatial sees, but in Pope Francis's eyes certain prestigious dioceses are no longer automatic guarantees of career advancement. Bergoglio "aims to undermine the game of factions competing to place their members" in important dioceses to ensure a purple hat, observed Luigi Accat-toli, an experienced connoisseur of the ecclesiastical world.[26]

Francis sent the incoming cardinals a letter to remind them that the cardinalate is not a promotion, an honor, or a decoration but simply a service and to invite them therefore to deny themselves "any celebra-tion alien to the evangelical spirit of austerity, moderation and pov-erty."[27] The Bavarian admirers of their new cardinal, Gerhard Müller, took the pope at his word, bringing bottles of Regensburg beer to the austere and venerable courtyard of the Holy Office and organizing there a simple and down-to-earth festive meal, driving away the phan-toms of the Inquisition with the odor of grilled sausages.

With his further nomination of cardinals in February 2015 Francis raised the profile of the southern hemisphere. Only one member of the Roman Curia received the red beret; the bulk of the nominees came from Latin America, Africa, Asia, and Oceania. No new cardi-nal was created from the United States, but Tonga Island now has a cardinal. In the next conclave, Europe will no longer have the major-ity of votes.

Quite unexpectedly there arrived on Pope Francis's desk in Febru-ary 2014 a severe admonition from the UN Committee for the Rights of the Child. After hearing from a Vatican delegation, the committee published a report requesting the Vatican to shed unsparing light on past crimes of sexual abuse and on the practice of transferring offend-ing priests from one parish to another. The document also urged the creation of agencies at every institutional level of the Catholic Church to protect minors and receive denunciations so that all those suspected of or responsible for abuse would be removed, without exception. The UN body recommended the obligatory reporting of denunciations to the authorities and, for the first time, an investiga-tion into the children of priests, who almost never know who their real father is.[28]

The Holy See protested because the report also touched on the questions of abortion, contraception, and the decriminalization of homosexuality, and gave insufficient weight to Benedict XVI's mea culpa in 2010, the operational measures taken by the ecclesiastical hierarchy in a number of countries, and the stiffening of the canoni-cal penalties at the behest of Benedict and Francis. It complained that the document had been drafted under pressure from nongovernmental organizations hostile to the church and that the committee had exceeded its terms of reference, interfering "with the doctrinal and moral positions of the Catholic Church."[29]

Still, self-justification apart, the Vatican spokesman Federico Lombardi did offer assurance that the Vatican will not refuse to engage with the UN committee and will be "receptive to justified criticism."[30] The UN Committee on Torture subsequently reminded the Vatican of its duty to ensure that all the victims of sexual violence will be indemnified. Pope Francis knew that the sexual abuse scandals that had bedeviled Ratzinger's reign could not be allowed to explode again on his watch. Already in December 2013, the privy council of cardinals had raised the prospect of creating a special commission for the protection of minors from abuse, supplying aid to victims, and finding ways to cooperate with the state authorities.

One the eve of Lent 2014, the editors of the *National Catholic Reporter*, the U.S. periodical that has followed with accuracy and honesty the scandal of clerical pedophilia and cover-ups since 1985, addressed an open letter to the pontiff, requesting him to wash the feet, on the upcoming Holy Thursday, of "those whose lives have been shattered by abusive priests." They acknowledged that "the church has done probably more than any other institution to institute norms and procedures for preventing abuse in the future." But, they went on, "for decades, church leaders denied that there was any problem; they lied about the numbers of people involved and fought, at enormous expense, disclosure of the dimensions of the problem. Not one of them has yet been held to account."[31] The pope's response on 22 March 2014 was to create a Vatican antiabuse committee headed by Cardinal O'Malley of Boston and including four men and four women, among them the Argentine Jesuit Humberto Miguel Yanez and a celebrated abuse survivor, the combative Irishwoman Marie Collins, who was raped by a priest at age thirteen. In July 2014, Pope Francis received six victims at the Vatican; they came from Germany, Ireland, and Britain, and he spent around half an hour speaking privately to each of them. During the mass celebrated on their behalf in Santa Marta, Francis emphasized a concept hitherto overlooked in the Vatican: accountability. Promising zero tolerance, the pope stressed that bishops have a duty to ensure the protection of minors, and "they will be held responsible discharging it."

As the months of the Bergoglio papacy passed, a sword of Damocles appeared to be dangling over the Vatican: the matter of the Polish archbishop and nuncio Józef Wesolowski, who was under investigation in the Dominican Republic for having sexually abused shoeshine boys he picked up along the waterfront promenade in the capital, Santo Domingo. The accusations were so specific that Pope Francis recalled Wesolowski to Rome in August 2013—an action that, in the eyes of many, amounted to spiriting him away to safety. But as events have shown, the Argentine pope was actually ruling with an iron fist.

In June 2014, Wesolowski stood trial before the Congregation for the Doctrine of the Faith, which stripped him of his functions and his clerical status. But Pope Francis did not stop there. Two months later, on 23 September 2014, the seventy-six-year-old former nuncio, who was living in a Roman convent and moving freely about the city, was summoned to the Vatican and arrested by the papal gendarmerie. The prosecutor for the papal state (whose official title is "promoter of justice") placed Wesolowski under house arrest in the Vatican palace occupied by the court and the gendarmerie, assigned him an official advocate, and notified him that he was to face criminal trial for sexual abuse and possession of child pornography (one hundred thousand videos and photographs of minors had been found on his computer).

The arrest, Father Lombardi stated, had taken place "at the express wish of the pope, so that a case this serious and sensitive may be dealt with speedily, with the just and necessary rigor, and with the institutions of the Holy See assuming their full responsibility."

In the Vatican, the shock was enormous. Never before had an archbishop been arrested within the papal state and made to stand criminal trial for sexual abuse. Pope Ratzinger, who had reduced no less than 884 priests to lay status for the abuse of minors during his pontificate, had always given bishops guilty of such offences the soft option of resigning discreetly. Even when faced with the crimes committed by Marcial Maciel, the founder of the Legionaries of Christ, whose victims had included young seminarians and one of his own offspring, Benedict XVI decided not to subject Maciel to a trial under canon law, "in light of the advanced age of the reverend Maciel and his poor health" (as the Vatican press office put it in an official communiqué of May 19, 2006). Maciel's sole punishment was forced withdrawal from public activity into a life of prayer; the protests of his victims went unheeded. Only after Maciel's death did Benedict XVI authorize a communiqué acknowledging his crimes, his immorality, and his "life without scruples or authentic religious sentiment."

And for that matter, in the case of the former archbishop of Boston, Cardinal Bernard Law—forced to resign for failing to publicly expose the pedophile priests in his diocese—John Paul II summoned him to Rome in 2004 and named him archpriest of the Basilica of Santa Maria Maggiore in order to keep him from having to appear in court in the United States.

Francis's decision to launch a criminal trial in the Vatican against a man with the status of archbishop and nuncio therefore marks an open break with the past. In 2013, he had already defrocked and stripped of his functions the auxiliary bishop of Ayacucho, the Peruvian Gabino Miranda Melgarejo. If a priest abuses a child, said the pope while returning from the Holy Land in May 2014, it is like celebrating a black mass. And he used the occasion to let journalists know that "there are three bishops under investigation."

Father Lombardi foresees that the criminal trial of Józef Wesolowski will take place during 2015. The whole affair has generated strong resentment in those sectors of the Roman Curia and the Catholic hierarchy accustomed for centuries to protect the ecclesiastical institution at any cost by stonewalling. The sociologist Mauro Magatti, a faculty member at the Catholic University of Milan and director of the Center for the Anthropology of Religion and Cultural Change, expresses the fear that they may succeed in isolating Francis—and the countervailing hope "that the clergy and the hierarchy will stand beside him" as he pursues this imposition of zero tolerance.

Not much is really known of the inner life of the man who is revolutionizing the Catholic Church. Every day he achieves greater media visibility as a potent figure, whom even nonbelievers instinctively recognize as a bearer of hope and humanity. His sayings are on everyone's lips. His smiling and determined face, his right hand raised in salutation, fills television screens. In Borgo Pio, close to the Vatican, there appeared a mural (later erased) depicting him as Superman in flight with a suitcase labeled "values." The U.S. magazine for gays *The Advocate* proclaimed him personality of the year, and *Rolling Stone* put him on its cover along with Bob Dylan's lyric, "the times they are a-changing." *Fortune* put him first on a list of the fifty most influential leaders on the planet. He has been the object of a book of drawings, a weekly publication entitled *Il mio papa*, and children's books entitled *Il Papa racconta ai ragazzi* (The Pope tells stories to children) and *Il nostro amico Jorge* (Our friend Jorge). A Salvadoran nun who unexpectedly gave birth to a child at Rieti proudly named him Francesco.

But his inner dimension eludes many. "Mario Bergoglio, priest," was how he liked to call himself before ascending the throne of Saint Peter. He was capable of spending a whole night confessing and regrets not being able to do so now. Prayer fills much of his life. He gets up at around 4:30 or 5:00 a.m. and meditates on scripture before celebrating mass. He recites the rosary in the afternoon and in the evening dedicates an hour to adoration of the Eucharist. His prayer deals with encounters, speeches, signals from his daily experience. "He is full of faces and names," say his friend Victor Manuel Fernández, rector of the Catholic University of Buenos Aires.[32] While praying, the pope has told his close friends, he often finds the solution to decisions he must make. There is a little room in the Santa Marta residence where the pope retires to pray before a statue of St. Joseph asleep; underneath it he slides the supplicatory notes sent him by the faithful.

His morning mass at Santa Marta before groups of the faithful—not selected guests, as with John Paul II—arises from his need to maintain direct contact, as a priest, with the people of God, around the Eucharist. When he enters the chapel dressed in his vestments, recognizable only by the white skull cap, one observes physically that Francis is reinterpreting his papal role as priest and witness of the gospel directed to humanity. Since his election, Francis has addressed not a category—faithful Catholics—but all the men and women of our time.

The rite at Santa Marta concentrates on the bare essentials, with long moments of silence and reflection. After he gives a brief homily or "morning meditation," Francis sits pondering silently in his chair while the Eucharist is distributed. He continues to observe silence after the communion. At the conclusion of the mass, he goes to sit in the pews for another meditative pause.

Within the restricted confines of the chapel, Bergoglio's strong spirituality stands out, a side of him less visible to the public. During the consecration, when he holds the host aloft, Pope Francis gazes at it with extraordinary intensity. His surroundings vanish, leaving only the white wafer upon which he appears to concentrate totally. The faithful in attendance feel the sense of the absolute that pervades the space. In that stark moment of concentration, which recurs when Francis fixes his gaze on the raised chalice, the pope might be anywhere—celebrating the Eucharist in the desert, like Teilhard de Chardin, or in a twentieth-century concentration camp.

There is a grave and serious dimension to Bergoglio, known to few but legible on his features when, celebrating the mass before large audiences, he abandons for a moment his public role, and his expression grows thoughtful and veiled with concern. It is as though in his mind's eye he is beholding the tragic aspect of life. Friedrich Hölderlin, the German poet he loves best, describes humanity in pain as

> Like water from cliff-top
> To cliff-top abounding
> Down through all the years to the dark.[33]

On the eve of his ordination as a priest, the thirty-three-year-old Bergoglio wrote in one of his prayers: "*I want* to believe in God the Father, who loves me like a son." At heart, his model seems to be one of the first companions of Ignacio de Loyola, Pierre Favre (St. Peter Faber, S.J.), who came from a peasant family and whom Francis himself canonized in December 2013. These are the qualities in Favre that Francis admires: "[His] dialogue with all, even the most remote and even with his opponents; his simple piety, a certain naïveté perhaps, his being available straightaway, his careful interior discernment, the fact that he was a man capable of great and strong decisions but also capable of being so gentle and loving."[34]

Francis is not someone who is always looking for the sunny side; he is free of superficial optimism. He is strongly aware of the ills and sins of the world, of the failings and errors that torment him like any other Christian. He has spoken of the devil ever since becoming pope. Evil is not an abstract concept for him; it is an active principle that corrodes the positive capacities of the person. When Jesus casts the devil out of a man possessed, he exclaimed one morning at mass in Santa Marta, it is not enough to say, as certain priests do, that he cured the man of a psychiatric disturbance. "We are not entitled to make it that simple." The passage from Luke's Gospel led him to suggest to the faithful that they undertake a serious examination of conscience. "Do I watch over myself? Over my heart? Over my feelings? Over my thoughts? Do I safeguard the presence of the Holy Spirit in me?"[35] The devil, he emphasized in his first meeting with the cardinals after his election, disseminates "pessimism, bitterness, discouragement." The pope has threatened members of the Mafia with the torments of hell: "That is what awaits you, if you continue on this road."

In recent decades, Francis has never exhibited his character as a Jesuit, although the reference to the depression caused by the devil is typical of St. Ignatius of Loyola. The aspect of Jesuit spirituality most characteristic of Francis is his "discernment": attentiveness in taking in and assessing "things great and small" in order to distinguish the signs of the Lord in daily reality and to follow in his footsteps.

Though Francis has a program, he in reality does not know the destination at which he will arrive. And although he is engaged in an enormous effort to reshape the Catholic Church, he does not pretend to determine the exact form it will assume in the end. "Being able to do the little things of every day with a big heart open to God and to others . . . inside large horizons" is the compass heading he steers by.[36]

Against those who think that change and reform can take place quickly, Francis objects that it takes time to prepare authentic change. It takes time to read "the signs of the times" is how the fathers of Vatican II would have put it. "Listening to the things that happen, the feeling of the people, especially the poor," is how Bergoglio puts it.[37]

This is the wellspring of the sense of calm that pervades him as he labors without pause—no vacations, no outdoors excursions like Wojtyla or regular strolls through the Vatican gardens like Ratzinger—to lay the basis for a renewed church. Francis arrived at the end of the first year of his pontificate with his face marked by fatigue. At times, his eyes are swollen with tiredness, and moments of weakness occasionally overcome him. "There is a lot of work, but I am content," he confided to an Argentine acquaintance who came to greet him. "Remember me," he added. To guard his health, he has cut back on his morning masses with the faithful at Santa Marta, no longer celebrating the rite on Wednesdays, Saturdays, or Sundays. But when he was still back in Buenos Aires and his auxiliary bishops were urging him to take a break for a couple of weeks, he listened with a frown and then responded vigorously: "And now why don't you all go to the devil?"

Francis is not unaware of the invisible water clock placed alongside his papal seat, but he carries on without being obsessed by immediate results. The church of the third millennium he has in mind is no longer monarchical but inspired by participation, a "harmony of differences." The model is no longer the pyramid or even the sphere, where all is uniform and every point is equal to every other. His model, he has explained, is "the polyhedron, which reflects the convergence of all its parts, each of which preserves its distinctiveness." It is a configuration that protects the individuality of each and in which, as he likes to stress, "even people who can be considered dubious on account of their errors have something to offer which must not be overlooked."[38]

It is impossible for one man to modify the church on his own. Francis is not isolated in terms of support: the enthusiasm of the laity for him is enormous—around 87 percent worldwide, 90 percent in Europe, 99 percent in Italy[39]—but the corps of ecclesiastics at whose head he stands has left him isolated, dragging their feet in the rear while he is out in front, leading the advance.

The Synod of Bishops in October 2014 was the first occasion on which the "Bergoglio line," which envisions the church as a field hospital dedicated to healing the existential hurts of the men and women of the early twenty-first century rather than promulgating anathemas grounded in abstract doctrine, was subjected to a real stress test.

As the day of the opening ceremonies drew near, the prevailing atmosphere was one of apparent optimism. The pontiff had uttered a reminder that "so many wounded people are asking of us what they asked of Jesus: closenessness, proximity"—the things that scribes, doctors of the law, and pharisees were unable to give them. In St. Peter's, Francis married twenty couples and gave them his solemn blessing; they included cohabiting partners and ones with a child from a previous marriage. The secretary-general of the synod, Cardinal Lorenzo Baldisseri, stated that "there is a door that has hitherto remained shut and that the pope wishes to open." *Avvenire*, the newspaper of the Italian bishops, forecast that the worldwide survey preceding the synod, in which once taboo questions such as communion for divorced and remarried persons, same-sex unions, and homosexual couples as parents of small children were broached, strengthened the likelihood that "certain pastoral practices may be reviewed."

In reality, starting with the consistory of February 2014 at which Cardinal Kasper had outlined the possibility of a penitential procedure that would make it possible to grant the Eucharist to remarried Catholics, opposition to the Argentine pope's strategy of compassion had begun to coalesce. On that occasion, according to the former president of the CEI, Cardinal Camillo Ruini, 85 percent of the cardinals present had reacted negatively.[40]

On the eve of the episcopal synod of October 2014, the opposition emerged into the open. Five cardinals, four of them from inside the Roman Curia, made their refusal public in a book entitled *Permanere nella verità di Cristo* (To remain in the truth of Christ). They emphasized that they were "united in firmly maintaining that the New Testament portrays Christ unambiguously prohibiting divorce and remarriage."[41]

Not since Vatican II had such a bold gesture been carried out. The five authors were anything but obscure: Gerhard Ludwig Müller, prefect of the Congregation for the Doctrine of the Faith; Raymond Burke, prefect of the the the Segnatura Apostolica, the Vatican equivalent of a high court of appeal; Carlo Caffarra, archbishop of Bologna; Velasio De Paolis, former president of the Prefecture for Economic Affairs; and Walter Brandmüller, former president of the Vatican Committee on the Historical Sciences. George Pell, a member of Pope Francis's privy council, was quick to side with them. Other sympathizers included Cardinals Angelo Scola of Milan, Thomas Collins of Toronto, and Marc Ouellet of Quebec, prefect of the Congregation of Bishops.

The stance of two important electors of Bergoglio at the conclave of 2013, Cardinal Timothy Dolan of the United States and Cardinal Sean O'Malley, was softer but substantially negative. "I do not see how there could be a radical shift (with respect to the divorced and remarried) without running counter to the church's teachings," said Dolan. O'Malley for his part had stated following the consistory in February that he could find "no theological justification" for change. Monsignor Georg Gänswein, Ratzinger's secretary, subsequently spoke up as well to stress that Catholics who chose to remarry were contradicting "what the Lord set down."

In opening the 2014 synod, Francis sent two signals. At the inaugural mass on 5 October, he spoke of "bad shepherds [who] load crushing burdens onto the shoulders of folk without lifting a finger to help them bear it." The next day, launching the sessions with the intention of transforming the synod into an instrument of collegiality, he urged participants to speak clearly and freely, "without trepidation" and without keeping silent for fear that the pope might "have a different outlook."

But the synodal fathers' freedom to speak out was offset by an unexpected blackout on the reporting of what it was they actually said. For more than forty years, the practice has been to supply the press with summaries of the speeches delivered by the bishops during synods, making it possible to track the course the assembly was taking on a daily basis. This time the secretary of the synod suspended that custom, and reporters were given briefings in which the identities of the speakers were suppressed. Paradoxically, it was Müller, the head of the Holy Office, who emerged as the champion of press freedom on this occasion, stating that "all Christians have the right to be informed about the statements of the bishops."

At the conclusion of the first week of general debates, the document *Relatio post disceptationem* (Report following the initial discussion, or, more informally, Interim report), written under the aegis of the general rapporteur, the Hungarian cardinal Péter Erdö, but in essence drafted by bishop Bruno Forte, special secretary of the synod, drew gasps of astonishment. The style, the substance, and the terminology of this interim report appeared to herald a new dawn in the way the church deals with the intimate lives of couples and varying sexual orientation.

Never before had anyone read in a document issuing from the ecclesiastical hierarchy a sentence such as this: "Homosexual persons have gifts and qualities to bring to the Christian community." It was the response to a question phrased this way: "Are we able to welcome these persons, guaranteeing them a fraternal space, in our communities?" Never before had there been such frank acceptance of the value of the homosexual couple as that seen in this passage: "While acknowledging the moral problems arising from homosexual unions, let it be noted that there are cases in which mutual support to the point of self-sacrifice constitutes a precious underpinning for the lives of the partners."[42]

At a press conference, the Filipino cardinal Luis Antonio Tagle (seen by some as a successor to Francis on the throne of Peter) related that while the debate was under way in the assembly, more than one participant felt the touch of "the spirit of the council" and of the pastoral constitution *Gaudium et spes*. "The image summoned up was that of a church not self-absorbed but heedful and engaged in dialogue with the contemporary world," was how Tagle put it.

The novel emphases contained in the *Relatio post disceptationem* of Monday, 13 October 2014, were remarkable. While acknowledging the stance of the opponents of change, it evoked the hypothesis of a "penitential path," at the conclusion of which divorced and remarried Catholics would be able to take communion. There was also an invitation to recognize the "constructive elements" inherent in civil marriage and cohabitation. Even in de facto unions, said the report, "it is possible to recognize authentic family values." Last, special attention was given to children living in families with same-sex parents—a family structure nowhere defamed or discredited in the document. It was a farewell to the stance of Wojtyla and Ratzinger, whose "nonnegotiable principles" are nowhere mentioned.

Nor was there even any mention of the concept of "natural law." On the contrary, the report presses the church to confront the whole theme of sexuality in the manner proposed by Cardinal Carlo Maria Martini a quarter of a century earlier. It uses concrete language: "The homosexual question compels us to a series of reflections about how to work out realistic pathways of affective growth and human and evangelical maturity, integrating the sexual dimension."

Within twenty-four hours, it seemed as if the document had been a mirage. Significant aspects of it were attacked by the conservatives, and it was revealed that the innovators were not a consistent majority. Those in a position to read all the draft versions of the speeches the bishops had sent to Rome prior to the synod stated that only four or five dealt with the topic of homosexual couples, which for that matter had not bulked large in the debates themselves either. From this perspective, the report had forced the issue. "It was a surprise," recalls one participant in the synod. As for communion for the divorced and remarried, opinion in the assembly had been more sharply polarized than the report allowed its readers to understand.

The conservatives struck back hard. Cardinal Müller rejected the overtures to change, commenting icily to reporters: "I am no longer part of the team in charge." The president of the Polish Episcopal Conference, Archbishop Stanislaw Gadecki, maintained: "This distances us from the teaching of John Paul II. In the report there are discernible traces of an antimatrimonial ideology." Cardinal Burke made the accusation that in the Vatican press room briefings "information is manipulated so as to highlight just one point of view, instead of faithfully relaying the various positions. A good many bishops do not accept the ideas of overture, but few people know this." Another critic was the South African cardinal Wilfrid Fox Napier, who requested emendations to the text. Within the African Episcopate especially, any suggestion of reassessing homosexuality is unwelcome. Indeed, Africans complain that the Western nations often make economic assistance conditional on the passage of pro-gay legislation.

The curial cardinal Robert Sarah, originally from Guinea and president of the Pontifical Council Cor Unum for Human and Christian Development, insisted that homosexual unions are a "gravely deviant form of sexuality" and denounced the attempt to bring the church to change its doctrine. Cardinal Ruini simultaneously put into circulation a text in which he drew attention to the apostolic exhortation of Pope Wojtyla *Familiaris consortio,* with its stress on "the practice, grounded in holy scripture, of not admitting to eucharistic communion those divorced and remarried." To be able to take the wafer, they must promise "to live in total chastity." It was an attempt to play the John Paul II card against Pope Francis.

Cardinal Fernando Filoni, too, a veteran Vatican diplomat and prefect of the Congregation for the Evangelization of Peoples, declared that a text such as the *Relatio post disceptationem* "would not receive my vote: it has to be modified and toned down in some respects." The newspaper *Il Foglio*, which has spearheaded ultraconservative revanchism in Italy since the election of Pope Francis, urged "resistance to this heretical tendency," lamenting that the *Relatio* contradicts both the Gospel and the catechism, robbing "the natural and divine order" of its value.

Faced with this tempest, the Vatican press room was forced to state that the report on the general debate was no more than a working document. At the same time, it put out a new version of the English translation of the paragraph dealing with the acceptance of homosexual persons. Where the text in Italian (the official language of the synod) spoke of "accepting," the English translation spoke of "caring for" gays.

Among the few persons who publicly stood up to this onslaught was Cardinal Christoph Schönborn, who praised the way ("marvelous, humanly and Christianly") in which two Viennese gay men known to him had supported one another during one's grave illness. Another was the president of the German Episcopal Conference, Reinhard Marx, according to whom it is impossible to say to someone, "'You are homosexual, you can't live the Gospel.' For me that is unthinkable." Cardinal Kasper had already stated, in an interview prior to the synod, that although absolutely impossible to equate to marriage, "homosexual unions, if lived in a stable and responsible manner, are to be respected."

During the second week of the synod, the discussion in the ten language-based working groups torpedoed and sank the most advanced formulations in the *Relatio* despite the interest they had aroused in public opinion. The synod's final document, which the pope published immediately, along with a breakdown of the votes cast for and against each proposition, is ambivalent.

Francis has opened a breach, exposing topics once taboo to unprecedentedly free debate. The synod acknowledges "valid elements" in human bonds that do not conform to Christian matrimony. The bishops assert that the church directs a loving gaze on those who "have entered into civil marriage, who are divorced and remarried, or who simply cohabit" since—a theologically important point—"the grace of God operates in their lives too" when partners take loving care of one another and tend to their offspring with affection and responsibility. The bishops also urge great respect for the divorced and remarried, who should be brought into parish life, "shunning any language or attitude that would cause them to feel discriminated." A way is opened for reforming the legal procedure by which Catholic marriage may be nullified, making nullification quicker and possibly free. Francis has already pushed this reform toward realization, creating an ad hoc committee even prior to the synod.

In the synod, all the paragraphs of the final document were approved by a majority of two-thirds. Only three—those dealing with communion for the divorced and remarried and with the homosexual question—failed to reach a quorum. The one on which the fewest participants voted (104 out of 183) is the one dealing with the penitential path leading to communion for remarried Catholics. There was hardly any greater degree of support for "further study" of the problem. In comparison to the interim *Relatio*, the assembly of bishops went into reverse gear on recognition of the value of life in a homosexual couple. The conservatives imposed a form of words that comes to a halt exactly where Cardinal Ratzinger drew the line when he was in charge of the Holy Office: respect and nondiscrimination for individuals, no concern for same-sex couples, and so implicit denigration of gay sexuality (which the 1992 declaration of the Congregation for the Doctrine of the Faith calls a "moral disorder"). Among the 62 votes against the very restrictive text of the paragraph on the homosexual question (out of a total of just 118 voters) are to be found many bishops of a reformist bent.

The experience of Vatican II, with all the fierce debate and adversarial dissension that attended it, serves as a reminder that in the Catholic Church it takes a long time to introduce a change of direction. That assembly existed as an institution for three years, and it took a lot of hard and patient work by Pope Paul VI to achieve the wide majorities of votes by which its texts were approved; the assenting voters at the time even included Bishop Marcel Lefebvre, later a notorious scismatic. Hence, this assessment by Bishop Joseph Kurtz, president of the American Episcopate, carries weight: "Francis was wise to establish a time frame of two years. As of right now we would not be prepared to take bold steps."

Apart from anything else, the episcopal synod of 2014 highlighted a wide range of approaches to family life. In many parts of Africa and Asia, the main concern of bishops is not so much individual decisions to divorce and remarry as things like the persistence of polygamy, arranged marriages, violence within families, and irregular situations caused by extreme poverty. One factor that made the synodal fathers hesitant to innovate was fearfulness at the prospect of suddenly overturning doctrinal positions that had stood rock solid for centuries. It is an attitude captured perfectly in a confidential remark made by Paul VI to the French philosopher Jean Guitton in relation to the ban on contraception: "An attenuation of the law would have the effect of bringing morality into doubt, and above all, showing that the church is fallible."

For the duration of the synod, and notwithstanding the tensions that burst forth in public, the Argentine pope retained his composure. Every day he showed up at the sessions with no special pomp, followed the debates attentively, went to the bar with the bishops to take coffee or a cold drink, and chatted with all and sundry—though it is true he was often seen scribbling notes to the general secretary of the gathering, Cardinal Lorenzo Baldisseri.

Francis believes firmly that debate needs to blossom within the church at every level and that bishops have to grow comfortable with the process of playing a part in formulating the strategic decisions the papacy must take on behalf of the institution. As the synod began, he gave an interview to the Argentine daily *La Nación* that included this forecast: "It will be a long synod, lasting a year probably. All I am doing is getting it under way. I was rapporteur for the synod of 2001, and there was a cardinal who instructed us as to what we could discuss and what we couldn't. That won't happen this time."

Francis's tranquility has been aided by the stance of absolute neutrality adopted by Joseph Ratzinger, despite a flutter of rumor to the effect that the most aggressive conservatives were trying to involve the pope emeritus in the opposition to his successor. In personal terms,

Francis is already out in front. In April 2014—according to testimony that has not been denied—he spoke on the telephone to a woman in Buenos Aires who had entered into civic marriage with a divorced Catholic and advised her to "go and take communion in another parish if the priest in your parish is withholding it." And in any case, as archbishop he was already encouraging the priests in his diocese to share the communion wafer with persons remarried or cohabiting.[43]

In retrospect, the first synod of the Catholic Church on the topic of family life—its participants including the presidents of 193 Episcopal Conferences, 23 representatives of the Oriental churches, and 25 heads of the dicasteries of the Roman Curia—revealed a pontiff with minority support inside the Vatican power structure and insufficient backing (to date) in the national episcopates. The synod of 1980—made up of bishops chosen by Paul VI still marked by the postcouncil ethos— had been more daring when on the topic of divorce and communion it had requested John Paul II by a large majority to study the system used in the Orthodox churches, where remarriage is accepted. The Polish pope, flanked by Ratzinger's Congregation for the Doctrine of the Faith, had ignored the proposal.

In certain respects, Francis has emerged more isolated within the ecclesiastical hierarchy than one might have foreseen. A comment from Cardinal Müller illustrates the irreducible nature of the clash at the highest levels of Catholicism. The image of the field hospital, he said, is a fetching one, but "the Church is not per se a health care facility; it is the house of the Lord" with its own divine laws.[44]

Perhaps this is why the pope, in celebrating the conclusion of the synod with a mass of beatification for Paul VI, evoked a God "who does not fear novelty! . . . who continually surprises us . . . leading us down unforeseen pathways." Still, ever since the conclusion of the first synod on the family, a section of the Curia has been gearing up for a showdown between Catholic conservatives and Catholic reformers at the upcoming synod of October 2015.

In the meantime, the pontiff understands how important it is to lower the average age of the clergy in the dioceses and above all in the Roman Curia to make room for personalities of a more open kind. Paul VI did exactly the same thing when, in order to gradually replace the bishops chosen by Pius XII, he ruled, for the first time in the history of the church, that diocesan bishops must retire at age seventy-five.

The new norms introduced by Pope Francis in November 2014 raise the pressure on bishops to retire upon reaching their seventy-fifth birthday. And it makes the same birthday the compulsory age of retirement both for cardinals who are heads of Roman dicasteries and cardinals holding a post by papal appointment. In particular cases, the pontiff reserves the right to ask any bishop to retire early after having "attentively listened to what he has to say, in fraternal dialogue."[45]

The first cardinal to be removed from the curia after the synod of October 2014 was Raymond Burke, age sixty-six, the spearhead of the conservative bloc. Francis stripped him of his role as prefect of the Segnatura Apostolica, the church's highest court, and made him patron of the Sovereign Military Order of Malta. A few days after the conclusion of the synod, Burke commented, "At this very critical moment, there is a strong sense that the church is like a ship without a rudder."

No revolution is painless, opposition always arises from within the ranks. Francis tastes weariness and concealed frustration every day. In November 2014, the Italian Episcopal Conference (CEI) startled public opinion by rejecting the candidacy of the bishop and theologian Bruno Forte for the position of vice president, whom the pope had personally selected as special secretary of the synod that had just ended. It was a move to undermine his role at the upcoming synod on the family in October 2015 and a sign of the influence of the Italian cardinals Scola, Ruini, and Caffarra, all of them opposed to granting communion to divorced and remarried Catholics. Nevertheless, the pope continues like an "unstoppable torrent," says Cardinal Leonardo Sandri, who marvels at the way Francis's drive has actually increased since leaving Buenos Aires. The extraordinary way in which he is tuned in to the laity is Pope Francis's shield against the criticism and the tacit sabotage coming from the ecclesiastical establishment. "This pontificate will yield many surprises," foresees Cardinal Tauran, who announced the results of the election that famous evening of 13 March 2013. "Francis has much courage and great spiritual resources."

He is not frightened by the terrorist threats of the ISIS "caliphate," which has stated its wish to "conquer Rome and break the crosses."

Habib al Sadr, the Iraqi ambassador to the Holy See, takes the view that "the pope is a target." Heightened security measures have been adopted in the Vatican, yet Francis seems unruffled in the face of danger, no matter what quarter it comes from. Juan Carlos Molina, an Argentine priest and an opponent of the drug trade, visited Francis, with whom he uses the informal "tu," at Santa Marta in November 2014. Molina said to him confidentially: "You are in a dangerous position. Watch out, they might kill you." Francis replied: "It is the best thing that could happen to me or to you."[46]

An example of the surprises the Argentine pope is capable of springing occurred on the second anniversary of his election. Francis announced an extraordinary Jubilee year to last from 8 December 2015 to 20 November 2016. In light of the resistance of part of the ecclesiastical hierarchy to his new pastoral approach, the Jubilee — deliberately scheduled to begin in the wake of the synod of October 2015 — will emphasize the key concept of Francis's pontificate: mercy.

In contrast to those whom he calls "the doctrinaires," the pope continues to proclaim a vision of a church that "flings its doors wide open" to sinners. He repeats the message tirelessly: "The way of the church is not to condemn anyone forever."[47] Nobody must be shut out from the mercy of God, he declared in announcing the Jubilee. In the bull indicting the Holy Year, he explicity rejected the tendency to fall back into legalism.[48]

Francis knows that the church cannot stand still or turn in on itself. In that case, he often says, "it falls ill." The church is a preserve of "old and tottering" structures that demand renovation, he has declared.[49] Hence, the pope intends to reawaken the same spirit of *aggiornamento*, "bringing up to date," in Catholicism that the council awakened in the 1960s. There are those who want to stifle the divine afflatus that inspired Vatican II and that still wafts forth, he has warned. Francis often invokes the assistance of the celestial breath in his undertaking. The Holy Spirit impels the church forward, but "this annoys some," he has said.[50]

Francis began the second year of his pontificate under the sign of the council, celebrating the canonization of John XXIII, who launched the great assembly destined to alter the face of the church, and of John Paul II, who did not recoil from announcing the faith in the era of secularization. Under the sign of ecumenism, Francis met with the heads of the Christian churches as the culminating moment of his voyage to the Holy Land in May 2014.

The pontiff who came from the ends of the earth is resolved to push on, transforming the Synod of Bishops into an assembly that will generate resolutions, valorizing the collegiality between the pope and the episcopate. In a church on the outskirts of Rome, he sketched how government should be conducted in a spirit of community. He was speaking of a parish priest, but what he said holds good for the high pontiff. The parish priest, he stressed, has the power to decide, but he decides through heeding; "he gathers counsel, he listens, he engages in dialogue."[51] Francis continues to regard clerical self-referentiality as a mortal sin—the attitude of those who "look on from above and afar; they reject the prophecy of their brothers and sisters, they discredit those who raise questions; they constantly point out the mistakes of others; and they are obsessed by appearances."[52]

The wager of Francis's revolution will be won or lost in the next few years. His adversaries are tenacious. They resist by creating invisible barriers of rubber around him and uttering ferocious offstage remarks, like the one made to Andrea Riccardi, the leader of St. Egidio, by an elderly cardinal: "Francis has brought the crowds back into the piazzas and the churches; his job is done. Let him leave now before he ruins the church."[53] It was not by chance that on the eve of Christmas 2014, Francis administered a stern rebuke to the Roman Curia, listing its "diseases" and denouncing the presence in the Vatican palaces of "the pathology of power . . . a superiority complex . . . narcissism . . . spiritual Alzheimer's." To these he added the tendency of the Curia to build walls around itself, and the temptation to believe itself capable of planning, regulating, steering, and confining the operations of the Holy Spirit.[54] The Argentine pope is aware of the widespread campaign to strip him of legitimacy. Even as we beat on against contrary headwinds, he told his fellow Jesuits, we must "all keep together" in the service of the church.[55] And so he stays the course.

The upshot might be a New Deal for the church like that of Franklin D. Roosevelt or an earthquake like the perestroika of Mikhail Gorbachev. The Argentine pope knows perfectly well that he is at the helm during an enormous change of course. "We are beginning a new stage in the life of the church" were his words to his friend the theologian Victor Manuel Fernández. Pope Francis has no illusions. A church that does not stand beside individuals, he thinks, and does not display the face of Jesus as love and salvation runs "the risk of dying."[56]

If he succeeds in transforming the Synods of Bishops into a permanent instrument of coparticipation in papal government, in making them into little councils that assist the church to chart its course on the ocean of modernity—involving the faithful, laymen, and laywomen—the revolution of Jorge Mario Bergoglio will become irreversible. "I only ask the Lord," the pope confided to an Argentine friend, as the third year of his pontificate loomed, "that this change, which I am pursuing for the sake of the church, at great personal cost, will endure, and not be like a light that suddenly goes out."

Francis has a vision, at which he hinted in the words he addressed to the cardinals a few days before the conclave: "I have the impression that Jesus has been shut up inside the church and that he is knocking because he wants to get out."

Notes

1. The Smell of the Sheep

1. M. De Vedia, *Francisco: El Papa del pueblo* (Planeta, 2013).
2. Pedro Baya, interview with the author.
3. J. Di Paola, interview with the author,
4. C. Martini Grimaldi, *Ero Bergoglio, sono Francesco* (Marsilio, 2013).
5. J. M. Poirier, editor of the magazine *Criterio*, interview with the author.
6. E. Piqué, *Francesco: Vita e rivoluzione* (Lindau, 2013).
7. E. Himitian, *Francesco: Il Papa della gente* (Rizzoli, 2013).

2. Francis's Fear

1. A. Tornielli, "Conclave: Scola, Scherer, and Oullet Are Front-Runners but the Race Is Still Open," *Vatican Insider*, 11 March 2013, http://vaticaninsider.lastampa.it. *Translator's note*: *Vatican Insider* publishes articles about the papacy from *La Stampa* newspaper in the original Italian as well as in English and Spanish translation. Because of the international interest in the papacy, other major Italian news organizations also maintain Vatican-oriented websites, at which it is possible, as in this case, to read English versions of articles cited by Politi in their original Italian version.
2. From the *Ordo rituum conclavis*.
3. A. Bagnasco, interview with the author.
4. See www.liberoquotidiano.it.
5. A. M. Vegliò, interview with the author.
6. E. Piqué, *Francesco: Vita e rivoluzione* (Lindau, 2013).
7. Pope Francis, *La mia porta è sempre aperta* (Rizzoli, 2013).

8. "Vatican: Conclave Won't Be Short as No Agreement on a Candidate Says US Cardinal," 8 March 2013, http://www1.adnkronos.com.
9. E. Himitian, *Francesco: Il Papa della gente* (Rizzoli, 2013).
10. L. Brunelli, "Così eleggemmo Papa Ratzinger," in *Quando il Papa pensa il mondo: I classici di Limes*, Rivista Italiana di Geopolitica, no. 1 (2009).
11. Ibid.
12. Himitian, *Francesco*.
13. C. Martini Grimaldi, *Ero Bergoglio, sono Francesco* (Marsilio, 2013).
14. Himitian, *Francesco*.
15. Pope Francis, audience with representatives of the media, 16 March 2013. The article at news.va, from which the English version of his words and the editorial interventions inside square brackets are taken, is entitled "Pope Francis: 'Oh, How I Wish for a Church That Is Poor and for the Poor!'"
16. D. Viganò, Convegno Aiart, Pavia, 25 October 2013.
17. Quoted in E. Scalfari, "Pope: How the Church Will Change," *La Repubblica*, 1 October 2013, from the English translation of the original article at the paper's website, http://www.repubblica.it.
18. Pope Francis, *Urbi et Orbi*, apostolic blessing, 13 March 2013.
19. Ibid. *Translator's note*: The official Italian and English texts do not indicate the pauses shown here by suspension points; they have been added to the Italian text by Marco Politi, and thus to this English translation, to convey with greater immediacy the manner in which the words were spoken.
20. "De una iglesia casi sitiada, con mil problemas, una iglesia que parecía un poco enferma, digamos, pasamos a una iglesia que se abrió." Quoted in M. I. Molina, "Pietro Parolin: 'Francisco cambió la percepción sobre la Iglesia,'" *Ultimas Noticias*, 4 August 2013.

3. The Coup d'État of Benedict XVI

1. Quoted in J. Frank, "Kardinal Joachim Meisner: 'Wie soll das gehen? Ein Papst im Ruhestand!'" *Frankfurter Rundschau*, 11 February 2013.
2. P. Poupard, interview with the author.
3. Benedict XVI, *Deus caritas est*, encyclical, 25 December 2005.
4. J. Ratzinger, *Münchner Kirchenzeitung*, 16 May 2002; cf. "Ratzinger hält Papst-Rücktritt für möglich," *Frankfurter Allgemeine Zeitung*, 16 May 2002.
5. J. Ratzinger, *Ordinariats Korrespondenz*, Munich, 14 August 1978.
6. Benedict XVI, *Light of the World: The Pope, the Church, and the Signs of the Times. A Conversation with Peter Seewald* (Ignatius, 2010).
7. Benedict XVI, homily, mass inaugurating the pontificate, 24 April 2005.
8. Benedict XVI, general audience, 16 January 2013.
9. Ibid.
10. G. Galeazzi, "Viene trascurata la componente sudamericana di Bergoglio," *La Stampa*, 8 October 2013, http://www.lastampa.it.

11. Benedict XVI, speech to participants in the forum organized by the Apostolic Penitentiary, 11 March 2010.
12. Benedict XVI, Angelus, 1 January 2011.
13. G. Galeazzi, "Pope Is Not Ill and Will Not Influence the Next Conclave, *Vatican Insider*, 12 February 2013, http://vaticaninsider.lastampa.it.
14. M. Politi, *Joseph Ratzinger: Crisi di un papato* (Laterza, 2011).
15. Frank, "Kardinal Joachim Meisner."
16. Benedict XVI, *Light of the World*.
17. "Il Papa alla tomba di Celestino V e il dono del pallio: Già pensava al rifiuto?" *Il Messaggero*, 11 February 2013.
18. A. Socci, "Dimissioni del Papa . . . Preghiamo che Dio ce lo conservi a lungo," *Libero*, 25 September 2011, http://www.antoniosocci.com.
19. See http://www.donboscoland.it.
20. Jean-Louis Tauran, interview with the author.
21. A. Tornielli, "Pope's Decision to Resign Came After His Fall in Mexico," *Vatican Insider*, 14 February 2013, http://vaticaninsider.lastampa.it.
22. Quoted in A. Riccardi, *Giovanni Paolo II* (San Paolo, 2011).
23. On the Vatican leaks scandal, see articles by M. Lillo in *Il Fatto Quotidiano* during 2012 and G. Nuzzi, *Sua santità: Le carte segrete di Benedetto XVI* (Chiarelettere, 2012).
24. Quoted in M. Politi, "Tutto Bertone parola e veleni," *Il Fatto Quotidiano*, 3 September 2013.
25. Quoted in L. Bettazzi, "Un giorno da pecora," Radio 2, 13 February 2012.
26. Benedict XVI, Declaratio, 11 February 2013.
27. Quoted in G. Galeazzi, "Vatileaks," *La Stampa*, 16 February 2013.

4. The Secrets of an Anti-Italian Conclave

1. Quoted in A. Beltramo Álvarez, "'Francis, the Champion of Mercy Who Will Not Yield on Doctrine,'" *Vatican Insider*, 28 April, 2013, http://vaticaninsider.lastampa.it.
2. Quoted in P. Rodari, "Gli ultimi quindici giorni di regno, l'attesa del successore," *Il Foglio*, 12 February 2013.
3. M. Lillo, "Complotto contro Benedetto XVI 'entro 12 mesi morirà,'" *Il Fatto Quotidiano*, 10 February 2012.
4. TMN News, 22 March 2013.
5. "Preti pedofili, la diocesi di Los Angeles pagherà 10 milioni di dollari a quattro vittime," *Corriere della Sera*, 13 March 2013, http://www.corriere.it.
6. *Il Quotidiano*, 20 February 2013, http://www.quotidiano.net.
7. See Reuters, http://www.reuters.com.
8. Quoted in "Les attentes des cardinaux avant le conclave," Documentation Information Catholiques Internationales (DICI), 15 March 2013, http://www.dici.org.
9. TMN News, 5 March 2013.

10. A. Tornielli, *La Stampa*, 12 March 2013, http://www.lastampa.it.
11. Benedict XVI, Ash Wednesday homily, 13 February 2013.
12. Benedict XVI, farewell address to the eminent cardinals present in Rome, 23 February 2013. In this passage, the pope quotes the Catholic priest and intellectual Romano Guardini.
13. Euro News, 12 February 2013.
14. R. Martino, interview with the author.
15. G. Marcó, interview with the author.
16. P. Baya, interview with the author.
17. E. Himitian, *Francesco: Il Papa della gente* (Rizzoli, 2013).
18. Quoted in P. Rodari, " 'Prima le riforme, inutile bruciare i tempi e a Ratzinger dirò di non farsi usare,' " *La Repubblica*, 6 March 2013.
19. Quoted in Sharon Otterman, "His Message in Rome: New York Isn't Sin City," *New York Times*, 14 February 2012.
20. Quoted in Jesús Bastante, "Cardenal Pell: 'Un buen candidato italiano siempre es favorito,' " *Periodista Digital*, 9 March 2013, http://www.periodistadigital.com.
21. P. De Robertis, *Quotidiano Nazionale*, 4 March 2013.
22. See http://www.quotidiano.net.
23. Quoted in N. Nuti, "Card. Wuerl: Papa USA come superpotenza," *News Cattoliche*, 5 March 2013, http://www.newscattoliche.it.
24. Quoted in M. Franco, "Papa, per il dopo Bertone avanza lo straniero," *Corriere della Sera*, 15 March 2013.
25. F. A. Grana, *La Chiesa di Francesco* (L'Orientale, 2014).
26. Cormac Murphy-O'Connor, Associazione Stampa Estera, Rome, 25 January 2014.

5. The End of the Imperial Church

1. Pope Francis, first greeting and apostolic blessing *Urbi et Orbi*, 13 March 2013.
2. Pope Francis, homily at Holy Mass with the cardinal electors, 14 March 2013.
3. Pope Francis, address to the Pilgrimage of Catechists, 27 September 2013.
4. Quoted in G. G. Vecchi, "Il Papa resta a vivere a Santa Marta 'Lì non sono isolato,' " *Corriere della Sera*, 29 May 2013.
5. Pope Francis, speech to the students of the Jesuit schools of Italy and Albania, followed by questions and answers, 7 June 2013.
6. Pope Francis, press conference during the return flight from Rio de Janeiro, 28 July 2013,
7. Pope Francis, quoted by A. Spadaro, S.J., in an interview originally published in *La Civiltà Cattolica* for 19 September 2013, and widely republished, translated, and discussed. This interview is quoted throughout from the English version entitled "Interview with Pope Francis," available at http://w2.vatican.va, where it is classified among the pope's "speeches" for September 2013.

8. Pope Francis, press conference during the return flight from Rio de Janeiro, 28 July 2013.

9. Pope Francis, audience with the media, 16 March 2013.

10. G. Filoramo, *La croce e il potere: I Cristiani da martiri a persecutori* (Laterza, 2011).

11. E. Scalfari, interview with Pope Francis, *La Repubblica*, 1 October 2013, available in English at the paper's website.

12. R. Allegri, *Messaggero di S. Antonio*, no. 7 (2000).

13. Quoted in M. Politi, *La Chiesa del no* (Mondadori, 2009).

14. A. Melloni, *Quel che resta di Dio* (Einaudi, 2013).

15. Quoted in "Francis: Look for Pastors Not Princes for Episcopacy," *News.va* (Official Vatican Network), 21 June 2013, http://www.news.va.

16. Adnkronos (news service), 16 November 2013.

17. M. Roncalli, *Giovanni XXIII* (Mondadori, 2006).

18. F. A. Grana, "Santa Sede, finisce l'era di Tarcisio Bertone: Alla Segreteria di Stato arriva Pietro Parolin," *Il Fatto Quotidiano*, 15 October 2013, http://www .ilfattoquotidiano.it.

19. Pope Francis, "Chirograph by Which a Council of Cardinals Is Established," 28 September 2013.

20. M. Voce, interview with the author.

21. Scalfari, interview with Pope Francis, 1 October 2013.

22. Ibid.

23. Spadaro, "Interview with Pope Francis." *Translator's note*: Here the Italian original and the official English translation, both published at the Vatican website (see note 7), are slightly at variance, and I have adapted the English to reflect accurately what Pope Francis said in Italian. He does indeed, as Politi remarks, avoid using the word *curia* in the passage quoted, referring merely to "i dicasteri romani," but the official English translation has him referring to "the dicasteries of the Roman Curia." In the original, he says that they may become censorious "quando non sono bene intesi"—that is, when there is a failure of self-understanding on the part of their personnel, but in the official English translation he is made to say, "when they are not functioning well."

24. Ibid. *Translator's note*: What the pope said is that "i dicasteri romani" are mediators, and that is how I translate the phrase. The official English translation makes him say that "the Roman congregations" are mediators. In fact, *dicastery* is a general term that comprises not just the congregations, but also the secretariats, tribunals, councils, offices, and commissions of the Roman Curia. Readers are referred to the excellent *Wikipedia* article "Roman Curia," which supplies references to the official sources, for more detail on these various dicasteries.

25. Quoted in C. Cardinale, "Rodriguez Maradiaga: 'Riforma della Chiesa, un'opera collegiale,'" *Avvenire*, 7 October 2013, http://www.avvenire.it.

26. Quoted in P. Farinella, *Cristo non abita più qui* (Il Saggiatore, 2013).

27. Voce, interview with the author.

28. Spadaro, "Interview with Pope Francis."
29. Quoted in R. Giusti, "Pietro Parolin: 'La renovación implica una vuelta al cristianismo primitivo,'" *El Universal*, 8 September 2013.

6. The Face of a Parish Priest

1. Quoted in S. Le Bars, "Six mois 'd'effet François' pour les catholiques," *Le Monde*, 6 October 2013.
2. Asca (news service), 18 December 2013.
3. Pope Francis, *Urbi et Orbi* message, 25 December 2013.
4. E. Olmi, *Lettera ad una chiesa che ha dimenticato Gesù* (Piemme, 2013).
5. N. Moretti, dir., *Habemus papam* (2011).
6. A. Spadaro, "Interview with Pope Francis" (English translation), *La Civiltà Cattolica*, 19 September 2013, http://w2.vatican.va.
7. A. Carrara, *Eco di Bergamo*, 9 March 2013, http://www.ecodibergamo.it.
8. Spadaro, "Interview with Pope Francis."
9. Ibid.
10. G. G. Vecchi, "Il Papa: 'Sono un peccatore e ogni 15 giorni mi confesso,'" *Corriere della Sera*, 20 November 2013.
11. Pope Francis, address to seminarians and novices, 6 July 2013.
12. Ibid.
13. Pope Francis, Radio Vaticana, 4 October 2013, http://www.radiovaticana.va.
14. *L'Osservatore Romano*, 3 December 2013.
15. E. Carpegna, *Sombras de tango* (Alberto Perdisa, 2006).
16. Pope Francis, homily, Holy Mass with Seminarians, Novices, and Those Discerning Their Vocation, 7 July 2013.
17. Quoted in Adnkronos (news service), "Papa: Nei seminari formare il cuore senno si creano piccoli mostri," 3 January 2014.
18. N. Gibbs, "Pope Francis, the Choice," *Time*, 11 December 2013.
19. Ibid.
20. M. Frukacz, http://www.zenit.org.
21. Quoted in G. G. Vecchi, *Francesco: La rivoluzione della tenerezza* (Rcs-Corriere della Sera, 2013).
22. Pope Francis, press conference during the return flight from Rio de Janeiro, 28 July 2013.
23. "Bergoglio al telefono: 'Sono il Papa.' Centralinista Vaticano: 'Sì e io sono Napoleone,'" *Blitz Quotidiano*, 21 March 2013, http://www.blitzquotidiano.it.
24. C. Tecce, *Il Fatto Quotidiano*, 13 June 2013.
25. *Porta a Porta* (television program), RAI Uno, 25 September 2013.
26. Quoted in "Il Papa lava i piedi a giovani detenuti: Anche due ragazze, una è musulmana," *La Repubblica*, 28 March 2013, http://www.repubblica.it.
27. Quoted in ibid.
28. Pope Francis, homily at Lampedusa, Sicily, 8 July 2013.

7. Walking with Unbelievers

1. Benedict XVI, address to the members of the Roman Curia, 21 December 2009.
2. J. Kristeva, quoted in "Julia Kristeva: The Humanism of the Enlightenment Must Dialogue with Christian Humanism," *AsiaNews*, 27 October 2011.
3. Benedict XVI, address at the meeting for peace in Assisi, 27 October 2011.
4. Quoted in M. Politi, *Il Fatto Quotidiano*, 20 March 2011.
5. Pope Francis, audience with members of the communications media, 16 March 2013; the switch from Italian to Spanish is noted in the official text, which is available in seven languages at the Vatican website.
6. E. Scalfari, "Le risposte che i due papi non danno," *La Repubblica*, 7 July 2013, and "Le domande di un non credente al papa gesuita chiamato Francesco," *La Repubblica*, 6 August 2013.
7. Pope Francis, "Letter to a Non-believer; Pope Francis Responds to Dr. Eugenio Scalfari," dated 4 September 2013, published in *La Repubblica*, 11 September 2013. *Translator's note*: The English text is from vatican.va; emphasis added by the author.
8. "Dunque, occorre confrontarsi con Gesù, direi, nella concretezza e ruvidezza della sua vicenda." Ibid. *Translator's note*: The translation from the original Italian is my own. The official translation, usually so faithful, is woolly here: "It is necessary, therefore, to look at Jesus from the point of view of the actual circumstances of his existence."
9. Ibid. Here the pope is quoting from his own encyclical *Lumen fidei*, which, as he acknowledges, was drafted largely by Benedict XVI.
10. Ibid., again quoting from *Lumen fidei*.
11. "La Chiesa, mi creda, nonostante tutte le lentezze, le infedeltà, gli errori e i peccati che può aver commesso e può ancora commettere in coloro che la compongono." Ibid. *Translator's note*: The translation is my own. The official translation drops the conditional form of words used by the pope and makes him state that these transgressions "are committed and are still being committed."
12. Ian Buruma, "Snowden and the Pope," 4 October 2013; the column can be found at the Project Syndicate website.
13. Quoted in Pope Francis and E. Scalfari, *Dialogo tra credenti e non credenti* (Einaudi and La Repubblica, 2013).
14. Quoted in ibid.
15. Ibid.
16. E. Scalfari, interview with Pope Francis, *La Repubblica*, 1 October 2013. *Translator's note*: The Italian text is available at the paper's website and in Francis and Scalfari, *Dialogo tra credenti e non credenti*. The English translation used here is also from the paper's website, but I have taken the liberty of modifying it slightly, using "mindset" rather than "way of feeling" to translate "modo di sentire" and using the gender-neutral pronoun *they* in the penultimate sentence quoted instead of the masculine singular used in the original.

17. A. Beltramo Álvarez, "Il giornalista: 'Ho aggiunto frasi che Francesco non aveva detto. Ma il suo segretario Xuareb mi ha dato l"ok,"'" *La Stampa*, 22 November 2013, http://www.lastampa.it.
18. J. Kristeva, interview with the author; subsequent quotations come from this interview unless otherwise indicated.
19. See Benedict XVI, address at the meeting for peace in Assisi, 27 October 2011.
20. J. M. Bergoglio and A. Skorka, *Il cielo e la terra* (Mondadori, 2013).

8. The Hidden Women Priests

1. M. Schmid, interviewed by the author, Effretikon, Switzerland. All quotations from Schmid come from this interview.
2. Pope Paul VI, *Gaudium et spes*, Pastoral Constitution on the Church in the Modern World, 7 December 1965.
3. Pope John Paul II, *Mulieris dignitatem*, apostolic letter, 15 August 1988. *Translator's note*: In the official English text, the word *genius*, used in the slightly unusual sense of "the prevalent character or spirit of something," is set off by quotation marks.
4. Pope John Paul II, *Ordinatio sacerdotalis*, apostolic letter, 22 May 1994.
5. Cardinal Joseph Ratzinger, *Letter to the Bishops of the Catholic Church on the Collaboration of Men and Women in the Church and in the World*, 31 May 2004, available at the Vatican website under the heading "Roman Curia," subheading "Congregations," sub-subheading "Congregation for the Doctrine of the Faith."
6. Pope John Paul II, *Mulieris dignitatem*.
7. Ratzinger, *Letter to the Bishops of the Catholic Church*.
8. L. Sebastiani, "Il concreto dello spirito due papi e 'la' donna," *Rocca*, 1 November 2013.
9. Benedict XVI, "We Have a Positive Idea to Offer," interview with German media representatives, 5 August 2006; English translation from the website of Deutsche Welle.
10. A. Spadaro, interview with Pope Francis, 19 August 2013, published in *L'Osservatore Romano*, 21 September 2013.
11. Pope Francis, address on the occasion of the twenty-fifth anniversary of *Mulieris dignitatem*, 12 October 2013. *Translator's note*: The official text in English at the Vatican website retains and glosses the term *servidumbre*.
12. A. Spadaro, "Interview with Pope Francis" (English translation), *La Civiltà Cattolica*, 19 September 2013, http://w2.vatican.va.
13. Pope Francis, press conference during the return flight from Rio de Janeiro, 28 July 2013.
14. Ibid.
15. Both Jewell and Thorn quoted in M. Fincher and C. Dunne, "Women Resistant to Pope Francis's Call for New Theology," *National Catholic Reporter*, 4 November 2013.

16. Quoted in G. Codrignani, "Caro Papa Francesco ti scrivo . . . ," *Il Paese delle Donne Online,* 9 October 2013, http://www.womenews.net.

17. Sister Ivone Gebara, "El Papa Francisco y la teología de la mujer: Algunas inquietudes," *Redes Cristianas,* 10 August 2013, http://www.redescristianas.net.

18. L. Scaraffia, "Una donna cardinale: Papa Francesco alle prese con l'ultimo tabù," *Il Messaggero,* 24 September 2013.

19. Quoted in P. Rodari, "Il cardinale Maradiaga: 'Via le poltrone di troppo e Ior sotto vigilanza, così cambierà la Curia,'" *La Repubblica,* 22 November 2013.

20. Quoted in P. Loriga, "'Donne cardinali? Serve molto di più di un titolo onorifico,'" *Città Nuova,* 8 November 2013.

21. Quoted in P. Loriga and M. Zanzucchi, *La scommessa di Emmaus* (Città Nuova, 2012).

22. *Annuarium statisticum ecclesiae* (Libreria Editrice Vaticana, 2001, 2011).

23. Congregation for the Doctrine of the Faith, *Doctrinal Assessment of the Leadership Conference of Women Religious* (8 April 2012).

24. Quoted in M. T. Pontara Pederiva, "LCWR Nuns: 'Catholic Church Is Profoetus but Keeps Silent on Other Essential Issues,'" *Vatican Insider,* 19 July 2012, http://www.vaticaninsider.com.

25. B. Baas, "Florence und Franziskus," *Publik-Forum.de,* 14 May 2013, http://www.publik-forum.de.

26. Congregation for Institutes of Consecrated Life and Societies of Apostolic Life, *Final Report on the Apostolic Visitation of Institutes of Women Religious in the United States of America* (8 September 2014).

9. Death in Front of the Vatican

1. Pope Francis, *Evangelii gaudium,* apostolic exhortation, 24 November 2013.

2. Rush Limbaugh, *Rush Limbaugh Show,* 27 November 2013, http://www.rushlimbaugh.com.

3. Jonathon Moseley, "Jesus Christ Is a Capitalist," *World Net Daily,* 1 December 2013, http://www.wnd.com.

4. Paul VI, *Populorum progressio,* encyclical, 26 March 1967.

5. Pope Francis, homily at Lampedusa, Sicily, 8 July 2013.

6. *Il Sore 24 Ore,* 17 July 2013, http://www.ilsole24ore.com.

7. *Il Sole 24 Ore,* 13 September 2013, http://www.ilsole24ore.com.

8. L. Campiglio, "Equità antidoto alla recessione," *Avvenire,* 25 January 2014.

9. Janet L. Yellen, speech, 17 October 2014.

10. S. Zamagni, "Ricchi sempre più ricchi," *Avvenire,* 1 February 2014.

11. *Der Spiegel,* 24 May 2012.

12. Quoted in A. Tornielli, "Mai avere paura della tenerezza," *La Stampa,* 15 December 2013.

13. Pope Francis, *Evangelii gaudium.*

14. Quoted in Ansa, "Papa: Elemosina deve costare e far male," Ansa (news agency), 4 February 2014.

15. Pope Francis, *Evangelii gaudium*.

16. Pope Francis, general audience, 5 June 2013.

17. J. Joffe, "Der Papst geht fehl in seiner Kritik am Kapitalismus," *Die Zeit*, 28 November 2013.

10. The Self-Critique of a Pope

1. A. Spadaro, "Interview with Pope Francis," (English translation), *La Civiltà Cattolica*, 19 September 2013, http://w2.vatican.va.

2. Adolfo Pérez Esquivel, interview, BBC Mundo (in Spanish), 14 March 2013.

3. N. Scavo, *La lista di Bergoglio: I salvati da Francesco durante la dittatura. La storia mai raccontata* (EMI, 2013), translated as *Bergoglio's List: How a Young Francis Defied a Dictatorship and Saved Dozens of Lives* (St. Benedict Press, 2014).

4. E. Himitian, *Francesco: Il Papa della gente* (Rizzoli, 2013).

5. I. Pérez del Viso, interview with the author.

6. F. Strazzari, *In Argentina per conoscere Bergoglio* (EDB, 2013).

7. Ibid.

8. L. Prezzi, *Il Regno—Attualita*, no. 16 (2000).

9. Quoted in Himitian, *Francesco*; the Spanish original is *Francisco: El Papa de la gente* (Aguilar, 2013).

10. Centro de Investigación y Acción Social.

11. E. Piqué, *Francesco: Vita e rivoluzione* (Lindau, 2013).

12. Spadaro, "Interview with Pope Francis."

13. J. Bergoglio, F. Ambrogetti, and S. Rubin, *Papa Francesco* (Salani, 2013).

14. Ibid.

15. F. Mallimaci, *Atlas de las creencias religiosas en la Argentina* (Editorial Biblos, 2013).

11. The Program of the Revolution

1. A. Spadaro, "Interview with Pope Francis" (English translation), *La Civiltà Cattolica*, 19 September 2013, http://w2.vatican.va.

2. Pope Francis, *Evangelii gaudium*, apostolic exhortation, 24 November 2013.

3. Pope Francis, address to the Consejo Episcopal Latinoamericano (CELAM, Latin American Episcopal Council) leadership, 28 July 2013.

4. Pope Francis, *Evangelii gaudium*.

5. J. M. Bergoglio, *Scegliere la vita* (Bompiani, 2013).

6. Spadaro, "Interview with Pope Francis."

7. Pope Francis, address to CELAM leadership, 28 July 2013.

8. Pope Francis, *Evangelii gaudium*.

9. Quoted in G. Galeazzi, "'Viene trascurata la componente sudamericana di Bergoglio,'" *La Stampa*, 8 October 2013, and at http://vaticaninsider.lastampa .it/.

10. Pope Francis, *Evangelii gaudium*.

11. Spadaro, "Interview with Pope Francis."

12. Ibid.

13. Pope Francis, presentation of Christmas greetings to the Roman Curia, 21 December 2013.

14. Pope Francis, *Evangelii gaudium*.

15. Cardinal Joseph Ratzinger, with Vittorio Messori, *The Ratzinger Report: An Exclusive Interview on the State of the Church* (Ignatius Press, 1985), 59, published the same year in Italian as *Rapporto sulla Fede*.

16. J. Ratzinger, speaking at the presentation of the motu proprio *Apostolos suos*, 23 July 1998, in English at http://www.tlig.org.

17. Quoted in G. G. Vecchi, "I nuovi eretici oggi aggrediscono l'uomo: Intervista a Gerhard Ludwig Müller," *Corriere della Sera*, 22 December 2013.

18. Spadaro, "Interview with Pope Francis."

19. Pope Francis, "Address of Pope Francis to Participants in the Plenary Session of the Congregation for the Doctrine of the Faith," 31 January 2014, at http:// w2.vatican.va.

20. Spadaro, "Interview with Pope Francis."

21. Pope Francis, *Evangelii gaudium*.

22. Pope Francis to H. E. Mr. Vladimir Putin, President of the Russian Federation, letter, on the occasion of the G20 St. Petersburg Summit, 4 September 2013.

23. Pope Francis, Invocation for Peace, Vatican Gardens, 8 June 2014.

24. Ansa (news service), 26 July 2014.

12. St. Peter Had No Bank Account

1. Cindy Wooden, "Anderson Says Vatican Bank Fired President to Increase Transparency," Catholic News Service, 29 May 2012, http://www.catholicnews.com.

2. Corte di Appello di Roma, sentence on the Calvi case, 7 May 2010.

3. Quoted in A. Tornielli, "IOR, scontro prima del conclave," *La Stampa*, 12 March 2013, http://www.lastampa.it.

4. M. E. Vincenzi, "L'avvocato dello IOR indagato per riciclaggio," *La Repubblica*, 28 March 2013.

5. "Inchiesta IOR, indagato per riciclaggio l'avvocato Michele Briamonte," *Il Fatto Quotidiano*, 28 March 2013, http://www.ilfattoquotidiano.it.

6. Quoted in M. Lillo, "Da suore e prelati bonifici milionari sui conti dello IOR," *Il Fatto Quotidiano*, 18 September 2013.

7. Ibid.

8. Quoted in ibid.

9. Quoted in D. Lusi and M. E. Vincenzi, "Nello IOR un sistema organizzato per sfuggire alle autorità di vigilanza," *La Repubblica*, 9 October 2013.

10. M. Lillo and V. Pacelli, "IOR, fuga di capitali verso la Germania. Svuotati i conti italiani," *Il Fatto Quotidiano*, 6 September 2013.

11. M. Lillo, "IOR, nell'archivio di Gotti Tedeschi trattative segrete tra Vaticano e Pdl," *Il Fatto Quotidiano*, 7 September 2013.

12. Quoted in F. Sarzanini, "Nomine, pressioni e trattative; le carte segrete di Gotti Tedeschi," *Corriere della Sera*, 5 September 2013.

13. Quoted in C. Bonini, " 'Troppi investimenti sbagliati e improduttivi' lo scontro IOR–Bertone sulle finanze del Vaticano," *La Repubblica*, 6 September 2013.

14. Quoted in "Pope: The Church Is Not an NGO and the IOR Is Needed 'up to a Certain Point' " (English translation), *AsiaNews*, 24 April 2013, http://www.asianews.it. *Translator's note*: These rather frank, impromptu words must initially have been reported by Vatican Radio, which the author cites, but since the original publication of his book they seem to have been scrubbed from any news source available at the Vatican website or News.va, the Official Vatican Network. The full report of the speech, from which I quote here, survives online (with an attribution to Vatican Radio) at *AsiaNews*, a Catholic website that publishes in Chinese and English, under the headline given here.

15. Pope Francis, morning meditation in Santa Marta, 11 June 2013.

16. Quoted in F. Marchese Ragona, " 'Doveroso per la Chiesa avere lo IOR.' Intervista al direttore generale Paolo Cipriani," *Il Giornale*, 14 June 2013.

17. Quoted in M. Politi, " 'Cacceremo i cattivi clienti, niente più conti a esterni,' " *Il Fatto Quotidiano*, 15 September 2013.

18. Pope Francis, press conference during the return flight from Rio de Janeiro, 28 July 2013. *Translator's note*: The sports metaphor used by the pope in Spanish ("pero estas cosas suceden cuando en el oficio de gobierno ¿cierto? uno va por aquí, pero le patean un golazo de allá y lo tiene que atajar, ¿no es cierto?") makes little sense in the official English translation ("But these things happen when you're in governance: you try to go in one direction, but then someone throws you a ball from another direction, and you have to bat it back. Isn't that the way it is?"). The translation here is my own.

19. Istituto Opere di Religione, *Rapporto annuale 2012*.

20. Quoted in Politi, " 'Cacceremo i cattivi clienti.' "

21. G. Nuzzi, *Vaticano spa* (Chiarelettere, 2009).

22. A. Tornielli, "Vatican Prelate Arrested as Part of IOR Inquiry," *La Stampa*, 28 June 2013, http://www.lastampa.it and http://vaticaninsider.lastampa.it.

23. E. Fittipaldi, "Un prelato godereccio—Vita, movida, soldi e affari di Monsignor Scarano," *L'Espresso*, 16 August 2013.

24. Quoted in M. Lillo and V. Pacelli, "Il 'sistema' Scarano–IOR tra denaro e agenti Segreti," *Il Fatto Quotidiano*, 3 July 2013.

25. Pope Francis, press conference during the return flight from Rio de Janeiro, 28 July 2013.

26. "Francis Issues Motu Proprio on Vatican Financial Information Authority," *Vatican Insider*, 18 November 2013, http://vaticaninsider.lastampa.it.

27. MONEYVAL, *The Holy See: Progress Report* (9 December 2013).

28. Quoted in "Scarano su operazioni sospette nel Vaticano: 'Apsa con tassi migliori dello IOR,'" *Il Fatto Quotidiano*, 2 October 2013, http://www.ilfattoquotidiano.it.

29. M. Lillo and V. Pacelli, "Saccomanni ammette: Il Vaticano non rivela i nomi dei riciclatori," *Il Fatto Quotidiano*, 7 December 2013.

30. "Bagnasco ripete: 'Lavoro oggi è la prima sofferenza,'" *Avvenire*, 24 May 2013.

31. Quoted in "Il Papa arriva al Centro Astalli senza scorta: 'I conventi chiusi? Diamoli ai rifugiati,'" *Corriere della Sera*, 10 September 2013, http://www.corriere.it.

32. G. Baldessarro, "Sequestri per 150 milioni alla 'ndrangheta c'è anche un hotel esclusivo a Roma," *La Repubblica*, 12 November 2013, http://www.repubblica.it.

33. R. Frignani and M. Proto, "Sequestrato il Grand Hotel Gianicolo: Proprietari vicini alla cosca dei Gallico," *Corriere della Sera*, 12 November 2013, http://www .corriere.it.

34. M. Politi, *Il Fatto Quotidiano*, 18 October 2013.

35. Ibid.

36. Quoted in I. Cimmarusti, "Fece sequestrare due confratelli; Superiore dei Camilliani arrestato," *Il Tempo*, 7 November 2013, http://www.iltempo.it.

37. "IDI, arrestato padre Franco Decaminada, 'Appropriazione indebita per 4 milioni,'" *La Repubblica*, 4 April 2013, http://www.repubblica.it.

38. "IDI, perquisizione in Vaticano incidente diplomatico sfiorato," *Il Messaggero*, 6 July 2012, http://www.ilmessaggero.it.

39. E. Fittipaldi, "Vaticano, il frate ha fatto crac," *L'Espresso e*, 27 October 2012.

40. I. Sacchettoni, "IDI, i soldi dell'ospedale in Congo per il petrolio," *Corriere della Sera*, 5 April 2013, http://www.corriere.it.

41. I. Sacchettoni, "Dalla farmacia dell'IDI i contanti per Decaminada," *Corriere della Sera*, 27 January 2013.

42. *Translator's note:* The pope's morning meditation on "the power of money" was delivered on 20 September 2013. At the Vatican website, it is reported and paraphrased in Italian and more briefly in English in the form in which it was printed in *L'Osservatore Romano*. Contrary to his usual practice, the author does not attach a footnote to his report of the meditation, dating it merely to "one September morning," and contrary to his equally strict practice, the quotations and paraphrase he gives here vary slightly from those at the Vatican website and have the pope denouncing the sins of "bishops and priests" more explicitly than in the official report, in which clerics are not singled out. I take the view, for what it is worth, that the author's report is highly likely to adhere more closely to what the pope said and meant on this occasion than the official report, which is highly likely to have been toned down.

13. The Enemies of Francis

1. Quoted in A. Riccardi, "Andrea Riccardi: 'No será fácil sacar a la Iglesia de su envejecimiento,'" *Criterio*, December 2013, http://www.revistacriterio.com.ar.

2. P. Deotto, "Il diritto dei fedeli di avere un po' di chiarezza dai pastori," *Riscossa Cristiana.it*, 12 November 2013, http://www.riscossacristiana.it.

3. Pope Francis, speech to heads of religious orders, *La Civiltà Cattolica*, 4 January 2014, http://www.laciviltacattolica.it, but also available at many other websites because the remark was widely reported.

4. Pope Francis, morning meditation at Santa Marta, 11 January 2014.

5. Quoted in G. Galeazzi, "'Viene trascurata la componente sudamericana di Bergoglio,'" *La Stampa*, 8 October 2013, http://vaticaninsider.lastampa.it.

6. Comment made at the blog *Apostati si Diventa*, 3 June 2013, http://www.apostatisidiventa.blogspot.it.

7. L. Verrecchio, "An X-ray of Francis' Interview," Tradition in Action, 24 September 2013, http://www.traditioninaction.org.

8. M. Castagna, "Tutti buoni, tranne i tradizionalisti," *Agere Contra*, 18 April 2013, http://www.agerecontra.it.

9. "Ich warte jeden Tag von Neuem, was heute anders sein wird." Quoted in "Benedikts Privatsekretär hadert mit Papst-Rücktritt," *Die Zeit*, 4 December 2013, http://www.diezeit.de.

10. R. de Mattei, "Re per diritto divino," *Il Foglio*, 28 March 2013.

11. S. Magister, "Lo strappo di papa Francesco," *L'Espresso*, 21 March 2013.

12. A. Gnocchi and M. Palmaro, "Questo papa non ci piace," *Il Foglio*, 9 October 2013.

13. Quoted in P. Mastrolilli, "Non si rende conto dei danni che sta facendo," *Vatican Insider*, 21 September 2013, http://vaticaninsider.lastampa.it.

14. P. De Marco, "De Marco su papa Francesco: 'In coscienza . . . ,'" *L'Espresso*, 2 October 2013.

15. Quoted in C. Martini Grimaldi, *Ero Bergoglio, sono Francesco* (Marsilio, 2013).

16. G. Valente, interview with the author.

17. Quoted in F. Marchese Ragona, "'Bertone corrotto, Tremonti omo': Le frasi choc della pr del Papa," *Il Giornale*, 10 August 2013, http://www.ilgiornale.it.

18. G. Laudadio, "Da Andreotti a Gotti Tedeschi, ecco chi è Chaouqui 'la lobbista di Francesco,'" *Formiche*, 20 July 2013, http://www.formiche.net.

19. S. Magister, "Ricca and Chaouqui, Two Enemies in the House," *Chiesa Espresso Online*, 26 August 2013, http://www.chiesa.espressonline.it.

20. S. Magister, "The Prelate of the Gay Lobby," *Chiesa Espresso Online*, 18 July 2013, http://www.chiesa.espressonline.it.

21. Pope Francis, press conference during the return flight from Rio de Janeiro, 28 July 2013,

22. Ibid.

23. F. Di Giacomo, *Il Venerdì di Repubblica*, 10 January 2014.

24. Quoted in B. Borromeo, "Papa Francesco, il pm Gratteri: 'La sua pulizia preoccupa la mafia,'" *Il Fatto Quotidiano*, 13 November 2013.

25. Pope Francis, homily at Piana di Sibari, 21 June 2014.

26. Quoted in "'Ndrangheta, boss dato in pasto ai maiali. Il killer: 'Che gioia sentirlo strillare,'" *Il Fatto Quotidiano*, 26 November 2013.

27. Quoted in C. Caporale, "'Ndrangheta, 200 detenuti al cappellano: 'Cosa veniamo a fare a messa se il Papa ci scomunica?'" *La Repubblica*, 7 July 2013, http://www.repubblica.it.

28. Pope Francis, press conference during the return flight from Rio de Janeiro, 28 July 2013.

29. Pope Francis, presentation of Christmas greetings to the Roman Curia, 21 December 2013.

30. A. Melloni, *Quel che resta di Dio* (Einaudi, 2013).

31. Quoted in M. Tulli, "Bregantini, 'Papa Francesco è santo ma rischia di restare solo,'" Ansa (news service), 18 December 2013.

14. The War of the Cardinals

1. A. Spadaro, "Interview with Pope Francis" (English translation), *La Civiltà Cattolica*, 19 September 2013, http://w2.vatican.va.

2. Pope Francis, morning meditation at mass in Santa Marta, 16 April 2013. *Translator's note*: The translation is my own. The Vatican website, www.vatican.va, publishes a full account of the homily in Italian, from which the author quotes and I translate, but only a brief summary in English from *L'Osservatore Romano*, which omits the quoted passages.

3. "Cardinal Donald Wuerl's Report at the Synod of Bishops," *Zenit*, 9 October 2012, http://www.zenit.org.

4. Benedict XVI, meeting with the parish priests and clergy of Rome, 14 February 2013.

5. Archbishop Gerhard Ludwig Müller, Prefect of the Congregation for the Doctrine of the Faith, "Testimony to the Power of Grace: On the Indissolubility of Marriage and the Debate Concerning the Civilly Remarried and the Sacraments," 23 October 2013, at the Vatican website, section "Roman Curia," subsection "Congregations," sub-subsection "Doctrine of the Faith."

6. Ibid.

7. Quoted in A. Tornielli, "Divorziati e risposati: 'Müller non può bloccare la discussione,'" *La Stampa*, 11 November 2013, http:///www.lastampa.it.

8. O. R. Maradiaga, from an interview that appeared originally in the *Kölner Stadt-Anzeiger*, 20 January 2014. The English translation is from http://www.imwac.net (the acronym stands for International Movement We Are Church).

9. Ibid.

10. Quoted in M. Matzuzzi, "Müller si spiega in buon tedesco ai ribelli di Monaco e Colonia," *Il Foglio*, 14 December 2013.

11. Quoted in E. Finger, "Was heißt Barmherzigkeit?" *Die Zeit*, 22 December 2013.
12. Quoted in M. Politi, "'Papa Francesco dà fastidio al malaffare.' Intervista ad Angelo Bagnasco," *Il Fatto Quotidiano*, 21 December 2013.
13. Quoted in P. Valentino, "'Il diavolo ai funerali di Ted.' La lite dei cardinali americani," *Corriere della Sera*, 11 November 2013, http://www.corriere.it.
14. Spadaro, "Interview with Pope Francis."
15. J. Westen, "Vatican Cardinal Burke Interviewed on Pope Francis: Says 'We Can Never Talk Enough' About Abortion," *Life Site News*, 13 December 2013, http://www.lifesitenews.com.
16. Quoted in A. Gaspari, "Il Card. Piacenza: Le donne prete, il celibato e il potere di Roma," *Zenit*, 18 September 2013, http://www.zenit.org.
17. Quoted in E. Pavesi, "La Chiesa e la bioetica: Monsignor Gerhard Ludwig Müller conferma la continuità della dottrina," *Osservatorio Internazionale Cardinale Van Thuân*, 12 December 2013, http://www.vanthuanobservatory.org.
18. See G. L. Müller, *Katholische Dogmatik* (Freiburg, 2003).
19. See G. L. Müller, *Die Messe* (St. Ulrich, 2002).
20. Pope John Paul II, *Familiaris consortio*, apostolic exhortation, 22 November 1981.
21. Spadaro, "Interview with Pope Francis."
22. Pope Francis, press conference during the return flight from Rio de Janeiro, 28 July 2013.
23. Pope Francis, in A. Spadaro, "Wake Up the World: Conversation with Pope Francis About the Religious Life," *La Civiltà Cattolica*, 4 January 2014.
24. Synod of Bishops, III Extraordinary General Assembly, Pastoral Challenges to the Family in the Context of Evangelization, Preparatory Document, 2013.
25. See Begegnung & Dialog," December 2013, http://www.begegnungunddialog.blogspot.com.
26. Quoted in "Archbishop Urges Catholics to Take 'Modern Life' Survey," 15 November 2013, http://www.bbc.com/news/uk. *Translator's note*: These comments are included in the article itself; in other words, they have not just been dredged up from the anonymous comment board "below the line."
27. Quoted in S. Falasca, "Baldisseri: La missione riguarda tutti," *Avvenire*, 17 December 2013.
28. P. Guerre, 4 December 2013, http://www.saintpothin.fr.
29. *Il Mondo*, 5 November 2013, http://www.ilmondo.it.
30. Quoted in "Archbishop Urges Catholics to Take 'Modern Life' Survey."
31. "Die Ergebnisse der Umfrage erzeugen und verstärken, auch wenn sie nicht repräsentativ sind, den Eindruck einer fatalen Situation. Eigentlich wissen wir schon lange darum. Vieles wurde verdrängt. Jetzt bietet uns Papst Franziskus auf mehrere Weisen die Chance einer klaren Wahrnehmung und dann auch einer entschlossenen Heilung der aufgezeigten Mängel." Quoted in "Auswertung des Fragebogens zur Außerordentlichen Familiensynode," Bistum Mainz (Mainz diocese) website, 18 December 2013, http://www.bistummainz.de.

32. "Umfrage zur Partnerschafts-, Ehe und Familienpastoral der katholischen Kirche—Ergebnisse," 30 January 2014, published online in pdf format by the Swiss Pastoral-Sociological Institute and in a communiqué by the Swiss Episcopal Conference, dated 4 February 2014, http://www.bischoefe.ch.

33. Ibid.

15. The Italian Knot

1. *Statuto della Consulta Nazionale delle Aggregazioni Laicali*, March 2009, http://www.chiesacattolica.it/.

2. Ibid.

3. Quoted in M. Politi, *La Chiesa del no* (Mondadori, 2009).

4. "Lettera del cardinale segretario di stato al nuovo presidente della Conferenza Episcopale Italiana," 25 March 2007.

5. G. G. Vecchi, "Dal Vaticano spinta ai cattolici per un partito d' ispirazione cristiana," *Corriere della Sera*, 15 July 2011.

6. G. Sporschill and F. Radice Fossati Confalonieri, "L'addio a Martini: 'Chiesa indietro di 200 anni,'" *Corriere della Sera*, 1 September 2012, http://www.corriere.it.

7. Ibid.

8. C. M. Martini, *La cattedra dei non credenti* (Rusconi, 1992). *Translator's note: Cattedra* means both a professorial chair and the chair of a bishop or pope—that is, the seat of authority in either case.

9. C. M. Martini and G. Sporschill, *Colloqui notturni a Gerusalemme* (Mondadori, 2008).

10. F. De Bortoli, "Il mendicante con la porpora," *Corriere della Sera*, 1 September 2012.

11. Quoted in M. Politi, "Da una parte l'amore dei fedeli dall'altra la freddezza del Papa," *Il Fatto Quotidiano*, 4 September 2012.

12. Every Italian taxpayer contributes an obligatory eight parts per thousand (*otto per mille*) of his or her annual income tax either to one of the organized religions, which he or she can designate, or to a state fund dedicated (in theory) to charitable spending. Not everyone indicates a choice, in which case the funds are distributed in proportion to the overall allocations of previous years. Of those who do indicate a choice, a strong majority direct the money to the Catholic Church, which accounts publicly for how the money is spent.

13. M. Bartolini, "Chiesa, 2mila miliardi di immobili nel mondo," *Il Sole 24 Ore*, 15 February 2013, http://www.ilsole24ore.com.

14. Pope Francis, profession of faith with the bishops of the Italian Episcopal Conference, 23 May 2013.

15. Pope Francis, address at the official visit of H. E. Mr. Giorgio Napolitano, president of the Republic of Italy, to the Vatican, 8 June 2013.

16. Pope Francis, address at his official visit to H. E. Mr. Giorgio Napolitano, president of the Republic of Italy, Quirinal Palace, 14 November 2013.

17. G. Napolitano, speech, 14 November 2013.
18. E. Bianchi, "Oggi alla Chiesa manca il respiro," *La Stampa*, 16 April 2011, http://www.lastampa.it. See also Giorgio Campanini and Saverio Xeres, *Manca il respiro* (Yet, 2011).
19. Quoted in M. Politi, "Gian Franco Svidercoschi: 'Questa chiesa autoritaria tra lotte per bande e privilegi,'" *Il Fatto Quotidiano*, 11 January 2013.
20. Pope Francis, address at his official visit to H. E. Mr. Giorgio Napolitano, 14 November 2013.
21. Quoted in Francesco Antonio Grana, "Cei, Galantino segretario. Il Papa alla sua diocesi: 'Scusate, ma ho bisogno di lui,'" *Il Fatto Quotidiano*, 30 December 2013.
22. *Comunicato finale del Consiglio Permanente CEI*, 31 January 2014.
23. Ibid.
24. Quoted in M. Politi, "Il cardinale Angelo Bagnasco: 'Papa Francesco dà fastidio al malaffare,'" *Il Fatto Quotidiano*, 21 December 2013.
25. CEI, *Linee guida per i casi di abuso sessuale nei confronti di minori da parte di chierici* (2014).
26. Quoted in P. Rodari, "'Io, violentata a 13 anni Francesco mi ha nominata perché non accada più,'" *La Repubblica*, 23 March 2014.
27. A. Castegnaro, G. Dal Piaz, and E. Biemmi, *Fuori dal recinto* (Ancora, 2013).
28. Quoted in E. Himitian, *Francesco: Il Papa della gente* (Rizzoli, 2013).

16. A Resignable Papacy

1. I. Pérez del Visto, interview with the author.
2. "L'indiscrezione: 'Papa Francesco si dimetterà come Benedetto XVI,'" *Il Libero Quotidiano*, 2 December 2013, http://www.liberoquotidiano.it.
3. Quoted in G. Galeazzi, "Il Papa a Seewald: In Vatileaks non ho fatto il sovrano assoluto," *La Stampa*, 17 February 2013.
4. Quoted in G. O'Connell, "Cardinal Onaiyken: The New Pope Cannot Ignore Islam," *La Stampa*, 13 March 2013, http://www.lastampa.it.
5. Pope Francis, press conference during the flight from Korea to Rome, 18 August 2014.
6. V. Alazraki, *Osservatore Romano*, 14 March 2015.
7. L. Accattoli, "Il calore dopo la dottrina. Otto pagine su ottanta sono opera di Francesco," *Corriere della Sera*, 6 July 2013.
8. Pope Francis, *Lumen fidei*, encyclical letter, 29 June 2013.
9. Farewell Address of His Holiness Pope Benedict XVI to the Eminent Cardinals Present in Rome, 28 February 2013.
10. Quoted in S. Izzo, "Papa: Confida a ex allievo, non immagini umilta' e saggezza Ratzinger," Agi (news service), 11 July 2013.
11. Quoted in A. Tarquini, "Kung: 'Chiesa e fedeli troppo distanti ora Francesco deve cambiarla,'" *La Repubblica*, 10 February 2014.

12. Pope Francis, press conference during the return flight from Rio de Janeiro, 28 July 2013.

13. E. Bianchi, "Caro Diogneto 53," *Jesus*, May 2013. This and other columns and writings by the same author may be read at the website of the monastery of Bose, of which he is prior: http://www.monasterodibose.it.

14. G. Carriquiry, Speech in the Sala Protomoteca of the Campidoglio, 19 February 2015.

15. L. Caracciolo, "Papa Francesco, la carta vincente della Chiesa," *La Repubblica*, 12 March 2014.

16. *Una Vox*, July 2014, http://www.unavox.it.

17. Pope Francis, homily at holy mass with the new cardinals, 23 February 2014.

18. All quoted in M. Politi, "Una voce dal sinodo: 'La Chiesa si penta,'" *Il Fatto Quotidiano*, 7 November 2012.

19. Quoted in ibid.

20. Quoted in ibid.

21. Congregation for Bishops, http://www.vatican.va/.

22. Press bulletin, 18 December 2013, http://www.news.va/en.

23. Pope Francis, address to a meeting of the Congregation for Bishops, 27 February 2014.

24. Quoted in "Il Papa: 'Famiglia, serve pastorale coraggiosa,'" *Avvenire*, 20 February 2014.

25. Pope Francis, morning meditation at Santa Marta, 28 February 2014.

26. L. Accattoli, "Il percorso di Bergoglio che supera le 'dogane,'" *Corriere della Sera*, 13 January 2014.

27. Pope Francis, letter to those who will be created cardinals at the upcoming consistory of 22 February, 12 January 2014.

28. UN Committee on the Rights of the Child, concluding observations on the second report of the Holy See, Geneva 2014.

29. Quoted in F. Lombardi, "Nota," Vatica Radio, 7 February 2014.

30. Ibid.

31. "Editorial: Francis, You Must Meet Victims of Clergy Abuse," *National Catholic Reporter*, 28 March–10 April 2014, and at http://ncronline.org, dated 6 March 2014.

32. Quoted in P. Rodari, "'Basta con i preti che vivono nel lusso: Vi spiego la rivoluzione di Francesco,'" *La Repubblica*, 21 October 2013.

33. F. Hölderlin, "Hyperion's Song of Destiny," trans. P. Hughes.

34. A. Spadaro, "Interview with Pope Francis" (English translation), *La Civiltà Cattolica*, 19 September 2013, http://www.vatican.va.

35. Pope Francis, "How to Rout the Demon's Strategy," morning meditation at Santa Marta, 11 October 2013. *Translator's note*: The translation from the Italian report, printed in *L'Osservatore Romano* and available at the Vatican website, is my own. The English summary, also printed in the newspaper and available at the website, is a much briefer and blander paraphrase.

36. Spadaro, "Interview with Pope Francis."

37. Ibid.

38. Pope Francis, apostolic exhortation *Evangelii gaudium*, 24 November 2013.

39. Bendixen and Amandi survey for Univision TV, February 2014.

40. M.Tosatti, "Concistoro segreto: Cosa accadde," *La Stampa*, 24 March 2014, http://www.lastampa.it.

41. Gerhard Ludwig Müller, Raymond Burke, Carlo Caffarra, Velasio De Paolis, and Walter Brandmüller, *Permanere nella verità di Cristo* (Cantagalli, 2014).

42. Synod 14, Eleventh General Assembly, *Relatio post disceptationem* of the General Rapporteur, Péter Erdö, 13 October 2014.

43. Quoted in S. Magister, "Communion for the Remarried. Francis Has a Yes 'In Pectore,'" *L'Espresso Online*, 8 September 2014, http://chiesa.espresso.repubblica.it.

44. G. L. Müller, *La speranza della famiglia* (Ares, 2014).

45. P. Parolin, "'Rescriptum ex Audientia Ss.Mi Sulla rinuncia Dei Vescovi Diocesani e Dei Titolari di Uffici di Nomina Pontificia," 3 November 2014, available at the Vatican website, section "Roman Curia," subsection "Secretariat of State."

46. Quoted in Elisabetta Piqué, "Molina dijo que el Papa alertó sobre las drogas," *La Nación*, 13 November 2014.

47. Pope Francis, audience with *Comunione e Liberazione*, 7 March 2015.

48. Pope Francis, *Misericordiae Vultus*, bull of indication of the extraordinary Jubilee of Mercy, 11 April 2015.

49. Pope Francis, morning meditation at Santa Marta, 6 July 2013.

50. Pope Francis, morning meditation at Santa Marta, 16 April 2013.

51. Quoted in S. Falasca, "Sinodale: Così è la Chiesa frutto maturo del concilio," *Avvenire*, 20 February 2014.

52. Pope Francis, *Evangelii gaudium*.

53. A. Riccardi, speech at the German embassy to the Holy See, 24 September 2014.

54. Pope Francis, presentation of Christmas greetings to the Roman Curia, 22 December 2014.

55. Pope Francis, speech at the Church of Jesus, 27 September 2014.

56. Quoted in G. Fazzini, "Victor Manuel Fernández: 'Il cuore del Vangelo al cuore della gente,'" *Credere*, 9 March 2014, http://www.credere.it.

Index